The IBM PC Programmer's Guide

W9-BIN-572

The Waite Group
James T. Smith

A Brady Book
Published by Prentice Hall Press
New York, New York 10023

The IBM PC AT Programmer's Guide

Copyright © 1986 by The Waite Group
All rights reserved
including the right of reproduction
in whole or in part in any form

A Brady Book
Published by Prentice Hall Press
A Division of Simon & Schuster, Inc.
Gulf + Western Building
One Gulf + Western Plaza
New York, New York 10023

PRENTICE HALL PRESS is a trademark of Simon & Schuster, Inc.

Manufactured in the United States of America

1   2   3   4   5   6   7   8   9   10

Library of Congress Cataloging-in-Publication Data

Smith, James, T., 1939–
    The IBM PC AT programmer's guide.

    Bibliography: p.
    Includes index.
    1. IBM Personal Computer AT—Programming.
I. Title.
QA76.8.I2594S59   1986   005.265   86-2334
ISBN 0-89303-580-7 (Paper Edition)

CONTENTS

This work is dedicated to my critic, friend, and wife, Helen.

Acknowledgement

I would like to acknowledge the influence of many colleagues in the academic and computer worlds who, intentionally or not, set me on course to the fascinating study reported here. A particular debt is owed to Richard Levaro of Blaise Computing Inc. who introduced me to the PC and showed me how to learn this material. That company's clients also provided important input. By their questions, they helped me answer mine: *what do you need to know to control this wonderful machine?*

Preface

This book discusses the IBM PC/AT personal computer, and its features, in detail, including DOS 3.0, the Intel 80286, and the PC/AT BIOS. Its major concern is *what you need to know* in order to have complete control of a PC/AT using DOS. This book provides extensive background on the IBM personal computers, DOS, and the Intel 8086 CPU family. While the emphasis is on the *new features* of the PC/AT, its 80286 CPU, and the operating system, many examples are given to familiarize you with the way the PC family and the 8086 family CPUs operate. Many programs illustrating 80286 instructions are selected from the PC/AT BIOS, and many short IBM Pascal programs show you how to use the BIOS and DOS interrupt services.

Limits of Liability and
Disclaimer of Warranty

The authors and publisher of this book have used their best efforts in preparing this book and the programs contained in it. These efforts include the development, research, and testing of the theories and programs to determine their effectiveness. The authors and publisher make no warranty of any kind, expressed or implied, with regard to these programs or the documentation contained in this book. The authors and publisher shall not be liable in any event for incidental or consequential damages in connection with, or arising out of, the furnishing, performance, or use of these programs.

Introduction

Concepts

* This book considers the *new features* of the PC/AT in detail, including DOS 3.0, the Intel 80286, and the PC/AT BIOS. * Its major concern is what you need to know in order to have *complete control* of a PC/AT running the DOS operating system. * It provides *extensive background* on the IBM personal computers, DOS, and the Intel 8086 CPU family.

If you are a programmer migrating or considering migrating to the PC/AT, then you need information about its hardware and software system organization and capability and how it is related to other computers. Because the PC/AT, the top of the IBM PC line, is more sophisticated than most personal computers, you may need guidance about more complex subjects than those covered in most books describing individual computers.

This book will help you find answers to many of the main questions that you face:

- What are the distinguishing features of the PC/AT and its Intel 80286 CPU and how do they relate to other computers and CPUs in the same families?
- How are these features supported by the PC/AT BIOS and the DOS 3.0 operating system? What hardware capabilities are not yet fully supported by DOS and other software?

This book is a compact information source, gathering in one place information about many details relating to the PC/AT. It provides the necessary background material about the PC and 8086 families and DOS, and it segregates description of the special features of the PC/AT, the 80286, and DOS 3.0 so that programmers with backgrounds in these areas can obtain quickly the information they need about the PC/AT in particular.

Examples of assembly language code from the PC/AT BIOS illustrate the use of the various types of 80286 instructions. The many BIOS and DOS services are clarified by short Pascal programs that access them via software interrupts. One of these examples shows how a BIOS service can help you make use of the vast extended memory of the PC/AT.

No book can ever include all the information that users of a computer system might need. For those topics that couldn't be covered here in complete detail, references are given to appropriate manuals. Moreover, some important topics that could not be covered at all are listed in the first chapter, then described briefly with full references in the final chapter.

About the Author

James T. Smith was born in 1939 in Springfield, Ohio. He holds degrees in mathematics from Harvard College, San Francisco State (SFSU), Stanford, and the University of Saskatchewan. His PhD and subsequent research work is in foundations of geometry. Since 1969 Smith has been a member of the Mathematics Department of SFSU, serving as its chairman during 1975–82. Smith's computer experience began with the UNIVAC I at Harvard and continued through service as a mathematician with the Navy in the 1960s. He was instrumental in setting up the Computer Science Program at SFSU and has taught many computer subjects, including computer graphics as a visiting professor at Mills College, University of Alaska, and California State University, Hayward. While writing this book, Smith was involved in IBM PC systems software development at Blaise Computing Inc. in Berkeley.

1

The PC/AT and This Book

Contents

In this chapter we shall consider in greater detail why this book may be useful to you. We shall explain how it is organized to give you quick access to needed information about the PC/AT, whether you are a newcomer to the PC family or already have PC experience and are now stepping up to this more sophisticated, top of the line personal computer. Moreover, we consider what information is *not* covered in this book, so that you will know what additional study is necessary to become familiar with all aspects of the PC/AT necessary for your application.

1.1 The flagship of the IBM PC family

Concepts

* Distinguishing features of the PC/AT * DOS 3.0 * PC/AT software

In 1984 IBM introduced the PC/AT, the flagship of its PC family of personal computers. This family now includes the original PC, the PC/XT, the PCjr, and the PC Portable. Like the earlier members, the PC/AT is based on a central processing unit (CPU) belonging to the Intel 8086 microprocessor family, and has an open architecture, admitting components designed and manufactured by other companies. The following new features distinguish the PC/AT as a far more capable and sophisticated computer than its predecessors:

Its Intel 80286 CPU is a true 16-bit microprocessor and runs several times faster than the 8088 CPUs of the earlier machines.

It can access up to 16 megabytes (MB) of main memory, with 256 or 512 kilobytes (K) on the mother board.

Many aspects of a multitasking operating system are implemented directly in hardware by the virtual memory management, protection, and task management provisions of the 80286.

A small battery-powered CMOS memory supports a nonvolatile clock/calendar and stores hardware configuration data. Through the PC/AT Basic Input Output System (BIOS), this clock provides timing and alarm services with resolution (1 millisecond) finer than that easily obtained on the earlier machines.

The PC/AT includes a 20-MB fixed disk drive with faster access time than the PC/XT fixed disk and a 1.2 MB high capacity diskette drive that can also read standard PC diskettes.

Eight expansion slots are provided for additional components available from IBM or other manufacturers. (Two of these must accommodate disk/diskette drive and display controller boards.)

Version 3.0 of the Microsoft/IBM Disk Operating System (DOS) was introduced to support the PC/AT. The new types of disk and diskette drives made this necessary. However, DOS 3.0 does not support the virtual memory management, protection, or task management features of the 80286. Moreover, the extended main memory, beyond the standard PC family 640 K base memory, is not easily accessible via DOS or the PC/AT BIOS. A year after the introduction of the PC/AT, new software that supports these features is beginning to appear, particularly the XENIX operating system. As such software becomes available, the PC/AT will assume a role as leader of the PC family for business, engineering, and scientific applications. Like the PC and PC/XT before, it provides a new standard for other manufacturers to emulate, and with its new operating systems, it will be host to entire libraries of new software.

1.2 How this book can help you

Concepts

* Who needs this book? Why? * What main questions does it consider? * What background does it assume? * How can you find information here about the new features of the PC/AT? * What background information is provided for programmers new to the IBM PC family? * Using reference manuals

---

To make best use of this book, you should have some familiarity with a few basic aspects of microcomputers. In particular, you should be familiar with

general concepts of computer organization and assembly language programming,

the use of an operating system,

programming in a higher level language.

You are *not* expected to be familiar already with the PC family, with the 8086 CPU family architecture, or with DOS. This book provides all necessary background material in these areas. The IBM Pascal language was chosen for higher level language examples because the organization of programs in that language so closely parallels the logic of the examples. For the convenience of programmers unfamiliar with that Pascal dialect, the programs are often documented line by line.

Organization of the book is based on two aims:

to provide necessary background material about the PC and 8086 families and DOS;

to segregate description of distinguishing features of the PC/AT, the 80286, and DOS 3.0 so that programmers with a background in these areas can obtain quickly the information they need about the PC/AT in particular.

Here is a general outline of the chapters, with the notations *background* and *AT* indicating that a chapter provides background information or a description of features new to the PC/AT.

Chapter	Type	Title
1	....	The PC/AT and this book
2	AT	A close look
3	AT	Main memory
4	Background	Introducing DOS
5	Background	DOS structure I
6	Background	Intel 8086 family traits
7	Background	DOS structure II: BIOS and DOS interrupt services
8	AT	DOS 3.0
9	AT	Intel 80286
10	AT	PC/AT BIOS
11	....	Important topics not covered in this book

If you are generally familiar with the use of a PC and DOS, you may skip Chapters 4 and 5. If you are already familiar with the 8086 family architecture and the instructions common to all 8086 family CPUs, you may skip Chapter 6. If you are already experienced in using software interrupts to obtain BIOS and DOS services, you may skip Chapter 7. The new features of DOS 3.0 are described in Chapter 8. The distinguishing features of the PC/AT are described as follows: Chapters 2 and 3 consider its physical details; Chapter 9 describes in depth the new 80286 instructions and its complex memory management, protection, and task management systems; Chapter 10 discusses the PC/AT BIOS in great detail, emphasizing features not present in the earlier PCs.

If you will only be using the DOS operating system, then some of the detail given in Chapter 9 concerning the Intel 80286 will not be immediately useful to you. However, using the PC/AT extended memory, available beyond the standard 640 K PC base memory up to a limit of 16 MB, involves some aspects of the 80286 memory management and protection systems described there.

In a number of areas, it is impossible to give complete detail. This book is not a reference manual. In fact, it is designed to make it easier for you to use a reference manual. Many details given in a reference manual obscure the basic concepts, particularly when they are merely applications of the same method to different situations, or when they correct earlier design errors. This book concentrates on the underlying concepts. You can't avoid manuals entirely— some necessary details just can't be provided elsewhere. Therefore, this book will refer to the manuals that give additional detail.

1.3 Assembly or higher level language?

Concepts

* Why does this book use a high level language to access low level services? * IBM Pascal

Many advanced features of the PC/AT and DOS involve concepts normally addressed in assembly language. Overuse of assembly language reduces clarity. An example might involve twenty lines of code, all to the unpracticed eye rather similar, only one or two of which are important. Much of the unimportant matter is repetitious. This book instead will rely as much as possible on a higher level language, IBM Pascal Version 2, to present examples. The IBM Pascal language was chosen because

the organization of Pascal programs closely parallels the logic of the examples,

the systems programming extensions in the IBM Pascal dialect are adequate for expressing the concepts in the examples and avoid much of the repetition.

For convenience of programmers unfamiliar with IBM Pascal, the programs are often documented line by line, in assembly language fashion.

IBM Pascal Version 2 is IBM's adaptation of Microsoft Pascal Version 3.2. The dialects are very similar, but this book uses some features of IBM Pascal not present in the Microsoft version.

1.4 Integrating hardware and software questions

Concepts

* Why does this book integrate hardware and software topics?

Although this book is aimed at programmers, it frequently emphasizes hardware. With microcomputers, the two are inextricable. In fact, a survey recently showed that many computer science graduates shun the microcomputer software industry because their education avoided hardware questions. As a microcomputer programmer, you may not assume that your programs will be run always with the same hardware or that someone else has taken care of the hardware differences. Moreover, you will probably have to write a program at some time that deals directly with peripheral equipment and the related input/output and interrupt controller chips. Finally, microcomputer programmers are often involved in acquiring microcomputer components. Familiarity with the hardware—even if only to the extent that you can recognize the components and discern which are connected to each other—will help you understand the software, and provide a basis for sound decisions. The software concepts in this book often reflect hardware considerations; the book tries to integrate rather than isolate them.

1.5 What important topics are not covered in this book?

Concepts

* What important topics would have been covered in this book had time and space permitted?

Ideally, this book would cover everything that you might need to know to have complete control of a PC/AT running the DOS operating system, independent of your particular application. Of course, reality never matches the ideal. Considerations of time and space have made it impossible to cover in detail a number of topics. These are described briefly in Chapter 11, with references to other literature should you need detailed information. The following list of topics not covered should indicate what further study you may need in order to undertake your intended tasks.

Topics not covered

- high level languages
- assemblers (80286 Assembly Language is used extensively to describe the CPU and BIOS, but no assembler is discussed.)
- object code librarian
- linker (Segment allocation, ordering, and combination are discussed briefly.)
- debugger
- program editor
- programming peripheral chips like the interrupt controller and timer
- selecting input/output equipment and controllers (Display controllers are described briefly.)
- acquiring additional memory

Finally, two new PC/AT operating systems were introduced just as this book was nearing completion: DOS 3.1 and XENIX. These are the first software products that really support the memory management, protection, and task management capabilities of the 80286. While their importance certainly merits inclusion in a book like this, time did not permit. Moreover, a thorough description of XENIX would require a book in itself. Adequate coverage of this software lies in the future.

2

A Close Look

Contents

This chapter will describe the various components of the PC/AT as they are delivered from your supplier and will consider some of the decisions you must make about storage capacity and peripheral equipment in order to set up a complete system. Special attention is given to the monitor and video controller. The external aspects of the system are depicted in detail, then you are given a guided tour of the system unit, visiting and inspecting many important internal components.

2.1 The major components of the PC/AT system

Concepts

* What versions of the PC/AT are available?   * What hardware and software come with the it?   * What kind of monitor and video controller do you need?   * What else will you have to provide?

Versions

The PC/AT is available in two versions. The more complete one has 512 megabytes (MB) main memory, a 20-MB fixed disk, a 1.2 MB high capacity diskette drive, a disk/diskette drive controller board, and a communications adapter board with a serial port and a parallel port. The stripped version has 256 MB of main memory, no fixed disk, and no communications adapter board, but it does contain the same high capacity diskette drive and disk/diskette controller board. The stripped version is unlikely to interest you unless you have found alternative suppliers for the missing components. Therefore, we shall ignore it. When we consider a PC/AT from now on, we mean a fully equipped model.

Notice that neither version includes a monitor, video controller, or standard 360 kilobyte (K) diskette drive!

Hardware and software shipped with the PC/AT

A fully equipped PC/AT has 512 MB of main memory on its motherboard (the main circuit board, to which others are attached). This is the maximum amount possible without adding a memory expansion board. The motherboard has eight slots to accommodate various kinds of expansion boards. Two of these are already occupied by a disk/diskette controller board and a communications adapter board with a serial and a parallel port. The latter board provides an interface for communication with printers, telephone lines, and other peripheral equipment. Also included are a 20-MB fixed disk, a 1.2-MB high capacity diskette drive, the keyboard, and power cord.

This list gives a good idea of one of the major differences between the PC/AT and the PC/XT, previously the top of the IBM line: *size!* The maximum main memory on the PC/XT motherboard is 256 MB, and its fixed disk and standard diskettes have capacity of 10 MB and 360 K, respectively. On the other hand, you will see later that inclusion of the new high capacity PC/AT diskette drive entails a serious problem of compatibility between the PC/AT and other IBM personal computers.

IBM ships with the PC/AT two manuals: *Installation and Setup* and *Guide to Operations*, references [19] and [18]. The latter includes two diskettes. The *Diagnostics* diskette contains software for initially setting up your system and for diagnosing any problems that may arise. The second diskette, *Exploring the IBM PC/AT*, is an effective and entertaining tutorial diskette. These two diskettes are the standard 360 K variety; the high capacity diskette drive will read them all right.

Much of the information in the *Installation and Setup Manual* is technical detail on the installation of various accessories. You should skim it to find out what's there and what sections you will have to follow closely to install your equipment.

Section 1 of the *Guide to Operations* goes with the *Exploring the IBM PC/AT* diskette. When your system is set up, you should step through that tutorial to get the feel of things. You may find it especially amusing if you have a color monitor! Section 2 gives detailed instructions for running the programs on the *Diagnostics* diskette. It's usually reassuring to step through these, too, soon after you've got your system running. Section 3 has some important tips about preparing your system for moving—particularly the disk and diskette drives.

Three BASIC language manuals, references [9], [10], and [11], are also delivered with the PC/AT:

BASIC Reference
BASIC Handbook: General Programming Information
BASIC Quick Reference.

These are provided to enable you to use the rudimentary BASIC Interpreter that is built into the PC/AT read-only memory. (The much more elaborate BASIC 3.0 system is supplied with DOS 3.0. It is fully described in these manuals.) Since BASIC is beyond the scope of this book, these manuals will not be discussed further.

You need a monitor and video controller board

You can't run a computer without a monitor and a video controller. IBM doesn't include them with the PC/AT, probably because there is no longer a *standard* IBM monitor or controller board. There are two familiar types of monitor-controller combinations that will work with the PC/AT.

The IBM Monochrome Display and IBM Monochrome Display and Printer Adapter This is the familiar green IBM monitor, and its original controller board. This controller produces the beautiful 9x14 dot matrix character set, but displays only text output. (You can construct boxes, etc., from special text characters.) Its parallel port provides a printer interface.

Compatible monochrome displays with green or amber phosphor are available from other suppliers. You can also find compatible controller boards, most of which add considerably to the functionality of the IBM board. One supplier's board, the Hercules, has itself become a standard that other enhanced monochrome controllers emulate. If you are considering buying a compatible monochrome monitor-controller combination from other vendors, you should consider these points:

There are only a few compatible monitors. They receive their power from the PC/AT power supply via a plug in the back of the system unit.

The character matrix is produced by the controller. The Hercules standard character set is identical to IBM's. Some boards use smaller matrices that produce inferior character sets.

Many controllers, including those following Hercules' standard, produce graphics output (usually about 720 x 350 pixels) on the monochrome monitor. However, these boards will not usually support software written for the familiar IBM Color/Graphics Adapter. (Some software products do have separate Hercules-compatible versions.)

In addition to providing monochrome text and possibly graphics output, some controllers can be switched to another mode that produces output compatible with the IBM Color/Graphics Adapter. With the nicest products you can switch mode via software. With the most awkward ones, you have to disassemble your computer to switch mode.

Some video controller boards include other features like a serial or parallel port, additional main memory, or a real time clock. The ports should work with the PC/AT. However, you should check very carefully any claim that expansion memory is compatible with the PC/AT! The clock is unnecessary, because the PC/AT already has one.

The IBM Color Display and IBM Color/Graphics Adapter board This is the familiar IBM color monitor with the glossy black background and its original controller board. This board has no functionality beyond video control, and it does that very badly. It produces an ugly and fatiguing 5 x 7 dot matrix character set, low resolution graphics (320 x 200 pixels) in four colors, and medium resolution (640 x 200) in two. Unfortunately, its inferior design influenced some other features of the PC (particularly the BIOS) so that even other vendors' improved versions must incorporate some of the bad features to ensure compatibility.

As with the monochrome monitor and controller, compatible equipment is available from other vendors. If you are considering such equipment, keep these points in mind:

The Color/Graphics Adapter and most compatible boards provide their video control signals in two distinct forms: *RGB* and *composite*. The RGB signal consists of separate Red, Green, Blue, and synchronization components and is transmitted via a nine pin D connector. Two connectors are provided for the composite signal, an encoded combination of the RGB components: an RCA phonograph jack and a four pin Berg connector. The phonograph jack can be connected to composite color and monochrome monitors. The Berg connector is provided for an optional radio frequency (RF) modulator. This device produces a degraded analog encoding of the composite signal that will drive a standard color or monochrome television.

Many compatible monitors are available, some less fuzzy than others. Normally, they do not receive their power from the PC/AT: you have to use another plug. Some of these monitors are monochrome, driven by the composite signal; they are *not* compatible with the Monochrome Adapter. They are useful if your primary interest is two color medium resolution graphics. The color monitors compatible with the RGB signal are called TTL (Transistor-Transistor Logic) monitors. Their input is digital; its values select colors from a discrete built-in color set. Use of a television set as a monitor is not normally recommended, since the picture quality is degraded by the RF modulation.

You'll probably have to tolerate the bad character set. (Include in your plans a budget for aspirin and new eyeglasses.)

Some, but not all, compatible controllers have conquered the awful flickering that you see when the IBM board scrolls. (This is not produced by the board, but by the PC itself, to avoid a still less appealing snow effect produced by the board.)

Some compatible controllers can produce higher resolution graphics output than the IBM board. However, software written for the IBM board cannot take advantage of this. Moreover, some monitors may not display it suitably.

In addition to providing output compatible with the Color/Graphics Adapter, some boards can be switched to another mode that is compatible with the Monochrome Adapter, perhaps even enhancing that to provide graphics on the IBM Monochrome monitor. With the nicest products you can switch mode via software. With the most awkward ones, you have to disassemble your computer to switch mode.

Some video controller boards include other features like a serial or parallel port, additional main memory, or a real time clock. The ports should work with the PC/AT. However, you should check very carefully any claim that expansion memory is compatible with the PC/AT! The clock is unnecessary, because the PC/AT already has one.

New IBM monitor and video controller boards Other vendors have developed video controllers that *greatly* enhance the functionality of the familiar IBM boards (and the price). These sometimes do not support software written for the standard boards. Their market is generally specialized computer aided design (CAD) or image processing applications. Often, they require a higher resolution analog RGB monitor.

Now, IBM is entering this market and supplanting its inferior Color/Graphics Adapter. The new **IBM Enhanced Graphics Adapter** board matches the functionality of the best combination Monochrome-Color/Graphics compatible video controllers. It provides text and graphics in both monochrome and color, with a better color mode character set, higher resolution, and more colors than the previous color board. This new product will probably become the standard video board for the PC/AT. To support the higher resolution, it requires a better monitor, the **IBM Enhanced Color Display.** Together, they also address the medium-resolution end of the CAD market. To enter the true high resolution part of that market, IBM has announced a new **Professional Graphics Adapter** board.

What else will you have to provide?

Many PC/AT systems will require some type of printer for output. Many varieties are available, and printer technology is changing rapidly. A survey of this equipment is beyond the scope of this book; for up to date details you should consult the periodical literature and a dealer. The PC/AT communicates with most printers via a parallel port, although some printers require a serial port. (A parallel port sends all the bits of a character code at once over separate wires. A serial port sends them one after the other, which takes about ten times as long.)

Many other input/output and communications devices such as digitizers, networks, or modems are available. Again, a survey of these is beyond the scope of this book; you should consult dealers and current periodicals for information. The PC/AT communicates with most of this equipment via a serial port.

You may need more than one serial or parallel port. If you don't get that with your video controller board, you may want to purchase a second IBM Serial/Parallel Adapter board or search for a memory expansion board that also has the required port. The built-in PC/AT BIOS software supports as many as two serial ports and three parallel ports. Special programming is required to handle more than that.

Although the 512 K motherboard main memory may seem large, the PC/AT is designed to accommodate applications with much greater need for memory. It is still 128 K below the standard main memory capacity of the IBM PC family. Beyond that, the PC/AT can support *15 MB of extended main memory!* Using extended main memory requires capabilities of the PC/AT's Intel 80286 central processing unit (CPU) that are not shared by other members of the PC family, and the software must be written specially for the PC/AT. Additional memory is available on memory expansion boards made by IBM and several other companies. The 128 K additional standard main memory can be purchased on a separate IBM board, or it can be obtained as part of the memory complement on compatible boards of much larger capacity from other suppliers. Some of these boards provide additional features—particularly serial or parallel ports.

Of course, you will have to provide a suitable working area for the computer and its servant. IBM supplies one neat item of this sort: a stand that will support the PC/AT in vertical position on the floor.

The additional hardware mentioned above is of course optional. However, software is not. The PC/AT is shipped with no software beyond the diagnostics and tutorial accompanying the *Guide to Operations* manual. You must purchase the operating system separately. Chapters 4, 5, 7, and 8 describe DOS 3.0, the principal PC/AT operating system. DOS 3.0 is shipped with the interpreter for the IBM Version 3.0 of the BASIC language.

If you intend to do serious programming for the PC/AT, you will need the *PC/AT Technical Reference* and *DOS 3.0 Technical Reference* manuals, references [20] and [15], which must be purchased separately.

2.2 Outside the PC/AT

Concepts

* Physical dimensions and requirements * What's the lock for?
* Is the PC/AT keyboard different from the familiar PC keyboard?
* Can the new high capacity diskette drive be used with standard diskettes?

The last section listed the various components of the PC/AT, as they are delivered from your supplier, and considered some of the decisions you must make about storage capacity and peripheral equipment in order to set up a complete system. Now let's walk around the outside of the computer and look at its external features in detail. In the next section, we'll climb inside it for a close look at the internal components.

Physical dimensions and requirements

As you can see from Figure 2.2.1, the system unit is styled somewhat differently from the older PC, but it is still recognizable as one of the family. It's about one inch larger in each dimension: 21-1/4" wide, 16-5/8" deep, and 6-3/8" high. (This is just enough difference that dust covers made for the older PC probably won't fit.) The PC/AT can use 50 or 60Hz a/c power either at 115 V, drawing 5 Amp maximum current, or at 230 V, drawing 2.5 Amp. You adjust it for 115 V or 230 V by setting a switch in back.

The power on/off switch is typically inaccessible at the right rear of the system unit.

The lock and keyboard

Unlike most personal computers, the PC/AT has a conspicuous lock in front. You can lock the cover onto the system unit, lock the power on or off, and disable the keyboard. Ridiculous icons identify the key positions. This kind of security is necessary for one of the principal intended uses of the PC/AT: it can serve as the central unit in a small network. Interference with its keyboard could inflict disaster on other network users.

Just as the world is getting used to the peculiar placement of some keys on the standard IBM PC keyboard, IBM changes again. The PC/AT keyboard is slightly different. The **Esc** key and the heavily used \ key have been moved to top right. This typist wishes they'd stay in one place! On the other hand, the troublesome ~ and **PrtSc** keys have been moved out of the way to upper left and far right. The **Enter, Shift, Ins,** and + keys are larger, making better

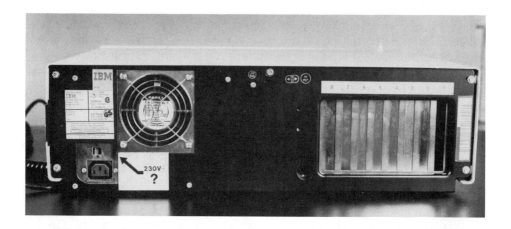

Figure 2.2.1 PC/AT exterior

targets. There is one new key, **SysReq,** that will serve an important function when networking software is available. The PC/AT keyboard is slightly larger than the PC keyboard: 20-1/2″ by 8-1/2.″ It has a cheaper, less solid feel than the older one. However, the new status indicator lights for the **CapsLock, NumLock,** and **ScrollLock** keys, and the new six foot keyboard cable are very welcome enhancements.

The PC/AT keyboard has several internal enhancements, and therefore is not compatible with other PC family keyboards.

Diskette drives

The PC/AT has a 5-1/4″ 20-MB fixed disk drive hidden inside and room for two 5-1/4″ half height drives accessible from the front. One of these drives, normally the upper one, is the new 1.2 MB high capacity diskette drive. The PC/AT is delivered with the lower slot empty. You can install any compatible half height unit. IBM's literature suggests another fixed disk drive or a standard 360-K diskette drive. The latter unit will probably be the more common, because the high capacity drive is unfortunately not entirely compatible with the standard units. Standard 360-K drives for the earlier PC's are wired slightly differently from those for the PC/AT and may require adjustment before installation.

The 1.2-MB high capacity drive is really intended as a backup device. (The effect of this intention on the diskette format is discussed in Section 8.3.) To store this much data, you need to obtain special high capacity diskettes. This drive also doubles as an input device: it can read standard 360-K diskettes (and the older 320-K and even single sided diskettes). However, it fails as a general output device. It can write the standard diskettes, and read the ones it's written. *However, standard diskettes written by the high capacity drive cannot be read reliably by standard drives!* In the author's experience, they can be read well only until they become about half full.

2.3 Inside the PC/AT

Concepts

* Why should you be familiar with the internal components?
* Power supply * Motherboard and expansion slots * Intel 80286 CPU chip * Provision for Intel 80287 Numeric Coprocessor chip
* Keyboard, Interrupt, and DMA controller chips * Timer and Clock/CMOS chips; oscillators * Principal monitor switch * Fixed disk and diskette drives and controller * Motherboard RAM and ROM

In this section we will climb inside the PC/AT and take a good look around. The aim is to visit all parts that a programmer may have to work with directly. Its modular design is stressed, for several reasons.

- You may need to consider various hardware configurations in order to find the optimum solution to your computing requirements.
- The ready availability of compatible modules from non-IBM sources means that two PC/ATs will rarely be exactly alike. If you are a serious PC/AT programmer, you must be aware of the differences.
- Software structure often mirrors hardware structure. Even if you aren't basically interested in the hardware, knowing how it's organized may help you understand the software.

So let's unlock the system unit, detach all its cables, remove five screws, lift off the cover, and jump in. We'll take a tour of the box, starting at the center of the back wall, going clockwise. Since some components are installed atop others, a map of the unit requires two Figures, 2.3.1 and 2.3.2. If you're physically unable to take the tour, you can refer to these.

Figure 2.3.1 represents the interior of the system unit as seen from above. The largest single component is the power supply at right rear. It converts your external 115-V or or 230-V electric power source into closely regulated low voltage power for the PC/AT components. It contains the external power connections and the on/off switch. The PC/AT power supply is larger than the older PC's: at 115 V it draws 5 Amp as opposed to the PC's 2.5 Amp. Moreover, at +5 V it supplies 19.8 Amp as compared to the PC's 7 Amp. This component generates more heat than the others in the system unit, so the fan is installed here. Its speed is variable and controlled thermostatically.

Attached at the center of the back wall is a second power source: a lithium battery that powers one chip on the motherboard even when the PC/AT is turned off. That chip, described in more detail below, contains the clock/calendar and a small amount of memory that remembers the configuration of your system.

The motherboard is the large circuit board mounted horizontally at the bottom of the system unit. It carries the CPU and memory chips and other closely related components. Expansion boards like communications adapters or video controllers are plugged into the motherboard. Because it lies partially under the power supply, disk drives, and expansion boards, you will need to refer to its map in Figure 2.3.2 for some details.

In the center rear are the motherboard connectors for the twelve multicolored lines from the power supply. Nearby is a strangely simple switch. When you turn on the PC/AT (boot it), this switch tells whether it should use the monitor attached to a monochrome video controller board or a color/graphics board.

Many of the principal chips are in this upper right quarter of the motherboard. You can find them in Figure 2.3.2 or by looking around you with a flashlight. The chips have model numbers painted on top. Here is a partial roll.

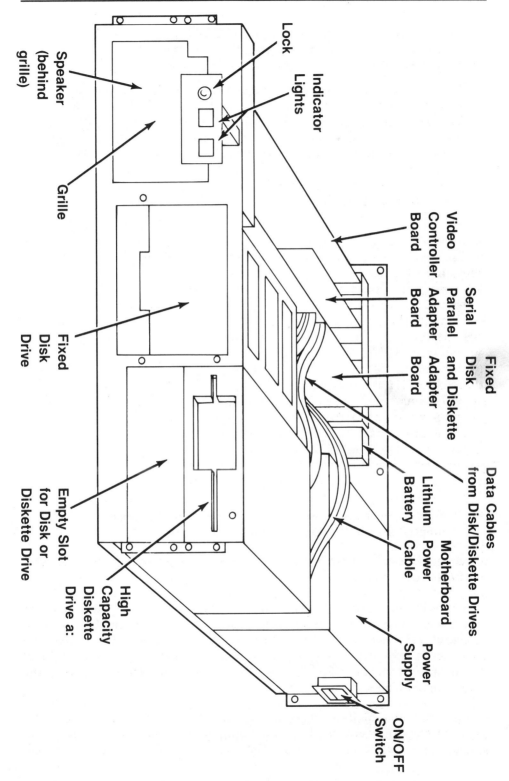

Figure 2.3.1 PC/AT system unit uncovered

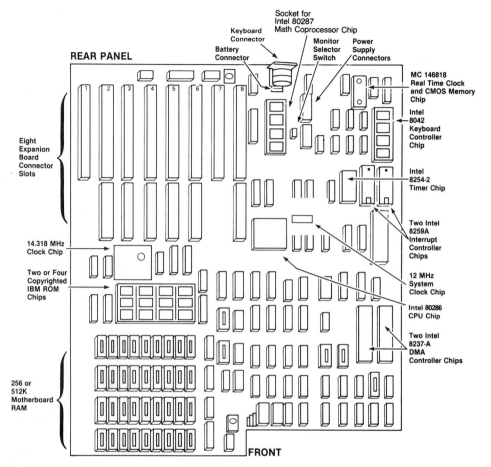

Figure 2.3.2 PC/AT motherboard

The Intel 80286 CPU chip, the heart of the PC/AT, about 1″ square, is appropriately near the center of the motherboard.

In a silver-colored container to the right of the 80286 is the 12 MHz System Clock.

A socket for an Intel 80287 Numeric Coprocessor chip is back near the power supply connections. If you install a coprocessor, the CPU can instruct it to do certain arithmetic calculations. You can do double precision integer arithmetic, floating point real arithmetic, and exact decimal arithmetic on the 80287 hardware far faster than you can execute the corresponding software routines on the 80286.

The Motorola MC146818 Clock and CMOS chip is attached at top right. This chip is powered by the lithium battery on the back wall, so it continues to operate even when the PC/AT is turned off. It contains the real-time clock/calendar, and 64 bytes of information about your equipment that the system needs every time you boot it. In older PC models, this information was saved by setting switches on the motherboard. The chip is clearly more convenient, since its contents can be set by software. (One motherboard switch remains, for monitor selection. If you could only set this by software, and your boot monitor quit, then you couldn't change to the other type of monitor!)

Hidden at right under the power supply is the long Intel 8042 Keyboard Controller chip. This is a small computer in itself, devoted to interpreting your keystrokes and sending the appropriate codes to the CPU.

Also on the right, partially hidden under the power supply, are two Intel 8259A Interrupt Controller chips. In the PC/AT, a device needing immediate software attention, like the keyboard or a communication port, can interrupt processing, cause execution of an appropriate service routine, and then let processing continue. The 8259As control this process.

The nearby Intel 8254-2 Timer chip provides timing signals for the CPU and various other devices, like the speaker.

Two Intel 8237A DMA (Direct Memory Access) controllers are located at right front, hidden under the diskette drive. These control the flow of information between memory and other units, especially the disk drives.

The 1.2-MB high capacity diskette drive is installed in the top righthand front area of the system unit. Visible on top is a circuit board with its own electronics. (This controls the physical operation of the disk, not the input/output operations. Those are managed by the disk controller, which we shall find later, at the other end of the flat, wide data cable.)

Underneath this drive is a slot for another of the same physical size (5-1/4" half height). Various diskette or fixed disk drives can be installed here, as long as they are compatible with the PC/AT and the right size for the slot. The *Installation and Setup* manual, reference [19], gives instructions for installing these. How marvellous that such delicate instruments can be made so simple to handle!

In the front middle is the 20-MB fixed disk drive. There is not much to see, since it's sealed against dust and other abominations. Its circuit board is underneath.

Behind the grille on the left front wall is the speaker, which may be disconcertingly loud, but can produce only one tone at once. You can't program PC/AT polyphony!

Just behind and below the speaker is the motherboard RAM (Random Access Memory). The minimum installion consists of thirty-six 64 K by 1 bit standard RAM chips. These are supplied by several companies. The author's were made by Mostek, except for one; the mysterious interloper said merely "Japan." In each byte of information the eight bits are labeled 0 through 7. An extra parity bit is stored with the byte to help detect storage and transmission errors. A single 64 K by 1 bit RAM chip stores bit 0 of 64 K bytes of information. Another chip stores bit 1, etc. Thus, nine such chips store 64 K bytes, so the minimum motherboard RAM installation amounts to 4 x 64 K = 256 K bytes.

To expand this to the 512-K RAM on a fully populated PC/AT motherboard, another 64-K chip is installed atop each of the base chips.

Behind the motherboard RAM, you see copyrighted IBM ROM chips and perhaps some empty sockets. The information in this ROM (Read-Only Memory) is permanently recorded. It consists of

- the Power On Self Test (POST) programs that test your equipment, causing a slight delay every time you boot your system;
- the BIOS (Basic Input Output System), a part of the operating system that communicates directly with and controls your peripheral equipment;
- a rudimentary version of the BASIC language interpreter.

The POST and BIOS code are listed in the *PC/AT Technical Reference* manual, reference [20]. IBM will sue companies that use copies of all or part of this code in their computers. Apparently IBM has two versions of the ROM, one that uses four chips and one that uses two more densely packed ones, leaving two vacant sockets. Either version contains 128-K bytes.

Behind the ROM, under a metal shield to protect us from radio interference, is another clock chip that oscillates at 14.318 MHz, providing timing signals for peripheral equipment.

In the left rear corner of the motherboard are eight connector slots for expansion boards. These can accommodate disk/diskette drive controllers, video controllers, serial/parallel ports, added memory, network controllers, modems, etc. They are numbered 1 to 8 from left rear to left center, with matching connector brackets on the rear wall and support brackets on the front. The rear brackets may contain connectors for cables to external equipment. All of these slots have the familiar 62 pin connectors like the PC. Six of them also have 36 pin connectors in front, which allow for full 16-bit data transfer—twice as fast as the older 8-bit PC transfer system.

Many standard PC expansion boards with 62 pin connectors will fit these slots and, if logically and electronically compatible with the AT, will work all right. However, some older boards (e.g., the IBM Color/Graphics Adapter board) will not physically fit any slots except those with short connectors.

Bulky data cables from the two or three disk/diskette drives connect to the IBM Fixed Disk and Diskette Adapter board, on the right side at top middle. Therefore, this board fits best in the rightmost slot, No. 8. The IBM Serial/Parallel Adapter board is short and needs only a 62 pin connector slot. Your video controller board requires another slot. This leaves five slots for future expansion.

The most common type of expansion board will probably be a memory board. A typical PC/AT compatible memory board, the *Advantage!*, made by AST Research Inc., requires a long slot, holds up to 3-MB additional main memory, and provides additional serial and parallel ports and a game device port. To install the full amount of memory, you must use a clip-on piggy-back board. This makes the memory board so fat that it spills into the neighboring slot. Thus it might fit best in Slot 6, with the short IBM Serial/Parallel board beside it in the short Slot 7.

We have arrived back at the starting point of our tour of the system unit. You should now have an intuitive grasp of its various components, how they work together to process your data, and how the system is modularized so that components can be developed independently. A clear picture of these relationships is beneficial to any programmer and particularly helpful to you when your programming involves close work with peripheral equipment.

3

Main Memory

Concepts

* How much memory can a PC or a PC/AT address? * How is it organized for use by the various hardware and software subsystems? * How does this organization relate to the physical arrangement of the memory chips?

In the last chapter you took a look at the hardware inside the PC/AT. Starting with Chapter 6, you will consider the Intel 80286 CPU in detail at the assembly language level. Until then, you will be concerned with installing and using the DOS operating system and executing programs. This doesn't require much knowledge of the underlying hardware organization. However, the question of the amount of main memory allocated to various subsystems will come up. In fact, the question of the total amount of main memory installed in the PC/AT and its location on the motherboard and expansion boards appeared already in the last chapter. Thus, it seems useful to consider this allocation now, instead of alluding to it several times in the next chapters on DOS.

The memory question is complicated by the fact that the PC/AT, or rather its Intel 80286 CPU, can operate in two modes. In one mode, called the *real* mode, the 80286 treats main memory just like the earlier members of the Intel 8086 family. When you boot the PC/AT, the 80286 starts operating in this mode, hence its main memory is allocated just as in the earlier members of the PC family. The second mode, the *protected* mode, is the principal distinguishing feature of the PC/AT and its CPU. In this mode, programs and data belonging to different users can be segregated in different parts of memory, protected from each other, stored on disk when not immediately needed, and automatically retrieved and restarted in main memory when called for. In protected mode, the PC/AT can use far more main memory than in real mode. We shall first consider main memory organization in real mode, since most allocation problems already occur there. Then we shall look at memory use in protected mode and finally at the physical arrangement of memory in the PC/AT.

In all members of the PC family, memory is organized into eight-bit bytes, each of which has a unique address. In the earlier members of the family, and in the PC/AT in real mode, the byte addresses are twenty bits long. (These addresses are constructed in a somewhat peculiar way from two sixteen-bit words, called the segment and offset parts of the address. This technique is described in Chapter 6. Until then it is only necessary to remember that addresses are, in fact, twenty bits long.) Since $2^{20} = 1,048,576$, earlier PCs and the PC/AT in real mode can address *one megabyte* of main memory.

Most PCs—even many PC/ATs—will not have this maximum amount of memory installed. Nevertheless, IBM has allocated the entire one megabyte of addresses somewhat rigidly to the operating system, to BASIC, and to your own programs. Figure 3.1 shows this allocation in detail. Note that the amount of memory occupied by DOS is given only approximately. This is necessary because DOS's size changes with different versions. The figure given is for DOS 3.0. As a result, the amount of memory allocated to your programs is not exactly known until you load DOS.

Several other features of this allocation scheme need interpretation. First, a rudimentary BASIC interpreter and the BIOS (a part of the operating system) are encoded in the ROM chips installed on the PC/AT motherboard, at addresses hex f6000 and above. Second, IBM reserves *specific* memory addresses for other custom ROM chips and for various video display buffers. Since one of the display buffers is always present and since DOS cannot use noncontiguous blocks of memory for your programs, you are barred from using much of the reserved memory for any purpose, even if some of the devices concerned are not installed. Actually, this is a major step toward software compatibility, even if it does irritate memory hungry users who produce their own software.

The reserved addresses for custom ROM memory have sometimes been used for device controllers encoded in ROM on expansion boards, and could be used by software systems encoded in ROM cartridges for other members of the PC family. Thus it's understandable that IBM reserved so much space (216 K) for ROM memory. But why is so much memory allocated to the video displays?

Some simple arithmetic shows why the displays need so much memory. In text mode, a standard 25 row by 80 column display consists of 25 x 80 = 2000 characters. Each character needs one byte for its ASCII code (there are $2^8 = 256$ different characters) and one byte for its attribute code. The attribute code indicates foreground and background color and whether the character is underlined or blinking. Thus 4-K bytes are needed for a standard text screen. The memory reserved for a video display will accommodate eight separate text screens, so that you can switch back and forth rapidly. While the IBM Monochrome Display Adapter board has only the 4-K memory for one screen starting at address hex B0000, some compatible boards have the entire 32-K memory installed.

Many users require a video controller with color graphics capability as well as a monochrome controller for text. IBM reserved disjoint memory blocks for them in order to make that possible.

Starting address (hex)	Memory block	Block size
00000	Interrupt vectors (See Chapters 6 and 7.)	1 K
00400	Temporary storage for the BIOS. DOS. and BASIC	.5 K
00600	Occupied by DOS 3.0 (See Section 5.3.)	About 35 K
About 09000	Available for your program	About 603.5 K
a0000	Reserved for displays*	64 K
b0000	Monochrome video controller display	32 K
b8000	Color/Graphics video controller display	32 K
c0000	Reserved for ROM*	216 K
f6000	ROM BASIC	32 K
fe000	ROM BIOS	8 K
		1024 K

* For example, the IBM Enhanced Graphics Adapter board has a 16 K ROM chip, containing a BIOS extension, with addresses in the range hex c0000 to hex c3fff. With the maximum amount of display memory installed, the Adapter can use the entire display buffer range hex a0000 to bffff.

Figure 3.1 PC/AT real mode main memory allocation

The IBM Color/Graphics Adapter has a maximum resolution of 640 x 200 pixels in two colors. These dots are either one color or the other, so require only one bit of memory each. This requires

640 x 200 / 8 (bits per byte) = about 16 K bytes.

However, to produce smooth animation, you need to store two whole pictures, so that you can alter one copy while displaying the other. Thus, Color/Graphics compatible controllers made by other manufacturers often require twice that amount of memory, the entire 32 K allocated.

Yet other video controller boards use the reserved memory somewhat differently. For example, a Hercules standard monochrome graphics board has a resolution of about 720 x 350 pixels, needing

720 x 350 x 2 / 8 = about 64 K bytes.

These boards use *both* blocks of display addresses, so cannot operate simultaneously with a Color/Graphics compatible board.

In summary, in earlier PCs and in the PC/AT real mode, memory addresses above hex A0000 are reserved for use by special hardware, leaving only 640 K standard memory for you to share with the operating system. In the PC/AT, this is called *base* memory.

In protected mode, the PC/AT uses an entirely different memory addressing technique. The important fact is that the protected mode addresses are 24 bits long. Since

$$2^{24} = 16,777,216$$

the PC/AT can address *sixteen megabytes* of main memory in protected mode. Any PC/AT memory above the one megabyte real mode limit is called *extended memory*.

You can use extended memory in two ways. The obvious way is to use software that is designed for the PC/AT's extended capacity. However, this software would be inherently incompatible with the other members of the PC family. When this book was being written, almost no such software had yet appeared. The second way is to incorporate into ordinary PC software some routines that shift the PC/AT into protected mode, move data to or from extended memory, then shift back into real mode. A technique for writing such software is described in Chapter 10. You can also use a routine of this type that is included with DOS 3.0: the **vdisk** virtual disk driver, described in Chapter 9.

With this overall organization in mind, we can review the physical memory layout inside the PC/AT system unit. The motherboard incorporates at least 256 K RAM, and if piggy-back chips are installed, it carries 512 K. The BIOS and BASIC ROM chips are also installed on the motherboard. The display buffer memory is installed on one or two display controller boards mounted in expansion slots. You can obtain expansion memory boards to add additional RAM. Of this, 128 K can be used to bring the PC/AT up to its full complement of base memory (512 K on the motherboard + 128 K = 640 K maximum). Expansion memory boards can also provide extended memory, addressed above hex FFFFF = 1 MB. A typical product, the AST Research Inc. *Advantage!* board, can carry up to three MB of RAM that can be allocated in any logical way to standard or extended memory. As many as five of these can be installed in the expansion slots.

4

Introducing DOS

Contents

This chapter introduces DOS with a brief overview and history. Its first section describes in detail the various manuals, diskettes, and diskette files that make up DOS, indicating where you can find information about them in this book or in other references. The second section gives step by step guidelines for installing DOS on a PC/AT. The steps necessary to reset the battery driven real-time clock are also included in this process and described here.

4.1 A quick look at DOS

Concepts

∗ What is DOS and how is it evolving?   ∗ What components are delivered with DOS 3.0 ?   ∗ What other manuals are useful?   ∗ What are the files on the DOS diskettes?   ∗ Which files are described in this book? Where?   ∗ Where can you find information on the others?

DOS (an acronym for Disk Operating System) is the principal operating system for the IBM personal computer family and a large number of other microcomputers with similar capabilities. An operating system consists of a set of programs that organize the data being processed and direct its flow, execute other programs (especially your application software), provide input/output facilities for all programs, and perform many other tasks helpful to programmers and computer users in general. DOS was developed by the Microsoft

Corporation, a software company with a wide selection of products, as a generic operating system suitable for many different computers. Microsoft licenses computer vendors like IBM to adapt DOS to their particular hardware, make other minor changes as appropriate, and market it under their own name. Thus, DOS for the IBM PC family is slightly different from DOS for other computers. However, the general structure and the appearance to users is maintained over the range of machines that run DOS.

DOS for the IBM PC has evolved rapidly, with major changes introduced in new versions released simultaneously with several advances in hardware. The first version, DOS 1.0, was short-lived because it supported only single sided 160 KB diskette drives. The market immediately demanded larger input/output media, so IBM began providing double-sided 320-KB diskette drives as standard equipment and DOS 1.1 to support them. Introduction of the PC/XT, with its 10-MB fixed disk, was accompanied by the appearance of DOS 2.0, a major extension of the DOS 1.1 functionality. DOS 2.1 followed soon after: its documentation was reorganized into a neater format, and several troublesome DOS 2.0 bugs were fixed. Most recently, DOS 3.0 was released with the PC/AT. This was necessary to support the new 1.2-MB diskette and 20 MB fixed disk drives. DOS 3.0 is really a transitional version, because it does not support many of the advanced features of the Intel 80286 CPU of the PC/AT. As this book nears completion, IBM is introducing DOS 3.1, which implements networking, an important 80286 application.

DOS 3.0 manuals

DOS 3.0 is supplied on two 360-KB diskettes with the following manuals. (Numbers in brackets refer to the bibliography at the end of this book.)

Application Setup Guide This booklet [12] shows how to use various IBM software packages with DOS.

DOS User's Guide This is a step by step introduction [16] to the most commonly used DOS commands. You may want to read it quickly before beginning to use DOS and to use it as a reference for a short while afterward. Because it's small, what is there can be found quickly.

DOS Reference This manual [14] gives a detailed technical description of all aspects of DOS likely to be helpful to the general user, plus three utility programs—debug, exe2bin, and link—commonly used by programmers.

There is also a *Quick Reference Card* [13] that summarizes the User's Guide.

If you intend to write involved programs using DOS, you will want to purchase another manual [15] separately:

DOS Technical Reference This contains *very* technical information useful mainly to programmers working at the assembly language level.

One other manual, the *Microsoft MS-DOS Operating System: Programmer's Reference Manual* [24], may be useful; it overlaps the IBM manual with the same name, but may contain additional (or corrected) material. No DOS 3.0 edition of the Microsoft manual had yet appeared when this book was completed.

If you are a serious DOS user running more than just one or two software packages, you should become familiar with the organization of the *DOS Reference* manual as soon as possible, to be able to find quick answers to the many questions that will arise. Greater familiarity will come as you search out solutions to each problem. Hardly anyone needs to become *totally* familiar with this book. If you are programming in assembly language, or using assembly language procedures to gain access to DOS services, you should browse through the IBM *DOS Technical Reference* manual. It will seem formidable at first, but some familiarity with its content may lead you to DOS services that help you solve your problems.

DOS diskettes

The two DOS diskettes are labeled DOS and DOS supplementary programs. Their files can be classified as follows:

DOS operating system	Programmers' utilities
General DOS utilities	vdisk source code
International keyboards	
Device drivers	BASIC interpreter
Editor	BASIC demonstration programs

The files on the left are for general use, while those on the right are of interest to programmers. The individual files are described below, with references to more detailed discussions in this book and others.

DOS operating system files
Three files form the heart of DOS:

```
command.com      ibmbio.com      ibmdos.com
```

They are loaded into memory when you start DOS and remain there to provide command services and control execution of other programs. The distinctions between these three files are described in Section 5.3. The two IBM files are *hidden read-only* files: they never appear on directory listings, and you may not erase or change them. The various DOS commands are described in Chapters 5 and 8 ; Chapter 8 is devoted to the new DOS 3.0 features.

General DOS utilities
A number of files contain programs that perform services closely related to DOS:

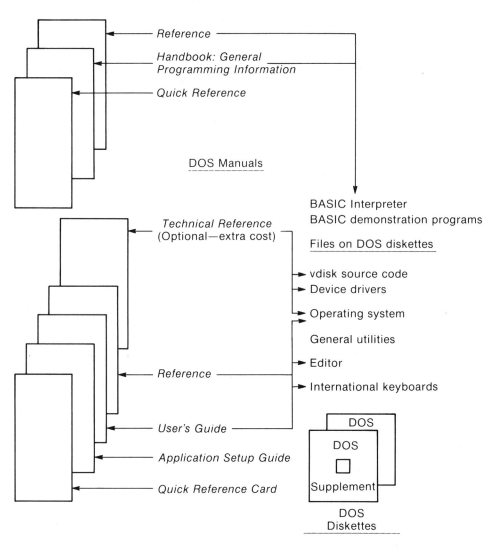

Figure 4.1.1 DOS and BASIC manuals and diskette files

```
assign   .com        find      .exe      print   .com
attrib   .com*       format    .com      recover.com
backup   .com        graftabl.com*       restore.com
chkdsk   .com        graphics.com        share   .exe*
comp     .com        label     .com*     sort    .exe
diskcomp.com         mode      .com      sys     .com
diskcopy.com         more      .com      tree    .com
fdisk    .com
```

*New with   DOS 3.0

You can think of these as part of DOS, but they are organized so that you don't have to load them into memory until you need them. They are described in some detail in Chapters 5 and 8.

International keyboards

DOS 3.0 supports keyboards arranged according to the conventions of several countries. The following **.com** files contain the necessary software.

```
keybfr.com       keybit.com       keybuk.com
keybgr.com       keybsp.com       select.com
```

The **select.com** program can help you install the right software, but it is not flexible enough for general use. The keyboards are described in Section 8.2.

Device drivers

Device drivers are extensions to the operating system that support specific devices. When you buy a new device such as a network, you may receive a driver that you must install. IBM supplies two drivers with DOS:

```
ansi.sys       vdisk.sys
```

The ANSI driver allows you to handle the keyboard and screen like an ANSI standard terminal. It is not discussed in this book; you can find a detailed description in the IBM *DOS Technical Reference* manual, Chapter 2. With the **vdisk** driver you can use part of main memory as a virtual disk. This is described in detail in Section 8.5.

Editor

DOS provides a primitive text editor:

```
edlin.com
```

You may want to use **edlin** for simple text processing because it requires little memory. It is also very general and can sometimes handle symbols in text files that other editors can't touch because they are regarded as special text control symbols. On the other hand, for complex text processing tasks you will probably want to install additional software. This book contains no description of **edlin.** You can find one in reference [25, Chap. 19] or [28, Chap. 7].

Programmers' utilities

The following three utilities are used by programmers to inspect areas of memory, debug assembly language programs, and to set up programs in **.exe** files ready for execution by DOS:

```
debug.com        exe2bin.exe        link.exe
```

Using **debug,** you can load a file or a program into memory, write the contents of an area of memory onto a file, and inspect or change an area of memory. You can load sequences of assembly language commands into memory in binary machine language form, and translate an area of memory back into assembly language form if possible. The **debug** program also lets you set the CPU registers and execute parts of assembly language programs, inspecting the registers as you proceed. Finally, it will do sums and differences in hexadecimal arithmetic. This book contains no detailed description of **debug.** You will find one in the *DOS Reference* manual, Chapter 10. Be prepared for frustration: neither the program nor the manual description is very friendly.

The **exe2bin** utility converts certain program files from the **.exe** format to **.com** format. These formats are discussed in Section 5.4 and the utility itself in Chapter 7 of the *DOS Reference* manual.

When you have compiled or assembled various units and procedures of a program into **.obj** files, you use the **link** utility to link them and perhaps other code from object code libraries to produce the **.exe** program files that DOS can load and execute. This book contains no description of **link**. You can find one in Chapter 9 of the *DOS Reference* manual. This linker was developed by Microsoft Corporation, and different versions are provided with various Microsoft language packages—Pascal, FORTRAN, C, and assembly, for example. The best documentation for this linker is in reference [23], the manual for the Microsoft Assembler Package, Version 3.0. Still other linkers are available from other software houses, with different features regarding library formats, program overlays, and so on. If you are developing software, you should find the best linker for your job, and be sure your documentation matches your software.

vdisk source code

IBM has provided with DOS 3.0 in file **vdisk.lst** the complete assembly language source listing of the virtual disk device driver **vdisk.sys** as a guide for systems programmers who need to write drivers for other equipment.

BASIC interpreter

Although the BASIC language is not a part of the operating system, IBM supplies with DOS 3.0 the two program files necessary to run IBM BASIC Version 3.0:

```
basic.com        basica.com
```

This book gives no description of BASIC. There are many introductory texts available. If you are generally familiar with the language, you will find the three manuals delivered with the PC/AT itself, references [9], [10], and [11], to be well organized and very helpful.

BASIC demonstration programs

A number of BASIC demonstration programs are also supplied with DOS:

```
art        .bas      comm     .bas      musica  .bas
ball       .bas      donkey   .bas      piechart.bas
circle    .bas      mortgage.bas      samples .bas
colorbar.bas      music    .bas      space   .bas
```

These serve as models for writing BASIC programs that use the various PC features, especially the Color/Graphics Adapter and the speaker. The colorbar program is also a good utility for choosing colors and for testing a color monitor.

4.2 Installing DOS on the PC/AT

Concepts

* How do you install or reinstall DOS on a PC/AT?   * How do you reset the PC/AT real-time clock?

A theorem of computer science states that

the hardest item to find in any manual is usually the one that describes what you have to do first.

The PC/AT is no exception. The relevant material is in the PC/AT *Installation and Setup* and *Guide to Operations* manuals, Chapters 1 and 4 of the *DOS 3.0 User's Guide*, and in Chapter 3 of the *DOS 3.0 Reference* manual. With some persistence, you can find out how to get your computer up and running, how to start DOS from the diskettes provided, and how to set up your fixed disk. But the *DOS 3.0 Reference* manual makes no reference to the others; it just assumes that DOS is already running. The *DOS 3.0 User's Guide* does not refer to the PC/AT manuals, and the important information in them is buried in masses of detail about installing optional equipment and diagnosing machine failures. Amazingly, the word "setup" is not found in the table of contents of the *Installation and Setup* manual! However, the needed information—a reference to the **setup** program—is indicated on the last page of that manual in Section 7, "Power-on self test," and in Section 2, "Testing your IBM Personal Computer AT," of the *Guide to Operations*. Even in those locations, the instructions for running this program are wrong!

The **setup** program must be used whenever various equipment options are installed or changed, like memory expansion boards, disk drives, display controller boards, and the battery that powers the real-time clock and the small system configuration memory. This obviously includes the first time that you start the computer! When you install DOS on the PC/AT, it is useful, or at least reassuring, to run **setup** again to make sure you know the list of equipment the computer recognizes. This discussion considers only that use of the program. If you need to install new equipment, follow the steps in the *Installation and Setup* manual in complete detail!

You should also use the **setup** program to change the time and date of the real-time clock—for example, when you change between standard and daylight savings time.

The **setup** program is on the *Diagnostics Diskette* shipped with the *Guide to Operations* manual. To run it, boot from that diskette. That is, place it in drive **a:** (the high capacity drive in the top slot), and turn the computer on or press the **Ctrl-Alt-Del** keystroke combination. To run **setup,** enter option **4** (not **F1** as instructed by the manuals). The program then leads you through some menus. First you can verify or reset the date and time on the real-time clock. Then you can verify the equipment installed: for example, the diskette and fixed disk drives, amount of motherboard memory, amount of expansion board memory, and choice of monochrome or color/graphics display controller board as the primary display (the one used whenever the machine is booted).

Presumably, **setup** says that you have Type 2 fixed disk drive **c:.** (Type 2 is the standard 20 MB PC/AT drive. The PC/AT BIOS recognizes, but does not necessarily support, fourteen different types.) If this is not the case, do not use these guidelines, but refer directly to the *DOS 3.0 Reference* manual and any manual that came with your equipment.

These guidelines also assume that you have backed up all files that you may already have stored on the fixed disk **c:.** This of course is no concern if you are installing DOS on a new system, but important if you are reinstalling DOS after some catastrophe has damaged an existing installation. If you are installing DOS on a system that will be running another operating system as well, do not use these guidelines, but refer directly to the *DOS 3.0 Reference* manual and any manual that came with the other system.

Now, to install DOS, insert in drive **a:** the *DOS* diskette (not the DOS Supplemental Programs diskette) that came with DOS 3.0. Turn on the power or reboot by entering **Ctrl-Alt-Del.** When the DOS prompt **A⟩** appears, DOS is in control and is asking you for a command. *Warning: what you do next will destroy any data previously saved on the fixed disk. Be sure you have backed up anything you may need again!* Enter **fdisk.** This will execute a DOS utility program to set up your fixed disk. That program communicates with you by means of menus. Select Option 1, **Create DOS partition,** and respond **yes,** you want to use the entire fixed disk for DOS. When **fdisk** is finished, the prompt will appear again. Now you want to format the disk. Enter **format c:/s/v,** and when asked, respond that it's all right to destroy any data already on the disk. This operation will record on the disk the directory information

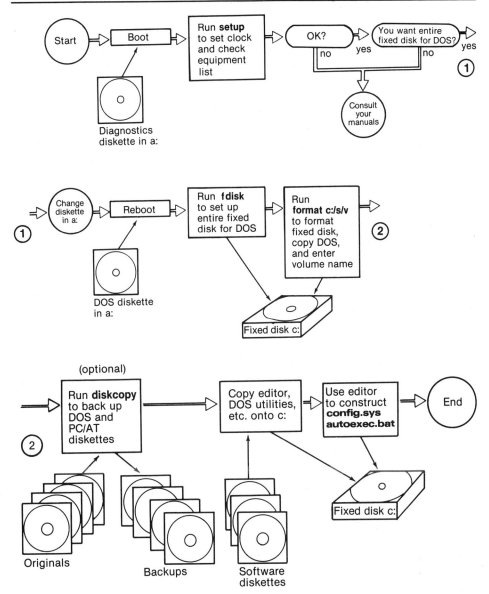

Figure 4.2.1 Installing DOS on the PC/AT

necessary to keep track of the file structure, copy three DOS files from the DOS diskette in drive **a:,** and ask you for a volume name for the fixed disk. Supply one, up to eleven letters long.

Now DOS is installed on drive **c:.** You no longer need to have a DOS disk-ette in drive **a:** when you turn on the power or reboot. One of the first things you should do is read the instructions for the **diskcopy** command in Chapter 7 of the *DOS 3.0 Reference* manual and use it to make backup copies of the two diskettes that came with DOS and the two that were shipped with the *Guide* *to Operations* manual. (This step is optional—you may have done it already.) Put the originals away for safekeeping.

You will probably want to follow the next few steps to get your software running under DOS. If this is new to you, you will want to read the manuals at the same time and proceed very slowly, so these steps could take several hours or days or weeks, depending on your experience and priorities. First, you will want to use the DOS **copy** command to load your word processor or text editor onto drive **c:** in order to create text files. The manual for your editing software will tell you which files you'll need. If you don't have your own editing software, you'll have to use the rudimentary editor **edlin** that you'll find on one of the DOS diskettes. When you become familiar with DOS you will decide which DOS utility programs you want to copy to **c:**; you will find these on the DOS diskettes, too. You may also want to load some utilities from other sources. Gradually, you will decide how you want your system set up, and design your **config.sys** and **autoexec.bat** files accordingly. You will create these with your editing software, and load them on drive **c:** with any other required files. (The **config.sys** and **autoexec.bat** files are described in Sections 5.3 and 5.4.) From then on, DOS will set up your customized system every time you turn on the power or reboot.

5

DOS Structure, I

Contents

This chapter is devoted to a general description of DOS, so that you will be able to understand easily the new features of DOS 3.0 detailed in Chapter 8 and even anticipate features of future operating systems for the PC/AT. Just outlining the standard features of DOS from a user's point of view would be insufficient. For one thing, you may be new to DOS or a veteran of its older versions. Moreover, such an approach would be short-sighted. DOS has grown rapidly over the past several years, and some of its features are accidental. To appreciate what may be coming next, you need some insight into the overall plan that DOS is trying to fulfill.

The first section considers the tasks that may be included in the "job description" of an operating system and discusses which are in fact addressed by DOS. Later sections discuss in conceptual terms DOS's approach to handling these tasks. In particular, in this chapter we will consider the DOS file system, how DOS configures your machine when you boot it, and its provisions for executing programs and directing data flow.

Several other types of DOS services, particularly input/output, are provided through software interrupts. Since understanding this technique requires some familiarity with programming at the assembly language level, discussion of these services is placed in Chapter 7. The intervening Chapter 6 is devoted to the Intel 8086 CPU and its instruction set and assembly language.

The new aspects of DOS 3.0 are discussed together in Chapter 8. Thus, if your aim is solely to learn about these new features, you might want to skip ahead to that chapter. However, you should realize that some of the new features are based on some of the more involved concepts covered in Chapters 5 through 7.

5.1 What is DOS for?

Concepts

* What kinds of tasks do operating systems do?   * Which of these tasks are handled by DOS?   * Different operating systems *vs* different versions of the same operating system

---

We'll begin our overview of DOS by considering first a number of tasks that may be included in the "job description" of an operating system. Some of these tasks are familiar to anyone who has used a microcomputer. Others are usually considered only on larger computers and have not been addressed yet by microcomputer operating systems like DOS. Still others are on the borderline; newer versions of DOS and other operating systems are beginning to deal with these tasks on the PC/AT. A catalog of tasks for an operating system generally contains at least the following items.

1. Organizing data into a file system.
2. Maintaining that system.
3. Directing the flow of data among the computer components and peripheral equipment.
4. Executing programs.
5. Keeping track of usage by individual accounts.

6. Setting up the computer when it is initially turned on and determining how it looks to users.

7. Allocating memory to programs.

8. Providing input/output facilities.

9. Providing means of interaction among programs and their environment.

10. Organizing the computer service accorded multiple users or tasks and preventing interference.

11. Recording and diagnosing system failures.

Tasks 1 to 5 are apparent to most end users of computer systems. Tasks 7 to 11 are familiar to programmers, but we try to keep this kind of thing hidden from ordinary people. All of these tasks are addressed by DOS except Nos. 5, 10, and 11. With the introduction of DOS 3.1, DOS is beginning to handle No. 10, as well.

In later sections we shall discuss, again in conceptual terms, DOS's approach to handling these tasks. It's the *conceptual* solution that's important. Different conceptual solutions mean *different* operating systems: for example, DOS, XENIX, and the UCSD p-System operating system have different conceptual frameworks. On the other hand, implementation of a single conceptual solution on different machines is subject to historical and commercial accident, and gives rise to different *versions* of an operating system, like PC-DOS and the various versions of MS-DOS for other machines.

5.2 DOS file system and related commands

Concepts

* DOS files and directories * Directory names and file names * Wild cards * Special device names * Volume and drive names * Issuing DOS commands; special keystrokes * Current drive and directories; command **cd** * Redirecting drive references with the **assign** command * Formatting, copying, and comparing volumes

---

DOS arranges data into a hierarchical system that reflects some of our intuitive ways of dealing with large amounts of information. For example, consider the organization of the Chapters One through Five of this book, shown in Figure 5.2.1. The data structure in Figure 5.2.1 is known as a *tree*. In computer science, trees are always depicted upside down, like the family tree in the *Encyclopaedia Brittanica* that lists the monarchs of England. The *root* is at the top and the *leaves* at the bottom.

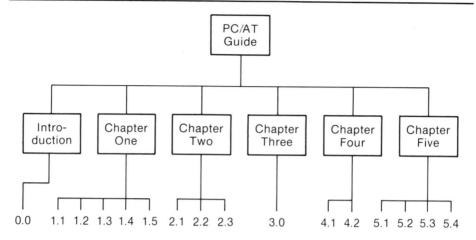

Figure 5.2.1 Tree structure of the Introduction and Chapters One through Five

DOS files and directories

DOS organizes information into *files* that correspond to the leaves of a tree. Several types of files are distinguished, but these differences have hardly any effect on general use of the file system. They will be discussed later, as necessary.

The files are gathered into *directories*, and directories into directories at higher levels until a *root directory* is reached. DOS file names are constructed by including character strings referring to all directories in the path from the root to a file and one indicating the file itself. This book was actually written on a PC/AT using DOS. Reflecting the structure of Figure 5.2.1, the text of this section was in a file called

c:\at_guide\chap_5\s05_02.ms.

The string **c:** is the name of the root directory on drive **c:** (the fixed disk drive), and **c:\at_guide** is the name of a DOS directory, a *subdirectory* of the root directory. In turn, **c:\at_guide\chap_5** is a subdirectory of **c:\at_guide**. For the exact syntax of the strings that make up a file name, consult Chapter 2 of the *DOS 3.0 Reference* manual, reference [14]. The most important things to remember are the maximum string lengths: eight characters, optionally followed by a period and up to three more characters.

In some descriptions of the DOS file system, the individual character strings like **chap_5** and **s05_02.ms** are regarded as directory and file names. That is misleading, because the same string can occur in the names of different directories or files. For example, consider the file name for the manuscript of this section and the name for a similar file containing its previous version:

c:\at_guide\chap_5\s05_02.ms
c:\at_guide.old\chap_5\a05_02.ms.

In this context, it doesn't make sense to speak of *the* file **s05_02.ms** in *the* directory **chap_5**. Nevertheless, when the context is clear, this technique provides useful abbreviations. For example, the directory and file might be referred to simply by

```
c:\at_guide\chap_5                chap_5
c:\at_guide\chap_5\s05_02.ms      s05_02.ms
```

if no other directory or file names under consideration ended with the strings on the right. When this abbreviation system is used, an unabbreviated directory name is often called a *path name*. This book will use such abbreviations often when the context is clear.

These abbreviations have been introduced as documentation aids. There is a way to use them on line with DOS, but that involves the notions of current drive and current directories. We will come back to this later.

Versions of DOS before 2.0 permitted only one level of directory: no subdirectories were allowed. That type of organization is not convenient for handling the amount of data that can be stored on large, media-like fixed disks. With Version 2.0, released simultaneously with the PC/XT, which has a 10-MB fixed disk, Microsoft supported subdirectories. This technique was adapted from Microsoft's XENIX operating system, which in turn was modeled on Bell Laboratories' UNIX system. UNIX' hierarchical file organization had proved extremely convenient, especially for time-sharing systems. Microsoft was apparently unable to incorporate all of UNIX' convenient file handling features, and DOS 3.0 is still noticeably deficient in some areas. For example, it is not always possible to handle all files in a given directory as a single unit. Moreover, in some contexts, DOS will not recognize a file name that includes a directory specification; you *must* use the abbreviation scheme just described, involving current directories.

Strings following periods in directory or file names, as in the examples **at_guide.old** or **s05_02.ms** (using the abbreviation technique of the last paragraph) are called directory or file name *extensions*. The DOS file system makes no attempt to interpret them. However, it is common practice to use an extension to indicate some attribute of the file—like "old version" or "manuscript" in these examples. This helps identify related files. Some other parts of DOS, notably the program execution subsystem, handle files differently depending on their file name extensions.

Some DOS functions can refer to *all* file names of a certain form. To describe classes of file names, DOS provides the *wild card* mechanism. The wild card characters **?** and * can be used in any file name to stand for any single character or any string of characters, respectively, except for symbols like \ and the period that have special meaning to DOS. Thus, in a file name, the string **s05_0?.*** can stand for any string consisting of **s05_0** followed by a single character, then optionally a period followed by a sequence of at most three characters (this sequence may be empty).

Special device names

DOS reserves the following file names for referring to special devices as though they were files:

aux	Same as com1.
com1 .. com2	Devices attached to serial ports 1 .. 2.
con	For input, the keyboard. For output, the screen.
lpt1 .. lpt3	Devices attached to parallel ports 1 .. 3.
nul	Dummy device for discarding output.
prn	Same as lpt1.

For example, the file name **prn** usually refers to the character stream going to the first parallel printer. This stream is handled like any text file except that its length is unbounded. You can use the **nul** device occasionally when you *must* specify an output device but you really just want to ignore the output.

Media and drives

The data in DOS files are recorded on media like diskettes or memory chips that are read and written by various devices like diskette drives or your computer's memory circuits. You can have multiple copies of a file on different media. Even though the recording techniques may be vastly different, DOS makes these files appear identical to you. Directories are entered along with the files on each medium, to indicate the file organization, and are recorded in more or less the same way as ordinary files. Directories also include the date and time of the last file modification. Each storage medium has exactly one root directory.

Since you may change the data in a DOS file, you may obtain on different media (for example, different diskettes) files with the same name but different data content. This can easily lead to confusion and error. Careful choice of file names and careful file updating and backup can help you avoid this problem.

Some devices, like diskette drives, permit interchangeable media, but others, like fixed disk drives, don't. It is useful to have names for interchangeable media, like individual diskettes. You can easily write a diskette's name by hand on its label. However, DOS can't read that, nor can any other program. Therefore DOS permits you to assign a machine-readable *volume name* to any data storage medium. DOS makes no real use of this name, because it is difficult for you to keep it consistent with a name you write on the label. Since one of DOS's aims is to let you handle in the same way data stored in files on different media, you may also assign volume names to non-interchangeable media like fixed disks.

DOS uses *drive names* **a:**, **b:**, etc., to refer to the devices that read and write file storage media. (The term suggests the most common device, the diskette drive, and may seem inappropriate for other devices.) The name of the root directory on the medium in a drive consists of the drive name followed by \.

Figure 5.2.2 represents some files on storage media in input/output devices, showing the various types of names.

Issuing DOS commands

So far in this section, we have been concerned only with nomenclature. From now on, though, you will be issuing commands using these names to do various tasks. You issue a DOS command by typing it and execute a program by typing its name, in each case followed by the **Enter** key. Programs are stored in files with extension **.bat, .com**, or **.exe**; the *program name* is the file name without the extension. To determine the exact syntax for executing DOS commands and utility programs you should refer to the *DOS 3.0 Quick Reference Card, User's Guide,* or *Reference* manual, references [13], [14] and [16].

When you execute a command, the DOS file **command.com** should be in the current directory on the current drive, as described in the next paragraph. Otherwise, you will have to use a path specification as described in Section 5.4.

A number of keystrokes have special meanings for DOS:

Ctrl-Break   Terminate execution of a DOS command. (This also terminates a program, but only at a point where the program itself requests a DOS service.)

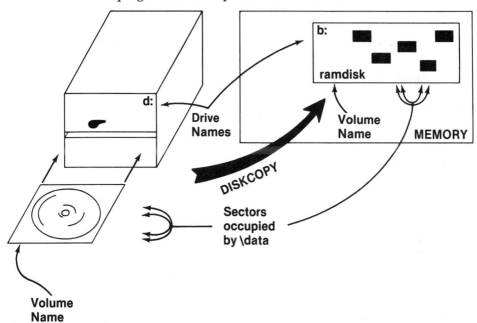

Figure 5.2.2 Files on media in drives

Drive **a:** is a diskette drive, into which is inserted a diskette with (optional) volume name **floppy1**. Drive **b:** is a portion of memory configured to operate like a diskette drive. Its medium, nonremovable chips, is given the (optional) name **ramdisk**. If the media sizes agree, DOS could execute a **diskcopy** command, which might copy a file **data** from noncontiguous diskette sectors to noncontiguous memory areas as shown.

Ctrl-C	Same as Ctrl-Break.
Ctrl-NumLock	Pause during DOS screen output, until you touch another key.
Ctrl-PrtSc	Route all DOS screen output to prn as well, until you enter this keystroke again.
Esc	Ignore the current command line and start a new one.
F1 .. F5	These are used for repeating DOS commands, perhaps with minor changes. Consult the *DOS 3.0 User's Guide*, reference [16, Chap. 2], for details.
Shift-PrtSc	Print the screen.

Current drive and directories

So that you needn't repeat the name of the same drive for many successive operations, DOS always regards one particular drive as the *current drive*. You may omit the drive name when issuing DOS commands referring to this drive. The DOS command **cd** can be used to ascertain the current drive, and the current drive can be changed merely by typing its name.

In order to provide systematic abbreviations for long file and subdirectory names, DOS always regards some particular directory on each input/output device as the *current directory* for that device. If you don't tell it otherwise, DOS assumes that the root directory is the current one. The command **cd** also serves to ascertain and change the current directory for a drive. If you have to tell DOS the name of a file in a current directory, and that directory is not a root directory, then you may omit the current directory name and a \ from the front end of the file name. Using the example mentioned several paragraphs earlier, if drive **c:** were the current drive, and **c:\at_guide** were the current directory on that drive, then you could refer to file

c:\at_guide\chap_5\s05_02.ms

by the abbreviation **chap_5\s05_02.ms**. If you change the current drive by entering the command **a:**, you still need not use the entire name for this file; you could use the abbreviation **c:chap_5\s05_02.ms.**

It's important to remember that each drive has a current directory and one drive is the current drive. You may omit the name of the current drive or a current directory from a DOS command. If you issue a DOS command that affects a file, but give neither drive nor directory name, then DOS will refer to the current directory on the current drive. Directory and file name abbreviations based on assumptions about the current directories and drive will be used extensively from now on in this book.

(It's possible for you to assign a current directory for a given drive, then manually change the medium so that the assignment no longer makes sense. DOS avoids confusion by checking for the *presence* of the current directory; if it is absent, then DOS regards the root directory as current.)

Under these abbreviation rules, the symbol \ can be used to name the root directory on the current drive. (For example, if the current drive is **c:**, then this root directory is **c:** and you may omit the drive name.) Two other very short abbreviations are provided. The period alone (or sometimes the empty string) refers to the current directory. For example, if the current drive is **c:** and the current directory on **c:** is **at_guide\chap_5**, then these commands all list this directory on the screen:

```
dir c:\at_guide\chap_5     dir at_guide\chap_5     dir.
                           dir c:                  dir
```

Finally, the symbol **..** is always used as the name of the parent of the current directory, if there is one. In this example, **..** can be used to refer to the directory **at_guide.**

Redirecting drive references with the assign command

A useful but dangerous DOS command is available to redirect input/output requests from one drive to another. You may want to use this to run on your PC/AT a PC program that expects input files on the current directory of a diskette in drive **b:**. You may have no drive **b:**, or you may want to speed input/output by placing these files in the current directory on the fixed disk drive **c:**. If you enter the command **assign b = c**, DOS will replace *every* reference to drive **b:** by one to drive **c:**. The command **assign** by itself will undo this provision. Warning: this is particularly dangerous if you really have a drive **b:** ! A careless command to erase something on **b:** (for example, its root directory) could be redirected to **c:** with disastrous consequences.

Formatting, copying, and comparing volumes

Data stored on different types of media are arranged by DOS so that they appear to you to have the same organization. The data in a single file need not be stored in contiguous parts of a medium. (If files were always stored in contiguous parts, the empty spaces created by erasing small files might not individually accommodate a large new file; you might be unable to store a new file, even though the medium had lots of free space.) DOS manages space allocation on a medium by means of a special file called a *file allocation table* (FAT). Each directory entry contains information leading DOS to an entry in the FAT. The FAT tells which areas of the medium, in what order, contain the corresponding data. Figure 5.2.3 illustrates this setup on a diskette medium.

Fortunately, end users are normally not concerned with the level of detail found in the FAT. DOS's function is to let you refer to files by their location in a directory on a medium in a device; DOS translates this method of address, using the FAT, into a physical location on the device.

DOS provides a utility program, **format**, that sets up the FAT for a new medium. If the medium is a disk or diskette, this utility also records some

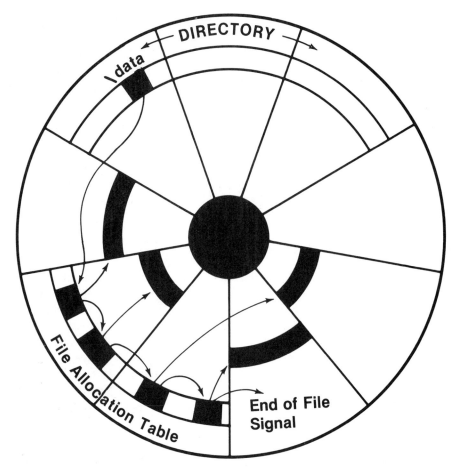

Figure 5.2.3 A file on a diskette

data dividing it into sectors; these are used by DOS, with the computer's timing signals, to locate data passing by the reading apparatus. Another utility program, **chkdsk**, is provided to check integrity of the FAT and repair it if that is desired and possible. (Malfunctioning programs can occasionally damage the FAT so that use of the medium is impaired.) The utility **recover** can be used to recover information from a physically damaged medium.

Like the three commands described in the last paragraph, several others are concerned with entire volumes. Commands **vol** and **label** allow you to ascertain or change the volume name of the medium in a given drive (**label** is a new DOS 3.0 feature). The DOS utility programs **diskcopy** and **diskcomp** will copy or compare entire volumes. To use these utilities you don't specify volume names, but just the drive names: they merely copy or compare the volumes currently on different drives, or volumes successively placed in the same drive.

Summary and examples of file handling commands

This section concludes with a summary and examples of all DOS file handling commands. Since command and program execution syntax are similar, no distinction is made between DOS commands and utility programs. Recall, however, that the commands are all built into DOS, whereas a utility program file must be present in the appropriate directory before it can be executed.

So far all the DOS commands discussed have been concerned with entire volumes of storage media:

assign   Redirect all references from one drive to another.
cd   Ascertain or change the current drive or the current directory for a given drive.
chdir   Alternate spelling for cd.
chkdsk   Check and perhaps repair a FAT.
diskcomp   Compare two volumes.
diskcopy   Copy a volume.
format   Format a new volume.
label   Change the name of the volume in a drive (new with DOS 3.0).
recover   Recover information from a damaged medium.
vol   Ascertain the name of the volume in a drive.

Here are some typical examples of their use:

cd c: Determine the current directory on drive c:.
cd at_guide   Change the current directory on the current drive to at_guide.
chkdsk a:/f   Check the FAT on the medium in drive a: and fix it if necessary.
diskcopy a: b: Copy the volume in a: onto the medium in b:.

DOS includes the following commands that process whole directories:

backup   Make a condensed backup copy of all files below a given directory, optionally omitting those that haven't changed since the last backup process.
dir   List a directory.
md   Alternate spelling for mkdir.
mkdir   Make a new directory ready to receive file entries.
restore Read backup copies made by the backup command.
rd   Alternate spelling for rmdir.
rmdir   Remove an old directory whose files have all been erased.
tree   List all files and subdirectories below a given directory.

Here are some typical examples:

dir c: List the current directory on drive c:.
md c:baby   Make a new directory called baby, an offspring of the current directory on c:.

DOS commands and utilities that operate with individual files include

copy	Copy a file.
del	Alternate spelling for erase.
erase	Erase a file.
find	List all lines in a text file that include (or, alternatively, do not include) a given string.
more	List a file, pausing after each screenful.
print	Send a file to a queue of files that will be transmitted to an output device simultaneously with subsequent computer operations.
ren	Alternate spelling for rename.
rename	Rename a file.
sort	Sort a text file according to the standard ASCII character sequence, starting at a given column.
type	List a file.

Here are some typical examples:

copy c:s05_02.ms a:	Copy file s05_02.ms in the current directory on c: to the current directory on a: .
print s05_0?.*	Queue for printing on prn all files fitting the given wildcard description.
rename c:x y	Rename file x in the current directory on c:, calling it y.
sort names /r/+10	Sort the text file names in the current directory on the current drive line by line in reverse alphabetical order, starting with column 10.

The **print** utility is a program of the type called *print spooler*. Unfortunately, its queue is maintained separately from the usual data stream en route to the output device. Thus subsequent computer operations involving that device will become confused with this queue, and output will not be transmitted correctly.

If you want maximum assurance that information written on a file is correct, you can use the **verify** command to set a software switch that will cause DOS to compare the result of any file writing operation against the original copy. This security is optional because it is so expensive in terms of input/output time.

You should remember that this section is just a *summary* of the DOS file handling capabilities. There is no attempt to give complete descriptions here, either of the command syntax or of the command functions. In fact, most of the commands listed here have features or special cases that were not mentioned. For detailed information on the individual commands, consult Chapters 2, 3, 5, and 6 of the *DOS 3.0 Reference* manual.

5.3 How DOS sets up your computer

Concepts

* Power On Self Test * The boot record loads DOS. * BIOS, device drivers and DOS layers * **ibmbio.com** and **ibmdos.com** * Resident and transient parts of **command.com** * Autoexec files * DOS memory utilization * **config.sys** file * ANSI device driver * Setting screen modes, the prompt, and the time and date

---

Booting DOS

Each time you turn on your computer or enter the keystroke **Ctrl-Alt-Del** for a cold or warm boot, DOS sets up various facilities for you and your software to use. Parts of this process are always carried out the same way, but others depend on your own options. Some of these optional initialization routines use the DOS feature known as an *autoexec* file, which will be discussed later in Section 5.4. However, the various steps that are carried out by an autoexec file are mentioned here individually.

The first phase of the boot process is the Power On Self Test (POST). The POST code is contained in Read Only Memory (ROM); it checks out many of the PC/AT's hardware subsystems, including all its memory. During the POST, you can see in the upper left screen corner a running tally of the amount of memory checked so far. This test may take considerable time if a great amount of memory is installed. After the POST, if no operating system is installed, control is transferred to the rudimentary BASIC interpreter contained in ROM, which awaits your input.

However, if DOS is recorded on a diskette that you have inserted in drive **a:**, or else on your hard disk **c:**, then the PC will begin reading DOS from that medium into memory. Actually, on *every* medium formatted by DOS there is a small portion of DOS called the *boot record*, which the PC will execute if that medium is in drive **a:** or **c:** during booting. If the rest of DOS is not present on the medium, the boot record will write a message to that effect. Otherwise, it will load more of DOS into memory. Besides the boot record, there are several parts of DOS to load:

the file **ibmbio.com,**
optional device drivers,
the file **ibmdos.com,**
the resident portion of the file **command.com,**
the transient portion of the file **command.com,**
the autoexec file processor in **command.com.**

DOS layers

One part of DOS is already present in your PC, the Basic Input Output System (BIOS). This code, along with the POST and rudimentary BASIC interpreter, is contained in the ROM. The BIOS contains assembly language programs for performing very basic tasks with the various components of the PC, like writing a character on the screen or reading a character from the keyboard. It forms a part of any PC operating system.

The other parts of DOS are arranged in layers over the BIOS. The inner-most, **ibmbio.com**, is the interface between the BIOS and DOS and is the first part of DOS loaded by the boot record. (Since the BIOS is an integral part of the PC, any PC operating system must contain a program analogous to **ibmbio.com**.) Since DOS cannot anticipate all the equipment that it will have to operate, it must be possible to extend the functions of the BIOS and **ibmbio.com** to support new devices. These extensions are provided by *installable device drivers*, which will be discussed in more detail later in this section. **ibmbio.com** loads the file **ibmdos.com** and any device drivers necessary, then **command.com.**

ibmdos.com is the heart of DOS: it contains the routines for file input/output, directory manipulation, memory allocation, and program execution. These work mostly by employing the BIOS via the **ibmbio.com** interface.

The outermost layer of DOS, **command.com**, interprets your commands and handles errors reported by programs and other parts of DOS. (For example, it provides the error message when you attempt to write on a write pro-

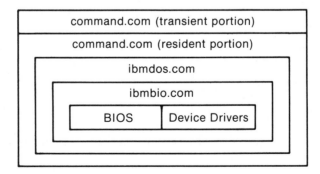

Figure 5.3.1 Layers of DOS

tected diskette.) **command.com** breaks your commands and the error handling tasks down into smaller units that are executed by the code in **ibmdos.com**. Just as it is possible to extend DOS at the inner level by installing device drivers for new equipment, it is possible (but unusual) to alter **command.com** to change the command repertoire.

Several DOS commands are available for setting up the appearance of the screen, interpreting the keyboard, and initializing the clock. You will probably want to execute some of these whenever you start up the PC, as well as some programs of your own that perform similar functions. These can be gathered together into a single *autoexec* program. If you put this in a file named **autoexec.bat** on the same drive with the DOS files, then it will be executed by **command.com** as soon as the latter is loaded. In Section 5.4 we will discuss **.bat** files in general.

The **command.com** program is split into parts because it is large and only part needs to be in memory at all times. Its autoexec file processor is discarded as soon as it is used, because it is used only once. Moreover, the command interpreter, called the *transient portion* of **command.com**, doesn't need to be present when other programs are running. When memory becomes scarce—for example, when several large programs must occupy memory at once—DOS releases for program use the memory area containing the transient portion. The remainder, called the *resident portion*, consists largely of error handling routines and code that reloads the transient portion when it's needed again.

The code for all DOS commands resides in **ibmdos.com**. Remember, however, that a number of DOS utility programs, like **diskcopy** and **chkdsk**, are used just like DOS commands. These programs are contained in separate files that are loaded into memory by **command.com** whenever needed. Their status is the same as that of any other program.

DOS memory utilization

Figure 5.3.2 shows the PC's memory utilization scheme when DOS is loaded. The amount of memory available for your programs is the total amount installed (up to 640 K) minus the size of DOS (including just the resident portion of **command.com**) minus the size of any device drivers. Figure 5.3.3 gives example statistics for three versions of DOS. These figures are part of the output from DOS command **chkdsk**. Clearly, increasing DOS functionality can lead to more severe memory requirements.

Configuration and autoexec files; setting up DOS

We mentioned above that the BIOS and its interface program **ibmbio.com** can be extended to handle new equipment by means of installable device drivers. These programs must satisfy very exacting standards set out in the *DOS 3.0 Technical Reference* manual, reference [15, Chap. 3], in order to interact properly with DOS. Several are supplied with DOS; others are provided by hardware vendors with PC compatible equipment. To cause a device driver to be installed with DOS, two steps are necessary. First, a file containing its code

Top of installed base memory (≤640 K)

Transient command. com
Area left for programs DOS uses this from the bottom up, and overwrites the transient command.com if necessary.
Resident command.com
Device drivers and miscellaneous DOS storage
ibmdos.com
ibmbio.com
Data area for BIOS and DOS

Bottom of memory (address 00000)

Figure 5.3.2 Allocation of memory available to DOS

must be accessible to DOS during the loading process. For example, suppose that file is **c:\drivers\equip.sys**. Second, the root directory of the drive containing the DOS files must include the text file **config.sys**, which must contain the line

```
device = c:\drivers\equip.sys
```

Once **ibmbio.com** has loaded **ibmdos.com**, it reads **config.sys**, then finds and loads any device drivers mentioned there. Finally, DOS finds and executes an initialization routine found at a standard location within each device driver. This sets up the equipment according to the needs of the driver. The **config.sys** file is also used to provide other information described later to DOS.

Two installable device drivers are provided with DOS, **ansi.sys** and **vdisk.sys**. The latter allows you to set up an area of memory to act like a disk, so that you can access information stored there in the usual way for disk files, but much faster. This driver is new to DOS 3.0 and will be discussed in detail in Section 8.5. The **ANSI.SYS** device driver allows you to control various screen features, like cursor position and color, and to redefine keystrokes to generate sequences of one or more ASCII codes. The codes for controlling

DOS Version	Total Memory Installed	Memory Available After DOS Loaded	Memory Used by DOS
1.1	655360 bytes	642860 bytes	12400 bytes
2.0	655360 ''	630784 ''	24576 ''
3.0	655360 ''	618496 ''	36874 ''

Figure 5.3.3 Memory used by versions of DOS

screen attributes resemble those for some CRT terminals that are termed "ANSI standard." Use of this driver is described in some detail in the *DOS 3.0 Technical Reference* manual [15, Chap. 2]. You should understand that although **ansi.sys** provides a convenient way to do some fairly complicated screen handling, its conventions conflict with ordinary BIOS screen handling, and hence it may interfere with software that uses the standard BIOS provisions to perform the same functions.

The **config.sys** file can contain some other statements that provide some very technical guidelines for DOS to follow in setting up your system. The most important of these are the number of 128 K buffers used in disk input/output and the number of files you can have open at once. Some new DOS 3.0 features of this sort are described in Section 8.3.

DOS provides several commands that you can use to set up the appearance of your screen. Command **cls** simply clears it and moves the cursor to the top left corner. You can use the **mode** command to switch screen output between Monochrome and Color/ Graphics Adapters when both are installed and to change the Color/Graphics Adapter between monochrome and color modes and between graphics and 40 and 80 column text modes. The **graphics** command sets up the printer driver so that you can use the **Shift-PrtSc** keystroke in graphics mode to produce a screen facsimile on an IBM printer. The **ctty** command can be used to switch screen and keyboard input/output to an external device accessed via a serial port. The **prompt** command can be used to set up prompts containing the date, time, current drive, current directory, and other informative text. DOS also has some commands to set the date and time of your computer's clock, in case you don't have a battery driven clock like the AT's or those commonly found on multifunction expansion boards. More commands of this type, new with DOS 3.0, are discussed in detail in Section 8.2.

You will probably want to gather various initialization commands like **mode** and **prompt** into your autoexec file. This file can also contain commands that execute programs, as described in Section 5.4. Hardware vendors often supply initialization programs to set up compatible equipment; these programs are intended to be executed by an autoexec file. Also, if you have installed a virtual disk device driver like **vdisk**, mentioned above, you will probably want to include in your autoexec file some DOS commands to copy files from diskette or hard disk to virtual disk so that they can be accessed more quickly. The author's autoexec file includes commands to set the prompt, initialize a printer spooler, set the screen text color, copy some word processor program files to a virtual disk, and set the default drive.

If you have a hard disk, you will want to install DOS there so that you needn't fuss with diskettes every time you turn on the power. Clearly, the first time you power up, you'll need to boot from a DOS diskette in drive **a:**. A utility program, **fdisk**, is provided with DOS to set aside a portion of your hard disk (usually the whole disk) as a volume for exclusive use by DOS, format it, and install the system files in its root directory. For details, see the *DOS 3.0 Reference* manual [14, Chap. 3]. The usual procedure for installing DOS on a PC/AT is described in Section 4.2.

Without a hard disk, you'll need to gather on one diskette the files **ibmbio.com, ibmdos.com**, and **command.com**. This can be done after booting from the original DOS diskette in drive **a:** by placing a blank diskette in drive **b:** and enter ing the command **format b:/s**. The three DOS files are copied automatically. Command **sys** can also be used to do this.

Remember, the **ibmbio.com** and **ibmdos.com** files are *hidden* files: they never appear on directories and cannot be overwritten nor erased (except when the whole medium is reformatted).

Whether you boot from diskette or hard disk, you will need to place in the root directory your **config.sys** and **autoexec.bat** files. Any device drivers or programs they refer to, as well as commonly used DOS utilities, must be put somewhere convenient, usually in the same root directory.

One last DOS command should be mentioned: **ver**. This command displays the version number of the installed operating system.

5.4 Program execution and data flow

Concepts

∗ DOS commands and program execution commands ∗ **Ctrl-Break, Ctrl-C**, warm and cold boots ∗ DOS environment; the **set** command ∗ **path** command ∗ Input/output redirection; piping and filters ∗ Batch files ∗ Batch file parameters and environment variables ∗ **echo, rem**, and **pause** commands ∗ **if, goto** and **for** in batch files ∗ Subprograms in batch files ∗ **.com** and **.exe** files; **exe2bin** utility

One of the major tasks of any operating system is to provide standard mechanisms for organizing and executing programs. This includes the commands you enter to execute programs and give them necessary information, methods for directing the flow of input and output data, and the organization of the files that contain programs. In this Section we will consider first the individual commands that execute programs and the provisions for directing data flow. Then we will see how to gather these together into batch files, which contain programs written in the DOS command language. Finally, we shall look at the organization of the files that contain machine language programs.

Command and program execution

The statements that you enter from the keyboard to execute DOS commands, DOS utilities, and programs in general are very similar. For DOS utilities like **format** or **diskcopy** this is not surprising, since they are just ordinary programs that happen to be provided with DOS. But the fact that DOS commands like **dir** and **copy** are invoked from the keyboard just like programs means that the DOS command interpreter (in **command.com**) must check everything you enter against the list of DOS commands, in order to determine whether it must just execute a command or go look for a file containing a program, then load and execute it.

A program ready for execution by DOS must be stored in a file whose name has extension **.bat, .com**, or **.exe.** We'll discuss the difference between these later. The *program name* is the name of this file without the extension. (Don't store two programs in files that have the same name except for the extension: you and DOS may get confused.) Here is the general syntax for the statement you enter to execute a DOS command or program. This is the DOS 3.0 syntax, which is easier to explain than the DOS 2.0 version. The restrictions enforced by DOS 2.0 are considered later under the heading **Path Command.**

> **DOS 3.0 command syntax:**
> command   command parameters

DOS 3.0 program execution syntax:
program name   program parameters

The parameters are character strings separated by delimiters (blanks, commas, semicolons, equal signs, or tabs). The only apparent difference between command and program execution syntax is that a program name, being a file name without the extension, can contain a path name. Here are two examples:

rename file_1.txt junk   a:games\tic_tac 4

Standard file name abbreviations are used with program files. Thus the command on the right executes program **tic_tac** in subdirectory **games** of the current directory on drive **a:** and provides this program some necessary information by means of the parameter **4** (e.g., play tic tac toe on a 4 by 4 grid). No path name may be used with the command on the left because **rename** is a DOS command, not a utility. When the entire path name is omitted, program execution syntax appears *identical* to command execution syntax.

It's nearly as important to be able to *stop* command or program execution as to start it. There are several ways to stop a command or program before it reaches a normal termination point. This need arises during ordinary operation when you realize you just asked the computer to do the wrong thing or during debugging when circumstances have caused you to lose control of your program. (Too often, debugging masquerades as ordinary operation!) Two keystroke combinations are provided—**Ctrl-Break** and **Ctrl-C**—that will let you terminate most programs and give control back to DOS. Often they don't immediately abort the program, because they can only take effect when DOS is providing certain services.

You can set up DOS to check for **Ctrl-Break** and **Ctrl-C** either when it performs *any* service or just when it does input/output via screen, keyboard, printer, or serial port. The latter choice would insure that programs can't be interrupted while doing long computations with no input/output. The DOS command **break** is used to determine the setting and change it; this command can also be entered in your **config.sys** file to set the default each time DOS is booted.

If a program isn't using DOS services, or if something has degraded DOS keyboard control, you can't terminate it with **Ctrl-Break** or **Ctrl-C**. A more drastic solution is necessary: a *warm boot*. Unless DOS has lost nearly *all* control, this will cause almost the same effect as turning the power off, then on again. You will lose the contents of main memory when you do that. (Ideally, you have saved everything you need!) When all else fails, do a *cold boot*: turn the power off, then on again. The principal difference between warm and cold boots is that the warm boot omits the sometimes lengthy POST memory check. You should realize that program termination by *any* of these methods can leave files in disarray (for example, only partially updated and therefore inconsistent). Be careful!

Environment

Before we continue with other aspects of DOS program execution mechanisms, it is useful to consider another DOS feature, the *environment*. This is an area of memory that DOS reserves for providing a program miscellaneous information that would not necessarily be known when its input files are prepared or when its execution command is given. The environment consists of character strings describing DOS *environment variables*. An environment variable name is just a character string that doesn't contain the symbols % or =; DOS converts any lowercase letters to uppercase. An environment variable value is *any* character string that doesn't contain the = sign.

Action	Effect
Ctrl-Break **Ctrl-C**	Back to DOS prompt. Memory is intact, except for the program that was terminated.
Ctrl-Alt-Del	Warm boot. Memory is lost (except possibly for some memory installed specially for virtual disks). The Power On Self Test (POST) is executed, except for the memory check. DOS is reloaded.
Turn power off then on	Cold boot. Like a warm boot except all memory is lost and the entire POST is executed.

Figure 5.4.1 How to stop command or program execution

The environment consists of strings of the form

```
environment variable name = enviroment variable value
```

which indicate the current values of the variables. You can inspect the environment by entering the DOS command **set**. You will see that it always contains at least two string variables,

```
COMSPEC = the drive and directory name for  command.com,
PATH = a path parameter, described in the next subsection.
```

Moreover, if you have entered a **prompt** command, its command parameter will be assigned to the environment variable **PROMPT**. The **COMSPEC** variable is used by DOS to find **command.com** when it has to reload the transient portion because some program overwrote it.

You can inspect the environment, and add, change, or delete environment variables by using DOS command **set**. Every program executed by DOS has access to the environment.

Path command

Frequently, you will want to work on two or more directories at once, perhaps widely separated in the file system tree. For example, on your fixed disk drive **c:**, you may want your Pascal source program files in a directory called **\pascal\work**, your compiler files in one called **\pascal\compiler**, and your DOS utilities with **command.com** in the root directory ****. You will probably be accessing the source files so often that you would like **c:\pascal\work** to be the current directory. Nevertheless, you will frequently have to access the files on the other directories. DOS provides a mechanism, the **path** command, so that you won't have to enter their full file names. For example, the command

```
path c:\;b:\pascal\work
```

makes it possible for you to execute DOS utilities in the root directory, or programs in directory **\pascal\compiler**, merely by entering their abbreviated names, without changing the current directory. In fact, the **path** command sets the value of the environment variable **PATH**. When you command DOS to execute a program, DOS looks first for a **.com, .exe**, or **.bat** file in the current directory (in that order), then finds the current path in the environment and searches each directory mentioned there, proceeding from left to right. If this long search is unsuccessful, DOS will tell you so. If you forget the current path command, you may just enter the word **path**; DOS will report the current path on the screen. It is common practice to include a path command in the autoexec file, so that frequently executed programs need not all be in the root directory.

DOS 2.0 and 2.1 *insisted* that you use the path command to execute a program not on the current directory of any drive. Thus, if you wanted to execute the program **pas1** in directory **\pascal\compiler** on drive **b:**, which was not the current directory on that drive, then with DOS 2.0 or 2.1 you would have to change that current directory with the command

cd b:\pascal\compiler

or else issue a path command

path=b:\pascal\compiler

before entering the execution command **pas1**. Under DOS 3.0, however, it is simpler: all you need do is enter

b:\pascal\compiler\pas1.

It is important to remember that the path is used only by the command processor in searching for a program file. DOS does not search for other data files.

Directing data flow

DOS provides some facilities for directing the flow of data to, between, and from programs. Of course, you could write a program to process the data in file **rst** and send its results to file **uvw**; and a second program to take input from file **uvw** and send output to file **xyz**. It doesn't require any elaborate DOS facility to do that. However, unless you already know about one of these programs when you write the other, you can't insure that the output file from the first and the input file to the second coincide. The solution to this problem is for programmers to use what DOS calls the *standard input and output devices*. DOS can then *redirect* program input and output to refer to any other files or devices. In fact, the standard DOS input and output devices are the keyboard and screen. However, the concept of standard device includes not only its physical form but also the standard procedures that DOS provides for controlling it. Thus, using standard input and output means using the DOS keyboard and screen input/output facilties described in Chapter 7. *If you do that,* then DOS will let you redirect your output to other devices as in the following examples.

   Example 1 If program **endmonth** writes a report on the standard output device—the screen—then the command

endmonth ⟩b:Jun_rept

executes the program and sends the output to file **Jun_rept** in the current directory on drive **b:**.

   Example 2 The command

endmonth ⟩prn

sends the report directly to the printer (**prn** is the DOS reserved file name for the character stream going to the printer.)

   Example 3 If program **chkbook** receives its input (debits and credits) from the standard input device—the keyboard—and writes its output on the screen, then the command

```
chkbook ⟨a:activity ⟩b:report
```

executes **chkbook** with its input coming from file **a:activity** and output going to **b:report**.

Example 4 Redirection can be used with DOS commands as well as programs. For example, the command **dir a: ⟩prn** lists on the printer the current directory on drive **a:**.

Sometimes you want to channel the output from one program or command directly to the input of another. This is called *piping*. To implement piping, the first program must use the standard output device and the second the standard input. A standard example is the use of piping to produce a sorted directory: the command

```
dir a: ¦ sort ⟩prn
```

first makes a listing of the current directory on drive **a:**; the pipe symbol ¦ sends this output to the DOS utility **sort**, whose output is redirected to the printer. DOS will create, use, and erase a temporary file to hold the piped data.

Obviously very convenient, piping has become a standard technique with other operating systems, especially UNIX. Many UNIX utilities, called *filters*,

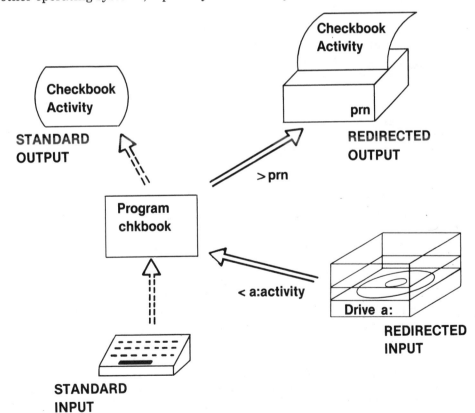

Figure 5.4.2 Input/Output Redirection

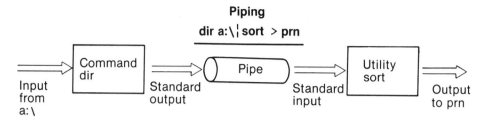

Figure 5.4.3 Piping

use both the standard input and output devices to facilitate piping. However, piping has not caught on yet with DOS, probably because the standard DOS screen output device is inflexible and slow compared with other screen output methods on the PC. Moreover, redirection and piping are not yet implemented as smoothly as they may be in the future. For example, since the **sort** utility is a filter, the simple command **sort** should accept keyboard input lines, for example

```
Smith ⟨CR⟩
Brady ⟨CR⟩
Waite ⟨CR⟩
⟨Ctrl-Z⟩ ⟨CR⟩
```

and produce the same lines in alphabetic order as screen output. This doesn't work, but the command **sort** ⟩**con** does. (The **Ctrl-Z** keystroke is the end of file indicator for keyboard input; **con** is the DOS reserved file name for character output enroute to the screen.)

Batch files

So far we have only discussed entering DOS commands one by one from the keyboard. In fact, you can gather any DOS commands into a *batch* file, i.e., a file whose name ends in the extension **.bat**, and execute it as described earlier, by entering its name without the extension. Thus a batch file really contains a *program* written in the DOS command language. An **autoexec.bat** file is a batch file that DOS executes automatically after booting.

To provide more flexibility, especially control over the order of executing the commands in a batch file, DOS provides a few commands and some control structures that are useful only in the context of a batch file. These features are considered in detail below, with a fairly complex example.

The echo, rem, and pause commands During normal execution of a batch file, when each command is executed, the DOS prompt (set by the last **prompt** command) is displayed and the command line is echoed on the screen. The DOS commands **echo off** and **echo on** serve to turn the prompt and echo off or back on. The echo command with any other parameter writes that parameter to the screen, even when the echo is turned off.

The DOS command **rem** identifies the rest of its line as a comment, not to be executed. Under normal operation, the **rem** line is echoed; the **echo** com-

Commands	Effect
echo	Turn on/off screen echo of commands. Write to screen.
for..in..do	For-loop.
goto	Jump.
if..then	Conditional execution.
pause	Pause, write a message, wait for any keystroke.
rem	Remark.
shift	Handle more than nine batch file parameters.

Constructs	Meaning
errorlevel	Status code set by a program.
exist	Does a given file exist?
= =	Are two strings equal?
not _	Negative.
: anything	Label
%1	Batch file parameter.
%%v	For-loop index.
%ABC%	Environment variable.
/c	Parameters for secondary command processor.

Figure 5.4.4 Commands and other constructs primarily for use in batch files

mand serves to hide the batch programmer's documentation from the user, while still displaying necessary information on the screen.

The DOS **pause** command displays its parameter, then the message **Strike any key when ready ...** and halts batch file execution until you comply. If you strike **Ctrl-Break** or **Ctrl-C**, execution of the file will terminate; striking anything else continues execution.

Batch file parameters A batch file refers to the parameters in its command line as %1, %2, etc. These are regarded as character strings, and can be concatenated with others. For example, consider this batch file **one.bat:**

```
echo off
echo twenty-%2
echo thirty-%1
```

If you execute this with the command **one two three**, it will display

```
the prompt line
echo off
twenty-three
thirty-two
```

If you omitted the **echo off** command, the display would be cluttered with more prompts and echoes. At most nine parameters can be dealt with this way; DOS has a clumsy provision—the **shift** command—for handling more parameters. The parameter name %0 always stands for the drive and file name of the batch file itself.

If .. then control DOS provides an *if ... then* control for batch files by using the words **if** and **not**, conditions, the command **goto**, and labels. A *label* is any string of eight or fewer characters. Including in a batch file a line consisting of : followed by a label merely serves to identify that place in the file; the line is not interpreted as a command and not echoed. The command **goto** followed by a label causes the DOS batch file interpreter to skip to the line following the specified label. Only three types of condition are possible:

```
errorlevel n        where n is a number;
exist name          where name is a file name (possibly including a
                    drive name) or abbreviation;
s == t              where s and t are any character strings (possibly
                    empty) or parameter symbols like %1.
```

Errorlevel is a DOS internal variable that can be set equal to a number n by a program (using DOS function hex 4c described in Chapter 7). An **exist** condition is true just when there is a file with the specified name. (DOS 2.0 and 2.1 allow only abbreviated file names with no \ symbols.) In evaluating an **s == t** condition, DOS is sensitive to upper and lower case: thus if parameter %1 is **Abc** then the condition **%1 == abc** is false. For any specified condition and command, DOS will interpret the *conditional* command statements

```
   if condition command
if not condition command
```

as you would expect. To use a condition to govern the execution of a series of commands, conditional statements like

```
if condition goto label
```

are employed.

Sample batch file Figure 5.4.5 shows a sample batch file that the author uses for Pascal compilation. Usually it is executed by a command like

```
compile test
```

This executes the programs **pas1** and **pas2** that constitute passes one and two of the compiler. With this command, the input to **pas1** is the source code file **test.pas**. If **pas1** succeeds, it produces some temporary files whose names are known to **pas2**. This second pass program then reads the temporary files and outputs two files named **test.obj** and **test.lst**—the object file and source code listing. Sometimes, however, the Pascal source code file name extension is not **.pas**. To compile source code in file **unit_one.imp**, for example, the command

```
compile unit_one imp
```

is used. The compiler then produces object and listing files **unit_one.obj** and **unit_one.lst**.

For-loops A primitive *for-loop* capability is available for batch files through use of the words **for ... in ... do ...**, batch file variables, and sets. A *batch file variable* consists of the symbols %% followed by a letter. A *set* consists of a sequence of character strings separated by commas and enclosed in parentheses. For example, the command

```
for %%v in (a,b,c) do echo %%v
```

will cause DOS to print lines consists of the single letters a, b, and c, interspersed with prompt lines. More usefully, the command

```
for %%f in (one.txt,two.txt) do if %1 == %%f type %1
```

will list the file specified by parameter **%1** provided it is one of the two mentioned in the set. You can also use file name wild cards: the command

```
for %%f in (*.*) do if not exist b:%%f copy %%f b:
```

copies to the current directory on drive **b:** all files in the current directory that do not already exist on **b:**.

In a **for** command, any command can be entered after the word **do** except another **for** command. The results may be bizarre if you enter a **goto** command there. For some reason, the syntax for entering a **for** command directly from the keyboard is slightly different: use single % symbols instead of double ones.

Accessing the environment A batch file can access the environment in much the same way that it accesses its parameters. For example, if **ABC** is an environment variable, then the string **%ABC%** denotes its value. This provides a way to implement subprograms in batch files, as in Figure 5.4.6. *Caution: this batch file feature is not documented,* probably because DOS doesn't behave correctly when you try to access a nonexistent environment variable, or to use a batch file parameter to give an environment variable name. (**%%1%** doesn't work!) *Take care!* (The feature was reported in Darryl E. Rubin, "Batch: A powerful IBM language," *Computer Language,* October, 1984, 31-35.)

The sample batch file in Figure 5.4.5 contained commands like **vx** that execute programs; **vx** is the program in file **vx.exe**. It is also possible for a batch file to execute another batch file. However, you must realize that once you leave the first batch file, you will not return to complete it once you start executing a second one. Instead, you will execute that one until it's done or calls yet another batch file, and eventually you will return to DOS. This feature is awkward, rather like BASIC program chaining. DOS provides an inelegant way around this problem. The program **command.com** has a parameter, a character string. If this string starts with /c, then **command.com** regards the remainder of the string as a standard DOS command line, and just executes it. For example, from your batch file you can call file **subprog.bat** as a subprogram with parameters **p** and **q** by using the command

```
        echo off

rem     Turn off echo to avoid cluttering screen.

        path c:\pascal\compiler
        cd c:\pascal\work
        c:

rem     Now the current drive and directory is  c:\pascal\work,
rem     and programs not here can be found in  c:\pascal\compiler.

rem     The following command is a cute way of determining if
rem     parameter %2 is absent, i.e. empty.  The simpler
rem     commands if %2 == goto choice_2 and
rem     if == %2 goto choice_2 leave something to be desired
rem     (and fail with DOS 2.0 )!

        if a%2 == a goto choice_2
        pas1 %1.%2,%1.obj,%1.lst;
        goto resume
        :choice_2
        pas1 %1.pas,%1.obj,%1.lst;

rem     The above code uses parameter %2 as a file name extension
rem     if it is present, else provides .pas as a default.
rem     If pas1 failed, it produced some error messages on the
rem     screen and set errorlevel ⊥ 1. In that case, it is not
rem     appropriate to execute pas2; just call in the editor.

        :resume
        if errorlevel 1 goto edit
        pas2

rem     Whether pas2 succeeds or fails, the next step almost
rem     always involves editing.

        :edit
        path b:\;c:\

rem     The editor is in the root directory of drive b: and most
rem     utilities are in the root directory of drive c:. Pause to
rem     permit reading the compiler's screen messages. Pause after
rem     the path command, so that if you break out here, the path
rem     will be OK. After a keystroke, get the editor (vx).

        pause
        vx
```

Figure 5.4.5 Sample batch file

```
echo This is in the 'main program' of a batch file.
set   RETURN=resume
goto subprog
:resume
echo This resumes operation in the 'main program'.
goto end
:subprog
echo This is in a subprogram to do something.
echo The next statement will get back to the 'main program'.
goto %RETURN%
:end
```

Figure 5.4.6 Batch subprogram using an environment variable

```
command /c subprog p q
```

Notice that this process requires DOS to load a *second* copy of **command.com**; this secondary copy then loads and executes **subprog.bat**. Moreover, **subprog.bat** has a new environment to go with the new command processor. It inherits all the environment variables from your batch program, but it can make no changes that effect *your* environment!

The secondary command processor feature, together with the possibility of accessing the environment, gives batch files nearly the same flexibility as or-

**MAIN
MEMORY**

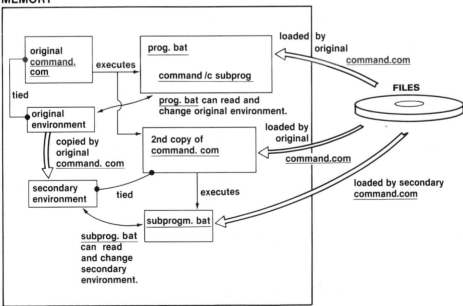

Figure 5.4.7 Using a secondary copy of command.com to execute a batch
subprogram.

dinary programs. However, this capability is implemented very awkwardly and should not be used unless thoroughly tested and documented.

Program file organization

So far we have discussed only one of the three types of program file, the batch file. Now we can consider the other two types, the **.com** and **.exe** files. These files contain machine language programs.

When DOS loads a **.com** or **.exe** program into memory for execution, it first builds a 256-byte table called the Program Segment Prefix (PSP) in the lowest portion of available memory, then loads the program immediately above the PSP and transfers control to the program. For full details about the PSP, see the *DOS 3.0 Technical Reference* manual, reference [15, Chap. 6]. However, a few facts about the PSP structure will clarify how DOS provides information to the program and controls its execution. Here is a brief list of the interesting PSP entries:

1. The address of the DOS environment for your program. This address is always in the same place relative to the start of your program, so you can find it and thus access the most recent **prompt** and **path** command parameters and also find **command.com**. This environment is actually a *copy* of the DOS environment at loading time, so even if your program changes it, DOS will return to its former environment when your program is done.
2. The complete drive and file name for your program. Thus you can find other files related to your program (e.g., in the same directory) even though their location is not explicitly provided in the execution command or in any program input.
3. The entire list of parameters entered with the command that executed your program.
4. The address of the next command that should gain control when your program terminates.
5. The original values of parameters essential to DOS that your program is allowed to alter (for example, the address of the routine that handles the **Ctrl-Break** keystroke).

The PSP also contains information about memory allocation, and areas used for transmitting data to and from DOS files.

Programs in **.com** files are independent of their location in memory and are written under the assumption that, when they start, the CPU registers will be set up in a certain specific way. They will run properly no matter where in memory DOS loads them. To execute a **.com** program, DOS merely has to build its PSP, copy the program into memory immediately above the PSP, set the CPU registers, and transfer control to the program.

On the other hand, an **.exe** program contains language that must be modified (in a standard way) to account for its exact location in memory, and the initial values for the CPU registers may depend on this as well. At the beginning of an **.exe** file is a Relocation Table that points to all the program instructions that must be modified, and contains the initial values for the CPU registers. To execute an **.exe** program, DOS has to build the PSP, load the program into memory, then modify the program according to the Relocation Table, set the CPU registers properly, and finally transfer control to the program.

Clearly, **.exe** files are bigger and load more slowly than **.com** files. DOS provides a utility program, **exe2bin.exe**, to convert certain **.exe** programs to **.com** programs.

6

INTEL 8086 Family Traits

Contents

So far in this book, we have surveyed the PC/AT hardware without going into low level detail like memory addressing, CPU registers, and CPU instructions. In the last two chapters we have been considering fundamentals of the DOS operating system without much reference to hardware. As a serious PC/AT programmer, you will be interested in the deeper aspects of the hardware and the operating system. In order to describe these it is now necessary to consider the CPU in greater detail. However, information about most new features of the CPU is not needed until much later, in Chapter 9. At this point, all we need is *overall familiarity* with the PC family CPUs.

The PC/AT CPU is the Intel 80286 microprocessor. Just as the PC/AT is a member of an evolving line of personal computers, the 80286 is one of a sequence of Intel microprocessors called the *8086 family*. All earlier members of the PC family and most so-called PC compatible computers used the earlier Intel 8088 CPU chip. Some compatibles have used the faster 8086 or 80186 chip.

As noted in Chapter 3, the 80286 features two modes of operation—real and protected. Most of its new characteristics have to do with the protected mode, which we don't need to consider until Chapter 10. Most of the information about the 80286 necessary at this point applies to the other CPUs just mentioned as well. That is why this chapter is called *Intel 8086 family traits*. In Section 6.1 we will consider the segment:offset memory addressing technique peculiar to the 8086 family. The various CPU registers are detailed in 6.2, and the different ways they are used with CPU instructions to access memory are described in 6.3. The instruction set is surveyed, class by class of instructions, in 6.4. Finally, the interrupt instruction, a special type of subprogram call, and the organization of an interrupt service routine (ISR) are outlined in 6.5. ISRs are a principal method for providing operating system services for your programs. A few special features of the 80286 are noted in this chapter, but most are discussed in Chapter 9 in the context of the protected mode of operation.

6.1 Segment:offset addresses

Concepts

* How is the PC/AT real mode memory organized into bytes, words, paragraphs, and segments?   * Why are bytes usually addressed as offsets relative to the beginning of a segment?   * How is a physical byte address related to a segment:offset address?

In Chapter 3 we saw that the standard main memory of the PC/AT in real mode, and all memory in older members of the PC family, is organized into eight bit bytes which have unique twenty-bit addresses. From now on we shall call these *physical* addresses. These computers can thus address at most

$$2^{20} = 1,048,576 \text{ bytes } = 1 \text{ Megabyte}$$

of standard memory.

When referring to specific bytes and to memory addresses, it's customary to use hexadecimal (hex) notation. One hex digit requires four bits, so a byte is represented by two hex digits. A twenty-bit physical address can be represented by five hex digits, so the physical addresses range from hex 00000 (low end) to hex FFFFF (high end).

Two other terms are used for small pieces of memory. A *word* is two consecutive bytes, i.e., sixteen bits or four hex digits. An *aligned* word is one whose first byte has an even physical address. The 80286 PC/AT CPU is designed to move data most efficiently to and from aligned words. For many programs, most data is organized into words or groups of words, and the 80286 will process these about twice as efficiently if the words are aligned. This consideration does not apply to earlier members of the PC family, which use the 8088 CPU. Finally, a *paragraph* consists of sixteen consecutive bytes, the first address of which is a multiple of sixteen. The possible paragraph addresses are distinguished by the fact that their physical address ends with hex 0. For example, physical address hex 43210 is a multiple of hex 10 = decimal 16, hence is the address of the first byte in a paragraph.

To facilitate modular, relocatable programming, memory is organized into large chunks called *segments*, and individual bytes are addressed relative to the beginning of a segment. If your data is stored in a single data segment and addressed relative to its beginning, then you or DOS can relocate this segment in memory just by changing the segment part of the addresses. If your program just refers to relative addresses—that is, to *offsets* relative to the current data segment—then it is independent of the actual location of the data. Similarly, if your program code is contained in a single code segment and all instruction addresses are given as offsets relative to the current code segment, then the program is independent of its own actual location in memory. When DOS loads for execution a program whose data and code are confined to single segments, it can search for appropriate free space, set the current data and code segment addresses, and execute the program without adjusting addresses further.

All segments contain hex 10000 = decimal 65536 = 64 K bytes and begin at paragraph addresses. They may overlap. In fact, most segments in use by a program usually do overlap. (Segmentation by itself is *not* a way to segregate different programs and/or data areas.)

The fact that segments must begin at paragraph addresses is the key to the segment:offset addressing technique used by the PC/AT in real mode and by all earlier members of the PC family. A segment:offset address of a byte consists of two words, the segment address and the offset, or relative, address, usually written like these examples:

```
segment: offset   segment offset
    address       address address


hex   1234: 5678    1234 5678
```

The physical address of the byte is obtained by multiplying the segment address by 16 = hex 10 and adding the offset. This is the same as shifting the segment address leftward one hex digit, or four bits, and adding the offset. The physical addresses for the above example and two others are obtained as shown in Figure 6.1.1.

As you see from these examples, the segment:offset address of a byte is not unique: *two different segment:offset addresses can refer to the same byte!*

6.2 CPU registers

Concepts

* What CPU registers are common to all members of the 8086 family? * How are they designed and what uses are intended for them?

Every CPU has a number of *registers*. These are high speed memory cells reserved for special functions and more closely connected with the organization of the CPU than the main memory. The design of the registers is inter-

segment: offset address	physical address calculation	physical address
hex 1234: 5678	12340 + 5678 ───── 179B8	179B8
hex 12B3: 4F26	12B30 + 4F26 ───── 17A56	17A56
hex 1000: 7A56	10000 + 7A56 ───── 17A56	17A56

Figure 6.1.1 Relationship between segment:offset and physical addresses

twined with that of the instruction set. You can think of the registers as facilitating the solution of certain programming problems and the instruction set as designed to permit easy and natural manipulation of the registers. On the other hand, you can view the instruction set as basic and the registers as the minimum amount of scratch pad memory necessary for them to perform their tasks smoothly and efficiently.

The Intel 8086 CPU family shares a basic register and instruction set. While there are minor incompatibilities among them, the newer members of the family, like the 80286 in the PC/AT, will usually execute programs written for the earlier ones like the 8086 or 8088. This comparison is valid for the 80286 only in its real mode of operation, however; in protected mode, the registers are used quite differently.

These basic 8086 family registers include

$$\begin{array}{rl}
4 \ \textit{data} \ \text{registers} & \text{AX, BX, CX, DX,} \\
2 \ \textit{index} \ \text{registers} & \text{SI, DI,} \\
2 \ \textit{pointer} \ \text{registers} & \text{BP, SP,} \\
4 \ \textit{segment} \ \text{registers} & \text{SS, CS, DS, ES,} \\
\text{the} \ \textit{Instruction Pointer} & \text{IP,}
\end{array}$$

and the *Flags* register. They are illustrated in Figure 6.2.1. The 80286 has some additional registers supporting protected mode operation; they are described in Sections 9.2 to 9.4.

The two letter mnemonic names of these registers are standard assembly language terminology. They are abbreviations for more elaborate full names, shown in Figure 6.2.1, that suggest how the registers are commonly used. While some registers have very narrow functions, others are general purpose and can be used almost at the programmer's discretion. We shall discuss each register in some detail, following Figure 6.2.1, to give you an idea of their function.

Notice first that the registers are each sixteen bits long. (In the 80286, some of these registers are greatly extended in length to support protected mode operation. However, in real mode, they operate exactly as in other members of the 8086 family.)

Data registers AX, BX, CX, DX

The four data registers AX, BX, CX, and DX are given distinctive names in Figure 6.2.1. However, they can be used almost interchangeably, and any special roles they play individually are assigned rather arbitrarily. Thus, their full names are not in common use; everyone uses the alphabetic mnemonics. Each of these can be regarded as a pair of eight bit registers that may be handled together or separately. The two parts are termed *high* and *low* and are systematically named:

$$\begin{array}{ll}
\text{AX} \ = \ \text{AH, AL} & \text{CX} \ = \ \text{CH, CL} \\
\text{BX} \ = \ \text{BH, BL} & \text{DX} \ = \ \text{DH, DL.}
\end{array}$$

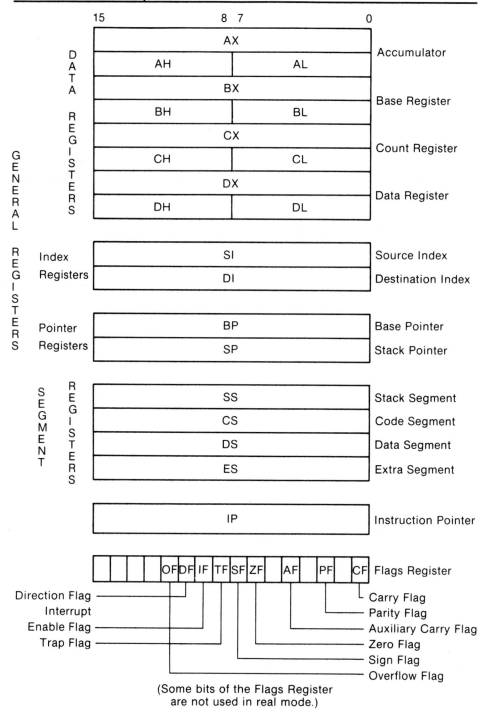

Figure 6.2.1 8086 family registers

These are general purpose registers, commonly used for temporary storage of data, particularly for intermediate results in calculations and for address manipulations.

Pointer registers

The two pointer registers BP and SP generally contain offset parts of addresses or data figuring in calculations of these offsets.

All 8086 family CPUs directly implement *stacks*. A stack is an area of memory managed like a stack of notes impaled on a spike. You can enter new data only by *pushing* it onto the *top* of the stack (adding a new memory cell to one end of the stack area), and you can retrieve data only by *popping* it from the top (reading the top cell and removing it from the stack area). Other stack entries are inaccessible for storage or retrieval. A stack is thus an *LIFO* storage mechanism (Last in first out). Stacks are particularly useful for storing information about nested processes that should be undone in the order opposite that in which they were executed, as in putting on and removing your clothing.

The Stack Pointer register SP often contains the offset part of the address of the top of a stack.

The logic of the overall 8086 family design is marred by a perversion. *Stacks are implemented upside down!* That is, stacks usually look like Figure 6.2.2. Remember, stacks grow *downward*, and the *top* of a stack is its *lowest* address in memory!

Index registers

The index registers SI and DI often contain addresses relative to the beginnings of memory cell arrays. For example, registers BX and BP might contain starting addresses of arrays S and D, and the Source and Destination Index registers SI and DI might be used to move data from S to D: the offset address of a source entry in S might be the sum BX + SI, and that of the destination entry in S would be BP + DI.

Segment registers

While the pointer and index registers generally store the offset parts of addresses, the segment registers handle the segment parts. Thus, if BX contains the starting offset address of an array, SI the index of an array entry relative to its start, and DS identifies the memory segment containing the array, then the physical address of the array entry would be

(hex 10)*DS + BX + SI.

The 8086 family design assumes that at any given instant a program may be dealing with, at most, four segments. Thus there are exactly four segment registers: one each for

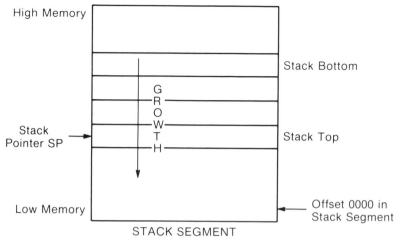

STACK SEGMENT

Figure 6.2.2 Family upside down stack

the program code: CS
the program stack: SS
the program data: DS

and one for data that might be stored in some other segment,

the extra segment: ES.

Instruction pointer

The Instruction Pointer register IP normally contains the offset address of the next instruction for execution. The complete segment:offset address is thus CS:IP. This register cannot be used directly by programs. However, jump instructions replace it by the target jump address, and procedure call instructions will push its content onto the stack for later use as a return jump address.

Flags

The Flags register is manipulated bit by bit. Only nine of its bits are in fact used, and each has a name, shown in Figure 6.2.1. The 80286 uses two more flag bits to support protected mode operation, discussed in Section 9.3.

Three of the flags have CPU control functions. The Direction Flag DF determines whether instructions that process arrays in memory proceed from low addresses toward high addresses or vice versa. This choice is critical, for example, when you move an array to a new location that overlaps its original site. The Interrupt Enable and Trap Flags IF and TF are used in connection with interrupts, a type of subprogram call described in Section 6.5.

There are six remaining Status flags:

```
OF   Overflow          ZF   Zero
CF   Carry             SF   Sign
AF   Auxiliary Carry   PF   Parity.
```

These report the designated aspects of the result of an arithmetic operation: whether the answer was so large it overflowed the computer's capacity, whether certain carrying or borrowing was necessary, and whether the result was zero, positive, negative, even, or odd. Since the flags can also be set directly by programs, they are also used frequently to report outcomes of other non-arithmetic operations.

6.3 Addressing modes and memory allocation

Concepts

* What addressing modes are supported by the 8086 family? * How are the registers used to implement them? * How are they indicated in assembly language? * Immediate, register, direct, based and indexed addressing * Default segment registers and segment overrides * How do you tell the assembler to allocate and initialize memory? * Segment classes and groups * Stack, public, common, and **at** segments * Entry points * How are the segment registers **SP** and **IP** initialized?

Most machine instructions perform some operation on one or more pieces of data, called its *operands*. Sometimes an operand is encoded in the instruction itself or stored in a register. When an operand is stored in memory, the instruction must determine its address. Although operand addresses are occasionally specified directly, most applications call for some manipulation of address data to compute the actual operand address. The methods used for this address computation are called *addressing modes*. Different modes have proved effective in different situations. For flexibility, the 8086 family CPUs implement a variety of addressing modes. In this section we will develop the terminology necessary for describing them and see how they are indicated in assembly language programs.

This book is neither an introduction to PC/AT assembly language nor a reference manual. The discussion of assembly language here is intended to give enough background for you to follow some examples in later chapters and to read the PC/AT BIOS code and other examples that appear in the technical literature. If you want to learn to program in this language, an excellent tutorial text is reference [22]. A more concise and advanced presentation is [27].

The standard assembler for the PC family is the *Macro Assembler* by Microsoft Corporation. IBM is licensed to distribute one version of this software. Warning: the 80286 CPU in the PC/AT has several instructions not shared by the other members of the 8086 family. These are not supported by all versions of the Macro assembler! Although the Macro manual [23] is an essential guide for the assembly process, it is nearly useless for learning about the language itself. This assembler is patterned after an earlier one, ASM86, developed by the Intel Corporation. For several questions, particularly memory allocation, the ASM86 manual [4] is a better reference; however, you must realize that the assemblers differ in some details.

As we discuss different addressing techniques we shall give examples, all involving a single type of instruction, the *move* instruction. By considering the assembly language form of this one instruction for the various addressing modes, you will be able to concentrate on addressing techniques without concern for the great variety of instruction types introduced in the next section. The move instruction always has the form

mov d, s

The mnemonic **mov** is the same for all addressing modes; the letters *d* and *s* are our symbols for the *destination* and *source* operands. (This one instruction thus subsumes both the load and store instructions of some other CPUs.) The source operand can be a constant, the content of any register except IP, or that of a memory cell. The destination can be any register except IP or CS or a memory cell. There are further restrictions, noted below, on register destinations. Moreover, no single **mov** instruction can move data *between* two memory cells.

The previous paragraph illustrates a terminological problem in describing addressing modes. Does "operand" refer to *data* that an instruction manipulates or to a *register or memory cell* where that data is stored? Although the former interpretation was used above, it proves inconvenient. Programmers rarely refer to the data itself because of the need for generality. In fact, the only common reference to an operand as data occurs when it is encoded in the instruction itself: no address is needed. From now on, except in this one case, *the word "operand" refers to a register or memory cell containing data that an instruction manipulates.*

Instructions have different binary codes corresponding to the different addressing techniques. Fortunately, *we* don't have to be concerned with those details. Assembly language provides suggestive notation for the various addressing techniques, and assemblers translate this into the proper binary mode. Although there are several assemblers for the 8086 family and their notations vary in some details, the fundamentals—all we need in this book— are the same. Occasionally, unfortunate programmers must inspect the binary code in memory to find out what went wrong with their software. Debugging tools are available (e.g., the **debug** utility provided with DOS or the more elaborate **symdeb** program included with the Microsoft Macro Assembler package) that will partially translate the binary instruction codes back to their assembly language forms.

Immediate and Register Modes

It's easiest to describe the **mov** instruction when it operates on constant data or register operands. Here are the assembly language statements for two typical situations:

```
mov ah,17h   Move hex 17 into register AH.
mov ax,bx    Move the contents of register BX to AX.
```

Most constants and registers are permitted when they make sense. When both source and destination are registers, they must have the same length. Some convention is necessary to clarify the effect of moving a byte constant into a word operand. Of course, a constant may not be used as a destination. The addressing modes illustrated in these two examples are called

register mode   when the operand is a register, and
immediate mode when the instruction operates on constant data, like hex 17 above; in this case the data is encoded in the instruction itself, and no address is necessary.

No immediate mode move to a segment register is permitted. To achieve that effect, use another register as intermediate storage.

How the assembler allocates and refers to memory locations

In other addressing modes, an operand is a memory cell, and the instruction must determine its complete segment:offset address. Before we can describe these modes and how to indicate them in assembly language, we must consider how the assembler, the linker, and the loader together allocate space in memory, initialize its contents, and arrange for programs to access it. It is important to distinguish between the first two tasks and the last. Several features of assembly language serve to define "chunks" of memory and indicate how the linker and loader should treat them. A different mechanism is used to set up the addresses so that your instructions can access this memory. Because the terminology is similar, you can easily confuse the two activities.

The official term for "chunk" of memory allocated by the assembler is "segment." Unfortunately, this usage of the word is only indirectly related to memory addresses and segment registers. Since both concepts play a role in this discussion, they become clearer if different terms are used. Therefore, we shall use the word "chunk" to mean an area of memory given a name by the assembler. A chunk can be as long as 64-K bytes. You identify a chunk by including in your assembly language program a statement like this:

```
my_data  segment  para  'my_info'
```

The identifier **my_data** is the name of the chunk and is used within your program to stand for the segment address of the first byte of this chunk in memory. The word **segment** is an assembly language pseudo-operation that defines chunks. The word **para** is an *alignment indicator*. It tells the linker that **my_data** must fall on a paragraph boundary, i.e., the physical address of its first byte must be divisible by hex 10. Other alignment possibities are

byte—no restriction,
word—divisible by hex 2,
page—divisible by hex 100.

The alignment indicator **para** is used as a default when none is explicitly mentioned. The string **'my_info'** is optional, the name of a *class* of chunks to which **my_data** will belong. The function of the class name will be considered later.

The size of a memory chunk is determined by the data or code placed there by the assembler (the initialization), and the position of an **ends** pseudo-operation. Consider the following example:

```
my_data        segment        byte 'my_info'
age            db             45
birth_year     dw             1939
name           db             'James T.  Smith'
salary         dw             ?
address        db             50  dup (?)
my_data        ends
```

The symbols **db** and **dw** are also *pseudo-operations*. They stand for *define byte* and *define word* and notify the assembler to allocate the appropriate amount of memory—one or more bytes or words—and perhaps to initialize it with the values specified. The **?** means to skip the initialization—just set aside the memory; **50 dup**() means fifty copies of whatever is in the parentheses.

If you want a chunk of memory to contain instructions, just place their assembly language code there, followed by an **ends** pseudo-operation. Code chunks are initialized by the familiar process of placing instructions in them. Figure 6.3.1 is an extract from the PC/AT BIOS listed in the *PC/AT Technical Reference* manual [20, pp. 5-32—5-51]. Its first line defines a chunk called **code**, given no special alignment. The word **public** is not a class name (no quotes), but a *combination indicator* that we shall discuss later. The single dotted line represents about a page of code irrelevant to this discussion. The next line is an instruction to clear interrupts, with a label, **mfg_boot**, that stands for the address of this line relative to the start of the chunk. Next is a *comment:* on any line of assembly language, anything following a semicolon is a comment, ignored by the assembler. The following instruction is an immediate mode move instruction: the symbol **disable_bit20** was defined several pages earlier in the BIOS to mean hex dd. The double dotted line indicates about eighteen pages of omitted code. The **ends** pseudo-operation indicates the end of this chunk, and the **end** indicates the end of a program. A duplicate of the first line of the Figure occurs shortly after that on the next page.

Now that the chunk *sizes* are specified, how is their *order* determined? In the **.obj** file the assembler passes to the linker all the chunk names and their class names. The linker assembles all the chunks in the order it encounters them, except that *chunks with the same class name are positioned next to each other*. All chunks with no class name are considered to belong to a single anonymous class. For example, if the linker encounters the following chunks in the order indicated at left, it will assemble them in the order at right:

order encountered		order assembled	
chunk	*class*	*chunk*	*class*
Abe	'Frosh'	Abe	'Frosh'
Bob	'Soph'	Ike	'Frosh'
Cal		Bob	'Soph'
Don	'Junior'	Gig	'Soph'
Eli		Cal	
Gig	'Soph'	Eli	
Ike	'Frosh'	Don	Junior'

The assembler will not allow you to assign the same chunk to different classes.

This is a simple rule, but it does not cover one situation: what does the linker do if it encounters two chunks with the same name and class? If the two chunks occur in the same program, then the second is simply regarded as an extension of the first. The situation is more complicated when you have two or more assembly language programs that you want to link together. There are several reasons why you might want to have segments of the same name and class in the two programs. You have seen an example already in Figure 6.3.1. Because these several situations must be handled differently, you must tell the linker your intention—via the assembly language. The device for this is the *combination indicator* that we saw earlier. (In the manuals, it's called the "combine type," reminding one of farm machinery.)

```
code            segment          byte public
mfg—boot:    cli
;degate address line 20
                mov              ah,disable—bit20

code            ends
                ends

code            segment          byte public
```

Figure 6.3.1 Assembly language examples*

*PC/AT Technical Reference manual [20, pp. 5-32.. 5-51].

If no combination indicators are given, the coincidence of name and class is regarded as an accident, and the chunks are kept separate: each program refers only to its own chunk. If you specify the indicator **public** as in Figure 6.3.1, the two chunks are concatenated into one large chunk, and each program has access to the whole thing. In this way, two programmers can independently build parts of the same program, provided they agree on the overall structure. There are four alignment indicators in all:

at   common   public   stack

The indicator **stack** is handled almost like **public**, except for one difference noted later. The indicator **common** causes chunks to be superimposed, with the same beginning and with length determined by the longest. In this way two programs can refer by different names to data in the same memory locations.

There are many ramifications of these assembly language techniques, which you will learn from texts and manuals when you need them. Figure 6.3.2 is an example of this kind of code taken from the PC/AT BIOS, reference [20, pp. 5-29 to 5-32]. Most of its features have been described above, but a few points remain to be covered. The assembler does not distinguish between upper- and lowercase letters. The **segment** pseudo-operations in this Figure use the **at** alignment indicator to specify absolute memory locations: the temporary storage area and color/graphics video controller display located at physical addresses hex 00400 and b8000, as described in Figure 3.1. The **label** pseudo-operations define the names on the left as labels standing for the addresses of the current location relative to the beginning of the chunk or group. The indicators in the **label** statements indicate not alignment, but the length of data items that the label will refer to (the third *word* after the label as opposed to the third *byte*, etc.).

The first piece of code in Figure 6.3.2 sets up the circular keyboard buffer that stores two-byte codes for your most recent fifteen keystrokes. When you strike a key, the keyboard controller interrupts the CPU to store this information. Your programs use it when they are ready. The buffer permits you to type ahead. If you fill it before your program has a chance to use the information, the BIOS will beep at you and ignore further keystrokes.

Now we know how big the chunks in a linked program are and in what order they are loaded into memory. Exactly *where* are they loaded? The chunks are assembled in order into the **.exe** file produced by the linker. It also adds the 256 byte Program Segment Prefix described in Section 5.4. When DOS loads the **.exe** file for execution, it determines the lower boundary of available memory and loads the file there.

We have still not discussed how the assembler, linker, and loader set up addresses so that your instructions can locate your data. The task is simplified by *relative addressing*. Whenever an instruction refers to an item in memory, it will determine the address relative to the start of a chunk. This is independent of the chunk's ultimate location. When you write your program, you have the information necessary to compute the relative address, and you build that

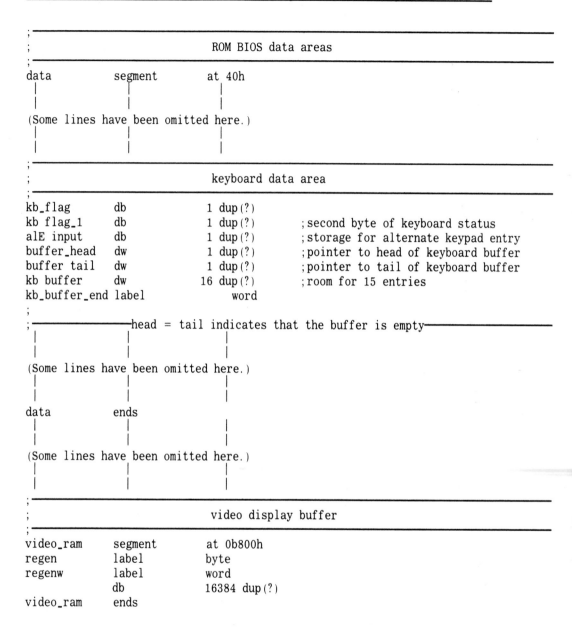

```
;─────────────────────────────────────────────────────────────
;                        ROM BIOS data areas
;─────────────────────────────────────────────────────────────
data            segment         at 40h
 |               |              |
 |               |              |
(Some lines have been omitted here.)
 |               |              |
 |               |              |

;─────────────────────────────────────────────────────────────
;                       keyboard data area
;─────────────────────────────────────────────────────────────
kb_flag         db              1 dup(?)
kb flag_1       db              1 dup(?)      ;second byte of keyboard status
alE input       db              1 dup(?)      ;storage for alternate keypad entry
buffer_head     dw              1 dup(?)      ;pointer to head of keyboard buffer
buffer tail     dw              1 dup(?)      ;pointer to tail of keyboard buffer
kb buffer       dw             16 dup(?)      ;room for 15 entries
kb_buffer_end label                 word
;
;─────────────head = tail indicates that the buffer is empty─────────
 |               |              |
 |               |              |
(Some lines have been omitted here.)
 |               |              |
 |               |              |

data            ends
 |               |              |
 |               |              |
(Some lines have been omitted here.)
 |               |              |
 |               |              |

;─────────────────────────────────────────────────────────────
;                       video display buffer
;─────────────────────────────────────────────────────────────
video_ram       segment         at 0b800h
regen           label           byte
regenw          label           word
                db              16384 dup(?)
video_ram       ends
```

Figure 6.3.2 Example assembly language memory allocation and initialization*

*PC/AT Technical Reference manual, [20, , pp. 5-29 .. 5-32].

into your code. The different ways of doing that constitute the various addressing modes. However, you don't know the ultimate addresses of the chunks, and your program can't determine them until DOS loads it for execution.

While it is convenient for you to use separate chunks for different kinds of data, this often leads to too many addresses that need to be determined when the program is loaded. Shortly, we shall see why the number of undetermined addresses should be kept down. There is a device, the **group** pseudo-operation, for cutting this number. An assembly language statement like

```
dgroup    group   my_data
```

assigns the chunk **my_data** to a *group* called **dgroup**. The assembler computes all addresses of items in chunks of the same group relative to the start of the *group*, not to the starts of their individual chunks. The linker also treats as a group any set of **public** chunks with the same name and class and any set of **stack** chunks with the same name and class. For simplicity in language, let's also consider as a group any single chunk that has not otherwise been associated with a group.

Thus only the addresses of groups of chunks remain to be determined by the loader. The positions of these groups relative to the beginning of the program are known, so the loader's task is simple. The assembler and linker record the occurrences of these addresses in your program for the loader to fill in. We will see later exactly how these addresses occur in your program.)

Segment specification

Now we can connect these rather abstract descriptions of memory allocation with the more concrete details of addressing. We have seen that, in order for addressing to be as independent as possible from the ultimate location of data in memory, most addressing is figured relative to the start of a group of chunks containing the data. This fits closely with the 8086 family segment:offset addressing technique. The segment addresses of groups are stored in segment registers that rarely need to be changed. These are used as the segment part of segment:offset addresses and the offsets within the group as the offset part. The major addressing effort is in determining the offset address of an operand.

This convention entails that offsets not exceed hex ffff; hence groups (and single chunks) may not exceed 64-K bytes in length.

Elaborate default conventions permit assembly language programmers to ignore the segment address most of the time. In some cases, using a specific register for the offset address calculation directs the instruction to find the segment address in a certain segment register. In other cases, the type of instruction indicates the default segment register. We will indicate the defaults as they come up. At the end of this section we will consider the *segment override* method of overriding these defaults.

When the assembler is ready to generate the binary code for an instruction that refers to a memory address, it has the following addressing information:

- it knows the offset part of the address relative to the beginning of a group; and
- it knows which segment register will be used for the segment:offset address.

However, it does *not* know to what addresses you will have set the segment registers. (To know that, it would have to be able to completely unravel the logic of your program before it was even assembled.) To provide this information you must use statements of the form **assume ds:my_data** or **assume es:dgroup**, where **my_data** and **dgroup** could be any chunk or group. The **assume** pseudo-operation does *not* cause any value to be placed in the indicated segment register; it merely provides information to the assembler. You must set the segment registers yourself. The **assume** statement does provide some redundancy that is used in error checking. If you attempt to use the wrong segment register to address a memory location—i.e., one which has not been related to the proper group by an **assume** statement, you will get an error message.

We have still not explained how your programs obtain the ultimate segment addresses of your groups. In order for your instructions to refer to the right groups when you access data, you must load the appropriate segment addresses into the segment registers. For example, if you want to set DS equal to the **dgroup** segment address, you must include in your program the statements

```
mov ax, dgroup
mov ds, ax
```

The first instruction is an *immediate* mode move of the segment address **dgroup** to the AX register. For some reason you may not make an immediate mode move to a segment register. How does the address **dgroup** get encoded in this instruction? The assembler identifies this instruction to the linker, and the linker passes on this information to the loader, noting that this address must be filled in by adding the program starting address to the known offset from the program start. Thus, DOS fills in the address **dgroup** when it loads the **.exe** file.

If you want to use the ES register, you will have to load it the same way.

You are expected to define a chunk with combination indicator **stack**. If you don't, the linker will object. The linker will concatenate all the **stack** chunks of each class and handle them as a group. It passes information about them to the loader, which will initialize the Stack Segment Register SS to the **stack** group segment address of the last stack group loaded and set SP equal to one beyond the highest offset in that group. This will cause the first item pushed onto the stack to go into the highest address in that **stack** group. From there, the stack will grow *downward*.

When DOS loads your **.exe** file, it sets the Code Segment Register CS equal to the segment address of the first group in your program, just after the Program Segment Prefix. You identify the entry point of your program by means of a label on its first instruction, then you repeat that label to the right of the **end** statement that terminates your program. This information is passed on to the loader, which initializes the Instruction Pointer IP so that CS:IP is the program entry point. If it were necessary to identify the **cli** statement in Figure 6.3.1 as a program entry point, then the corresponding **end** statement would be **end mfg_boot**. (BIOS entry points are in fact determined some other way.)

With this background on the way the assembler and DOS allocate and refer to memory locations, we can now consider the remaining addressing modes.

Direct addressing

The simplest way for an instruction to access an operand in memory is through *direct mode* addressing. The offset address of the operand is encoded directly into the instruction, and the segment address is assumed to be in the DS register, unless you override this default. In some cases, you may have determined the offset *a priori*, for example as hex 1234; the instruction that moves to register AX the word beginning at that offset is

```
mov ax, [1234h]
```

The brackets are necessary to distinguish this addressing mode from immediate mode. This situation is rare, however. Unless you are referring to particular BIOS or DOS storage areas, you will rely on the assembler to determine the addresses of your data in memory, using the **db** or **dw** pseudo-operations as described above. The following lines define a word variable called **salary** and move it to register AX:

```
salary dw ?
          :
(lines omitted)
          :
mov ax, salary
```

If you had defined **salary** as a byte variable, you could move it to AH or AL, but not AX.

The assembler can do simple arithmetic. Occasionally, you may see a statement like

```
mov ax, salary+2
```

The + sign does not signify an operation in the program being constructed; it is a directive to the assembler to add 2 to the offset **salary** before assembling it into the binary code for the **mov** instruction. The resulting instruction moves to AX the word that begins 2 bytes after **salary**, i.e., the next word in memory.

Note that direct addressing can be used for the source or destination operands, but *not both*, because the **mov** instruction cannot be used to move data
between memory locations.

Indirect addressing

Some assembly language applications involve considerable address manipulation to determine which data in memory are the operands for certain instructions. It is often convenient to place the offset address of an operand in a
register: this is called *indirect mode* addressing. Four registers can be used for
indirect addressing:

BX, BP, SI, DI.

For example, the statement

mov ax, [bx]

moves to register AX the word whose offset address is in BX, while

mov [di],ch

moves the contents of register CH to the byte whose offset is in DI. Determina-
tion of the segment address for an indirect mode operand is slightly more complicated than for direct mode. Unless you override the default, the segment
address for the indirectly addressed operand is assumed to be

```
in  DS  if  the  offset  address  is  in  BX,  SI,   or  DI
        (as above), or
in  SS  if  the  offset  address  is  in  BP.
```

The latter default convention permits concise instructions for indirect addressing of stack entries.

In the example **mov [di],ch** above, the assembler determined that a *byte*
was to be moved because CH is a byte register. Had the source operand been
immediate rather than direct, the assembler might not have had sufficient
information to determine its length. For example, should the assembler interpret the statement **mov [di],1** as "move hex 01 to the *byte* whose address is in
DI ", or as "move hex 0001 to the *word* whose address is in DI "? In fact, the
assembler will reject this statement as ambiguous. The proper forms for the
two possible interpretations are

```
mov byte ptr [di],1
mov word ptr [di],1
```

Note that indirect addressing can be used for the source or destination operands, but *not both*, because the **mov** instruction cannot be used to move data
between memory locations.

Based and indexed addressing

The *based* and *indexed* addressing modes are very similar, intended to permit convenient location of array entries in memory. The offset address of the operand is the *sum* of a direct address encoded in the instruction, plus the contents of one of the registers BX, BP, SI, or DI. If the Base Register BX or Base Pointer BP is used here, the mode is called *based*. If an index register SI or DI is used, it is called *indexed*. (The difference in terminology stemmed from other CPUs whose index and base registers were used quite differently.) If BP is specified, then the default segment address is in the Stack Segment Register SS; otherwise it is in DS. For example, suppose you defined a fifty byte array

```
byte_array   db   50 dup (?)
```

Then you could move its sixth entry to register AX with the instruction

```
mov si,5
mov ax,byte_array[si]
```

Alternative notations for **byte_array[si]** are **[si]+byte_array** and **[si+byte_array]**.

The last, and most involved, 8086 family addressing mode is a combination of based and indexed addressing, naturally called *based indexed* mode. The offset address of the operand is the sum of two or three quantities: the content of one of the base registers, that of one of the index registers, and (if indicated) a direct address that is encoded into the instruction itself. If the Base Pointer BP is specified, the default segment address is in SS; otherwise it is in the Data Segment Register DS. For example, the instruction

```
mov [bp][di],ch
```

adds the content of BP and DI to obtain the offset address of a byte in memory, gets its segment address from SS, then moves the content of CH to that byte. The instruction

```
mov ax,byte_array[bx][si]
```

adds the contents of BX and SI to the offset **byte_array** to obtain the address of a word, gets its segment address from DS, and moves that word to AX. The following alternative notations have the same meaning:

```
byte_array[bx][si]
byte_array[bx+si]
[byte_array+bx][si]
```

Note that based or indexed addressing can be used for the source or destination operands, but *not both*, because the **mov** instruction cannot be used to move data *between* memory locations.

Segment overriding

In all the above examples, the segment address of an operand was obtained from a segment register according to a default convention that depended on the use of the BP register. You may override this convention by explicitly specifying a segment register. For example, the instruction

```
mov ax, es: [bx]
```

moves to register AX the word whose segment and offset addresses are in ES and BX, respectively. The assembly language override specification actually places a one-byte machine instruction code called a *segment override prefix* to be placed ahead of the code for the move instruction.

6.4 Survey of 8086 family instruction set

Concepts

* 8086 instruction types: – Data transfer – Sequence control – Arithmetic – Processor control – Bit manipulation – String manipulation
* Input/output port addressing   * Use of Flags Register

In this section we shall survey the common instruction set of the 8086 family. The PC/AT's 80286 CPU has a few more instructions, which will be considered in Chapter 9. The aim is not to teach you to program in assembly language, but to help you read assembly language programs, particularly the PC/AT BIOS and device drivers. We will consider each instruction category briefly, giving general descriptions of its members. Proper use of some instructions requires more detailed knowledge that you can gain easily from manuals and texts. If you want to learn 8086 assembly language programming from the ground up, Lafore's primer, reference [22], is well arranged and very instructive. Scanlon's text [27] is faster and more advanced. Even if you are following one of these, you will need a manual: the most appropriate are the Intel *iAPX 86, 88 User's Manual* [7] and *iAPX 286 Programmer's Reference Manual* [5]. The relevant parts of the manuals are very well written.

The instruction set is divided into six major categories:

Data transfer	Sequence control
Arithmetic	Processor control
Bit manipulation	String manipulation

Data transfer instructions move single units of data from one register to another or between registers and main memory. *Arithmetic* instructions perform addition, subtraction, multiplication, and division on eight- or sixteen-bit un-signed or signed integers. *Bit manipulation* instructions give you access to in-dividual bits in your data. *Sequence control* instructions change the ordinary sequence of instruction execution, permitting you to implement branching and looping, and to invoke subprograms. Under the category *processor control* are gathered some instructions that manipulate the Flags register and some miscellany. The final category, *string manipulation* instructions, includes some fast instructions for moving and comparing entire strings of bytes or words. These categories are considered in order below. As you read through this, you will gradually gain enough information to follow the assembly lan-guage programming examples included with the discussion. Taken from the PC/AT Basic Input Output System (BIOS) and Power On Self Test (POST), which are stored in ROM and listed in the *PC/AT Technical Reference* man-ual, they illustrate nearly all types of instructions.

Data transfer instructions

The first category of instructions moves data from one place to another in the CPU, memory, or an external device. Its members can be further grouped as follows:

```
mov     push     xlat     in
xchg    pop               out

lea     lds      lahf     pushf
        les      sahf     popf
```

Move and Exchange Instructions **mov** and **xchg** move data from a source operand to a target operand, or exchange data in two operands. The operands can be immediate, registers, or memory cells, addressed in any mode, with some exceptions:

- You may not move or exchange *two* memory cell operands. Thus a mem-ory to memory move requires an intermediate register: to move a word from location **init_val** to location **count**, for example, you might write

```
mov ax, init_val
mov ax, count
```

- No immediate operand may be a destination.
- The CS register may not be a destination.
- You cannot move an immediate operand to a segment register: to clear the DS register, for example, you might write

```
mov ax, 0
mov dx, ax
```

These restrictions apply to all instructions that have source or destination operands.

Push and pop These instructions let you push data onto a stack or pop it off in just one operation. Recall that SS:SP is always assumed to be the address of the top of a stack, and that the stack grows downward. (It is *upside down!*) The **push** instruction decrements SP and stores its single operand in SS:SP. The **pop** instruction moves data from SS:SP to the operand, then increments SP. These instructions always move *words*, so only word registers may be used as operands, and *SP is always decremented or incremented by two*. The operation of these instructions is illustrated by Figure 6.4.1. Note that these operations provide another way to move a word between memory cells: to move a word from location **init_val** to location **count**, for example, you might write

```
push init_val
pop count
```

Translate The **xlat** instruction provides a very concise table lookup facility. Suppose you had stored byte values $b_0,...,b_n$ in consecutive addresses starting at cell **table**. Here, n must be ⟨ 256. If you store the address of **table** in register BX, then you can load a table entry b_k into register AL simply by loading k into AL and executing this instruction. For example, these instructions load b_4 into AL:

```
mov al,4
xlat
```

In and Out These two instructions provide input and output operations between register AL or AX and one of the 64 K possible input/output ports of the CPU. The ports are conduits between the CPU and external devices. It's not

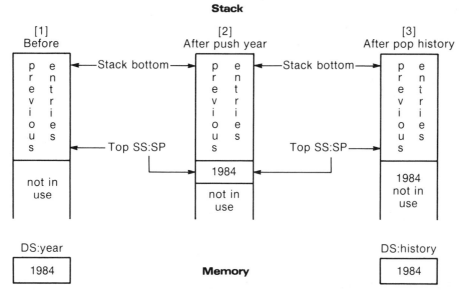

Figure 6.4.1 Operations PUSH and POP

likely that you have that many physical ports, but all your ports have sixteen bit *port addresses*. (Note: on the PC/AT only the first 1024 of these port addresses are actually available.) Each device usually has several CPU port addresses. For example, the parallel printer port LPT1 on the IBM Monochrome Display Adapter has three CPU port addresses:

port address (hex)	*function*
3bc	Output a byte for printing
3bd	Input a printer status byte
3be	Output a printer control byte

Some CPU ports transfer bytes, some transfer words. You must accordingly use the AL or AX register. The addressing mode for the port operand is either immediate or indirect via the DX register.

A good example of the use of **out** instructions is the technique for programming the Motorola 6845 video controller chip, the principal component of both the IBM Monochrome and Color/Graphics Adaptor boards. This chip has eighteen one byte registers R0 to R17 that hold certain video control parameters—for example, the cursor shape and location. The CPU sends values to these Parameter Registers by using two additional 6845 registers, the Index and Data Registers. The Index Register is connected to a one byte CPU port whose port address is hex 3b4 for the Monochrome board or hex 3d4 for the Color/ Graphics board. The Data Register is connected to CPU port hex 3b5 or 3d5, respectively. To send a value to a 6845 parameter register, the CPU must first send its number—0 through 17—to the 6845 Index Register, then the desired value to the Data Register.

Figure 6.4.2 is a fragment of the PC/AT BIOS video control routine that uses this technique. It is listed in the *PC/AT Technical Reference* manual [20, p. 5-130]. We haven't yet discussed a few features that appear in this code. After the initial comments is a label **m16:** that identifies the location of the next instruction so that the assembler can set up various kinds of jump instructions. About a page earlier, a BIOS routine that sets the video mode had stored at offset **addr_6845** the correct CPU port address, hex 3b4 or 3d4. Thus the source operand in the first **mov** instruction is addressed in direct mode. For some reason, the 6845 Parameter Register number comes to this routine via the AH register. It must be moved down to AL for the **out** instruction. The **out** instructions use indirect addressing via the DX register. The **inc** and **dec** instructions increment or decrement the specified register by one. The **jmp $ + 2** jump instructions merely waste some time to allow the 6845 to read a CPU port: **$ + 2** means "2 bytes after this location," i.e., the location of the next instruction. This routine first sends the value in the CH register to the specified 6845 register. Then, after the second **out** instruction, it repeats itself, sending the value in the CL register to the next 6845 register. (This would cause a problem if you set AH = 17 to send a value to 6845 register

R17; but you wouldn't, because that register is used to send you the light pen position.)

Moving addresses Three instructions are used to move addresses. The **lea** Load Effective Address instruction moves the offset address of its source operand (relative to the segment address of its group) to the indicated register. The **lds** and **les** instructions—Load Data Segment and Load Extra Segment—load two words from the source operand to two registers. The low order source word is regarded as an offset address and loaded into the specified destination register. The high order source word is regarded as a segment address and loaded into the DS or ES register. For example, if you had stored offset and segment addresses of some data table at memory locations with offsets **haya** and **haya+2**, then instruction **lds si,haya** would set up DS:SI as the segment:offset address of the table.

Moving flags The CPU Flags register is used to control the CPU status and to inform you of the results of many operations. To use it you need to be able to move it around. Four instructions are provided. Instructions **lahf** and **sahf** move some of the individual flag bits to and from the AH register. They are obsolete relics from the Intel 8080 and 8085 CPUs. The more flexible **pushf** and **popf** push and pop the entire Flags register onto or from the stack. To change a flag, for instance, you may use **pushf**, pop the stack to a register, manipulate the appropriate bit in the register, push the register, then use **popf**. More direct methods are available for most of the flag bits.

```
; This routine outputs the cx register to the 6845
; registers named in AH.
m16:
        mov     dx,addr_6845    ; address register
        mov     al,ah           ; get value
        out     dx,al           ; register set
        inc     dx              ; data register
        jmp     short, $+2      ; io delay
        mov     al,ch           ; data
        out     dx,al           ;
        dec     dx
        jmp     short $+2       ; io delay
        mov     al,ah
        inc     al              ; point to other data register
        out     dx,al           ; set for second register
        inc     dx
        jmp     short $+2       ; io delay
        mov     al,cl           ; second data value
        out     dx,al
```

Figure 6.4.2 Fragment of PC/AT BIOS video controller*

*PC/AT Technical Reference manual [20 , p. 5-130].

Arithmetic instructions

The arithmetic instructions perform addition, subtraction, multiplication, division, and some related housekeeping tasks on two operands. In some cases, the one-bit Carry Flag is used as a third operand. Except in one case, the result of the operation replaces the value of the destination operand. The arithmetic instructions can be further classified as follows:

```
add         inc         mul         aaa
sub         dec         div         aas
            neg                     aam
adc                     imul        aad
sbb         cmp         idiv
                                    daa
                        cbw         das
                        cdw
```

Several number representations are supported by these operations. The most fundamental are the eight- and sixteen-bit binary representations, with ranges 0..255 and 0..65535, respectively. For signed binary arithmetic, eight- and sixteen-bit twos complement representations may be used, with ranges −128..127 and −32768..32767. The same sixteen bits can represent different numbers in the two systems; Figure 6.4.3 shows how they correspond.

In some applications, simple arithmetic must be done with great volumes of data already encoded as decimal digits using the ASCII or some other BCD system. The overhead of translation to and from binary representation can be avoided, at the expense of efficiency in arithmetic operations, by using unpacked or packed decimal representation. In the former, one decimal digit is stored per byte in binary form in the low order four bits with the high order

8 bit				16 bit			
unsigned binary		signed binary		unsigned binary		signed binary	
hex	dec	hex	dec	hex	dec	hex	dec
00	0	00	0	0000	0	0000	0
::	:	::	:	: :	:	: :	:
ef	127	ef	127	efff	32767	efff	32767
f0	128	-f0	-128	f000	32768	-f000	-32768
::	:	::	::	: :	: :	: :	::
ff	225	-01	-1	ffff	65535	-0001	-1

```
In memory, the numbers look
like this, but you can use the
other systems to refer to them.
```

Figure 6.4.3 Correspondence between signed and unsigned numbers

four bits set to 0011. In the latter, two decimal digits are stored per byte, the high order digit in binary form in the high order four bits and the low order digit in the low order four.

Most of the arithmetic operations affect various flags— i.e., bits in the Flags register. These provide you with information about the outcome of the operations. You may need that in order to handle error situations, or combine the 8086 arithmetic operations for multiword higher precision or real number arithmetic, or to implement some less standard operations. The CPU sets the Overflow Flag OF = 1 to indicate that an operation produced a value outside the range of the representation used. The Carry Flag CF indicates that an operation produced a carry from the high order bit of the result or required a borrow into it. The Zero Flag ZF indicates that an operation produced the result zero. The Sign Flag SF is set equal to the high order bit of the result; in unsigned arithmetic, this means that the result was negative. The CPU sets the Parity Flag PF = 1 to indicate that the number of 1's among the low order eight bits of the result is odd. This has little use in arithmetic, but is good for performing parity checks on data. The Auxiliary Flag AF is used mainly in decimal arithmetic: it indicates a carry from or a borrow into bit 3 of the destination operand (this bit: 0000 0000 0000 1000).

Binary addition, subtraction, and comparison Unsigned and signed addition are identical operations, as far as the underlying bit patterns are concerned, if you ignore the carry bit. For example, consider Figure 6.4.4. Therefore, the same addition instruction supports both representations. This is true for subtraction as well. Instructions **add** and **sub** perform both signed and unsigned addition and subtraction.

To perform multiple word higher precision addition, you may break the addends into single words, added individually from right to left. However, these single word additions need one more addend: the carry bit from the sum of the words on the right. A similar situation obtains in the case of subtraction. Two instructions are provided for implementing multiple precision addition and subtraction: **adc** and **sbb**. For instance, the result of the **adc** operation is the sum of its two operands plus the value of the Carry Flag.

The Negative operation **neg** replaces its operand by its (twos complement) negative. Warning: **neg** won't compute the negative of the largest negative number because it's not representable!

signed decimal	eight bit unsigned binary representation	unsigned decimal representation	
15	0000 1111	15	
-37	1101 1011	221	
-22	1110 1010	236	
3	0000 0011	3	
-1	1111 1111	255	
2	1 0000 0000	2	(mod 256)

Figure 6.4.4 Signed and unsigned addition

Often in programming you must compare two numbers a and b, taking different action according as a ⟩ b, a = b, or a ⟨ b. This is usually implemented by subtracting, then determining whether a - b is positive, zero, or negative. Since you don't need the exact value of the difference, the Compare instruction **cmp** is provided to subtract two operands, setting the flags as usual. But **cmp** does *not* replace the destination operand with the result: it performs a *nondestructive* comparison. Usually, you will follow a **cmp** instruction with a jump based on the flag values.

Warning: comparing numbers by this method takes care, because the Sign Flag interprets numbers as negative if their high order bit is 1. Here is an example, using eight bit arithmetic:

```
a  =  hex 22   =   0010 0010
b  =  hex FA   =   1111 1010
```

You might expect to find a ⟨ b, but if you compute -b and add, you'll get

```
  a  =  0010 0010
 -b  =  0000 0110
a-b  =  0010 1000  ⟩  0
```

The secret is to look at the Carry and Overflow Flags as well as the Sign Flag. See the discussion of the conditional jump instructions below.

It is so frequently useful to count upward or downward, adding 1 or -1 to a number of modest size, that two instructions have been provided: **inc** adds 1 to its operand and **dec** subtracts 1. These Increment and Decrement operations are done *modulo* 28 = 256 or 216 = 65536 depending on the length of the operand—8 or 16 bits—and the Carry Flag is never set (but the Overflow Flag may be).

Multiplication and division Two multiplication instructions, **mul** and **imul**, are provided for unsigned and signed arithmetic, respectively. Each has only one operand, the source. If the source is a byte, it is multiplied by the byte in register AL, and the resulting word is placed in AX. If the source is a word, it is multiplied by the word in AX, and the resulting 32-bit product is placed in DX and AX (high order word in DX). Immediate addressing mode is not allowed. Flags CF and OF are set alike and indicate that the product is longer than the source operand. The other flags convey no information about these operations.

A good example of programming with the arithmetic instructions is found in Figure 6.4.5, a fragment of the PC/AT BIOS video control program [20, p. 5-131]. A few aspects of this code need discussion. First, it is an assembly language *procedure*, so it must commence with a **proc** statement giving its name and the type of **call** statement used to invoke it. Moreover, it must return to the calling program via a **ret** statement and end with an **endp** statement. These will be discussed again later under the heading *Program transfer instructions*. Since this procedure will use the BX register, it saves the register value on the stack at the onset and restores it with a **pop** at the end. Next, it saves the input AX value in BX so that it can use AX for multiplication.

When it last set the CRT mode, the BIOS stored the appropriate number of columns (40 or 80) in the byte variable **crt_cols**. The **mul** instruction then computes the row number times the number of columns (characters per row). It must use the address prefix **byte_ptr** to indicate that the operand is a byte rather than a word. The **xor** instruction sets BH = 0 (explained below under the heading *Bit manipulation instructions*). Next, the column number is added to the product, and the result multiplied by two, because each character requires two bytes—an ASCII code and an attribute byte. Multiplication by two is most easily accomplished by another bit manipulation instruction **sal** that shifts the AX register left one bit. This procedure thus computes the formula.

```
video memory offset = 2*(row * no. of columns + column).
```

Division is somewhat like multiplication. Two instructions, **div** and **idiv**, are provided for unsigned and signed arithmetic, respectively, and each has only one operand, the source. If the source is a byte, it is divided into the word in register AX, and the quotient and remainder are placed in AH and AL, respectively. If the source is a word, it is divided into the 32-bit dividend in DX and AX (high order word in DX), and the quotient and remainder are placed in AX and DX, respectively. Negative nonintegral quotients are truncated toward zero. Immediate addressing mode is not allowed. The flags convey no information about these operations.

If the quotient exceeds the capacity of the register indicated above, the CPU issues an **int 0** interrupt instruction. (These are discussed in Section 6.5.) If

```
position
   This service routine calculates the regen buffer address of a
   character in the alpha mode.
input
   ax = row, column position
output
   ax = offset of char position in regen buffer
```

```
position proc near
        push bx                  ; save register
        mov  bx,ax
        mov  al,ah               ; rows to al
        mul  byte ptr crt_cols   ; determine bytes to row
        xor  bh,bh
        add  ax,bx               ; add in column value
        sal  ax,1                ; *2 for attribute bytes
        pop  bx
        ret
position endp
```

Figure 6.4.5 Fragment of PC/AT BIOS video control program*

*PC/AT Technical Reference manual [20 , p. 5-131].

you are running under DOS, this will cause your program to terminate and DOS will display the message **DIVIDE OVERFLOW.**

For a divide instruction the dividend is always twice as long as the divisor (the source operand). Thus it's useful to be able to construct the proper two-byte representation of a one-byte dividend or the two-word representation of a one-word dividend. This amounts to filling a register with copies of the sign (high order) bit of the short dividend. Two instructions are provided: **cbw** fills register AH with copies of the sign bit of AL, and **cwd** fills DX with copies of the sign bit of AX.

Decimal arithmetic The remaining arithmetic instructions,

```
aaa    aas    aam    aad    daa    das,
```

are used with the standard ones to implement unpacked and packed decimal arithmetic. You may consult an Intel manual for information concerning their use.

Bit manipulation instructions

A number of instructions provide means to deal with individual bits. They can be grouped as follows:

```
not        test       shl/sal    rol
and                   shr        ror
or
xor                   sar        rcl
                                 rcr
```

These instructions generally affect the flags in intuitive ways, as described next. However, for some details you should consult an Intel manual.

Logical instructions The **not** instruction reverses all the bits (switches 0 and 1) in its single-byte or word operand. The **and**, **or**, and **xor** instructions perform the indicated operations bit by bit on the source and destination operands, and place the result in the destination operand. For example,

	and	*or*	*xor*
	0000 1111	0000 1111	0000 1111
	0011 0011	0011 0011	0011 0011
	0000 0011	0011 1111	0011 1100

Since *xor*-ing any value with itself yields zero, this instruction can be used handily to clear registers: **XOR BH,BH** clears register BH in Figure 6.4.5.

Test This instruction is rather like the Compare instruction **cmp**. It performs the **and** operation on the source and destination operands and sets the flags accordingly, but does *not* replace the destination operand. Normally, one of the operands is a byte or word of flags bits, the other is a mask with bits set just at the flag bit positions you care about. After the **test** instruction the Zero

Flag ZF = 1 unless one of your interesting flags bits was set. You can then execute a jump instruction on the basis of the ZF value.

Shift and rotate instructions These instructions move bits around within a byte or word. They have two operands, the first of which is best called the *target* operand; the other can be named n. If you want $n = 1$, you can specify it as an immediate operand. Otherwise, you must move it into the CL register and specify CL as the second operand. The Left Shift instruction has two names: **shl** and **sal**. It shifts bits of its target operand leftward n places, filling on the right with zeros. Its Right counterpart is **shr**. The *Arithmetic* Right Shift **sar**, however, fills on the left with copies of the target operand's original sign bit.

The Left and Right Rotate Instructions **rol** and **ror** regard their target operand as a circular structure, so that bits shifted off one end appear at the other. The Left and Right Rotate with Carry instructions **rcl** and **rcr** operate the same way, except that the Carry Flag is regarded as a bit in the target operand, just to the left of its sign bit. Figure 6.4.6 shows some eight bit examples of the shift and carry instructions.

In binary arithmetic, you can use left and right shifts to multiply and divide by powers of two. However, you must take particular care in dealing with negative numbers: the results may not be what you expect.

```
instruction     CF     target

                c    stuvwxyz   (Each letter representa a bit.)

shl target,1    s    tuvwxyz0
shr target,1    z    0stuvwxy
sar target,1    z    sstuvwxy
rol target,1    s    tuvwyxzs
ror target,1    z    zstuvwxy
rcl target,1    s    tuvwxyzc
rcr target,1    z    cstuvwxy
```

Figure 6.4.6 Examples of shift and rotate instructions

Sequence control instructions

The 8086 family CPUs provide a great variety of sequence control instructions: unconditional jumps, conditional jumps, loops, and procedure and interrupt calls and returns. The last type, procedure and interrupt calls and returns, will be discussed in the Section 6.5. The others can be arranged as follows:

jmp	31 conditional jump instructions beginning with **j**	**loop** **loope**/**loopz** **loopne**/**loopnz**

Jumps and labels The unconditional jump instruction **jmp** transfers control to some target instruction instead of obtaining the next instruction as usual from the next memory cell. The mechanics of the transfer are simple: the values of the Code Segment and Instruction Pointer Registers CS and IP are replaced by the segment:offset address of the target instruction. CS is replaced only if necessary. How do the assembler, linker, and loader determine the correct target address from your code? This is done using labels of various sorts. A *label* is a symbol in the left hand column of an assembly language program that serves as a name for that particular location in memory. If you can assume that a label refers just to an offset relative to a segment address assured to be in the CS register when it is the target of a jump instruction, then the label is termed *near*. Jumps to near labels require the CPU to change only the IP register. The assembler regards a label as near if it is followed by a colon or if it is part of a near **proc** statement. (The latter is a type of procedure declaration discussed in Section 6.5.) If your program indicates that no such assumption is warranted, then the label is termed *far*, and the assembler sets up the binary instruction code so that the CPU changes both the CS and IP registers.

The unconditional jump instruction **jmp** has one operand, its destination. Almost all addressing modes except immediate are valid. If direct addressing is used, the assembler encodes a near or far jump depending on the context in which the operand—a label—is defined. In the other modes, the target is not completely specified by the program, but is computed from data in registers. The assembler has no direct way of knowing whether a near or far jump is required, so you must include the symbols **near ptr** or **far ptr** in the instruction to indicate your intention. For example, the **jmp** instruction below transfers control to the instruction at label **target1**, **target2**, or **target3** according to the value in register SI. Since the assembler has no simple way of relating the **target** addresses to that of the **jmp** instruction, the latter must include a near or far specification.

```
addr      dw      target1, target2, target3

          jmp   near ptr addr[di]

target1..........  ⎫  These labels
target2..........  ⎬  could be
target3..........  ⎭  defined anywhere.
```

A special *short* form of the near **jmp** instruction may be used when the target label lies in the range $-128... $+127$, where $ indicates the address of the **jmp** instruction. If you know that the label **cake:**, for example, lies in this range, you can specify this more efficient instruction by writing

```
jmp short cake
```

You can even use one of the symbols in the range $-128... $+127$ to specify a target a certain number of bytes back or ahead. This is not easy, because you have to study the manual in detail to find out how long each instruction is. One case is common, however: since a **jmp short** instruction is two bytes long, the instruction **jmp short $ + 2** just jumps to the next instruction. It requires fifteen clock cycles to do essentially nothing, so is frequently used in the PC/AT BIOS to waste just a little time. For example, fifteen cycles is apparently just enough time to allow some external devices to read data sent them by a CPU **out** instruction and prepare to receive the next transmission.

Conditional jump instructions In concept, conditional jump instructions are similar to the unconditional jump; they execute the jump if some condition is met, else do nothing. However, their implementation for the 8086 family CPUs differs in one major aspect from the **jmp** instruction: they permit only direct addressing, and the destination operand must be a label in the short label range. There is a great variety of conditional jump instructions, shown in Figure 6.4.7. Two sets of jumps based on numerical comparison are given, one for unsigned arithmetic, using mnemonic letters **a** and **b** for *above* and *below*, and one for signed arithmetic, using mnemonic letters **g** and **l** for *greater* and *less*. After a **cmp** instruction to compare source and destination operands and set the flags, you execute the jump appropriate for your problem and the type of arithmetic you are using. For example, to jump to label **target** in case the signed integer in AX is less than or equal to that in BX, you may write

```
cmp ax,bx
jle target
```

The conditional jump instructions only inspect the Flags, and the condition AX $\leq$ BX corresponds to different Flag settings depending on the kind of arithmetic used. In some cases, alternative names are provided for the same instruction. For example, since AX $\leq$ BX is equivalent to not (AX $\rangle$ BX), the **jle** instruction above could be written **jng.**

Figure 6.4.8, another example taken from the PC/AT BIOS video control routines [20, p. 5-132], illustrates the use of a **jz** conditional jump with a **test** instruction. This routine turns off a display attached to the IBM Color/Graphics Adaptor board before scrolling the screen. (This prevents unsightly snow due to bad design of the Adaptor.) The routine uses registers DX and AX for scratchwork, so it saves them on the stack and restores them later with pops. Two CPU ports are involved: hex 3da and 3d8, which are attached to the Status and Control Registers of the Motorola 6845 video controller chip on the Adaptor. The routine repeatedly inputs a byte from the status register and performs a **test** instruction to inspect bit 3 ($8 = 2^3$) until that bit = 0. This condition means that the CRT beam is turned off while moving from the bottom CRT line to the top. (This happens sixty times each second.) When the beam is off, the CPU sneaks in and turns off the monitor by outputting a hex 25 code to the control register. (If you turn off the monitor at other times, you may see it bounce.)

Loops The loop instructions combine a decrement operation with a comparison and a conditional jump. You can use them for controlling three varieties

For use with unsigned arithmetic	Jump if this condition is satisfied	After cmp d,s the condition means	Jump if this condition is satisfied	For use with signed arithmetic
ja /jnbe	CF = 0 & ZF = 0	d > s	OF = SF & ZF = 0	jg /jnle
jae/jnb /jnc	CF = 0	d ≥ s	OF = SF	jge/jnl
jb /jnae/c	CF = 1	d < s	OF ≠ SF	jl /jnge
jbe/jna	CF = 1 or ZF = 1	d ≤ s	OF ≠ SF or ZF = 1	jle /jng
	CF = 0 means d ≥ s ZF = 0 means d ≠ s		SF = OF means d ≥ s ZF = O means d ≠ s	

General use			Mnemonic letters:	
je /jz	ZF = 1	d = s	a above	j jump
jne/jnz	ZF = 0	d ≠ s	b below	l less
jo	OF = 1		c carry	n not
jno	OF = 0		cx CX register	o overflow, odd
js	SF = 1		d destination	p parity
jns	SF = 0		e equal, even	z zero
jp /jpe	PF = 1		g greater	
jnp/jpo	PF = 0			
jcxz	CX = 0			

Figure 6.4.7 Conditional jump instructions
(The slash symbols / indicate different names for the same instruction.)

```
; 80x25 color card scroll
push dx
      mov   dx, 3dah        ; guaranteed to be color card here
      push ax
n8:                         ; wait_disp_enable
      in    al, dx          ; get port
      test al, 8            ; wait for vertical retrace
      jz    n8              ; wait_disp_enable
      mov   al, 25h
      mov   dx, 03d8h
      out   dx, al          ; turn off video
      pop   ax              ; during vertical retrace
      pop   dx
```

Figure 6.4.8 Fragment of PC/AT BIOS video control routine*

*PC/AT Technical Reference manual [20 , p. 5-132].

of *for* loops, with the counter variable in the CX register. They are similar to conditional jump instructions in that they permit only direct addressing, and the destination operand must be a label in the short label range. Although two of the loop instructions use the Zero Flag set somewhere in the body of the loop, none of the loop instructions themselves alter any flags. The counter variable is treated as an unsigned integer. The simple **loop** instruction decrements CX by 1 and jumps to the target (the start of the body of the loop) unless CX = 0. This implements a downward *for* loop as follows:

```
target:  ....                    for i: = CX downto 1 do
         (something)                 something
         loop target
```

Figure 6.4.9, a fragment of the Power On Self Test (POST), gives a good example of a **loop** instruction. This routine adds all the bytes in a 64 K block of ROM, and sets ZF = 0 just in case the sum is zero. When programs and data are stored in ROM, a checksum byte is included in each 64 K block to ensure that this sum is zero. Thus the Figure 6.4.9 POST routine checks the integrity of the data in the ROM. On entry to this routine, the Data Segment Register DS must contain the segment addresss of the 64 K block to be tested. The routine clears CX and AL, then adds all 64 K bytes to AL using the **loop** instruction. The final **or** instruction doesn't change AL but does set the Zero Flag appropriately. The segment override on the **add** instruction seems unnecessary.

The **loope** instruction, also named **loopz**, decrements CX by 1, then jumps to the target if CX $\neq$ 0 and ZF = 0. This implements a variety of *while* loop that is sometimes written as a downward *for* loop with a *break*. Equivalent IBM Pascal versions of a **loope** statement are shown in Figure 6.4.10.

The **loopne** instruction, also named **loopnz**, is similar, but it reverses the ZF test.

```
                 ros checksum subroutine

                 assume cs: code,  ds: abso
post3:
ros_checksum      proc near     ; next ros module
                  sub  cx,cx    ; number of bytes to add
                                ; is 64k
ros_checksum_cnt:
                  xor  al,al    ; entry for optional ros
                                ; test
c26:
                  add  al,ds: [bx]
                  inc  bx       ; point to next byte
                  loop c26      ; add all bytes in ros
                                ; module
                  or   al,al    ; sum = 0?
                  ret
```

Figure 6.4.9 PC/AT POST fragment*

*PC/AT Technical Reference manual [20 , p. 5-67].

Processor control instructions

The 8086 family processor control instruction category is a miscellany. Its members can be grouped further as follows:

```
nop       wait       stc       std       sti
          esc        clc       cld       cli
hlt       lock       cmc
```

```
                    target:   ....
                              (something)
                              loope target
```

```
for i := CX downto 1 do          while (CX ) 0) and (ZF = 0) do
  begin                            begin
    something;                       something;
    if ZF ≠ 0 then break             CX := CX - 1
  end;                             end
```

Figure 6.4.10 Equivalent Pascal versions of a loope statement

The **nop** instruction does nothing. Its only use is to hold a place for some instruction that you might want to insert later without disturbing any addresses. Instruction **hlt** halts the CPU until it is reset or receives certain hardware interrupts (discussed in Section 6.5). The three instructions **wait**, **esc**, and **lock** are used when the CPU must work closely with another CPU or external device; consult the *i286 Programmer's Reference Manual* [5] for details.

Setting flags The remaining processor control instructions manipulate certain flags, i.e., bits in the Flags register. Instructions **stc**, **clc**, and **cmc** set, clear, and complement (reverse) the Carry Flag CF. This flag is often used to transmit error status information not necessarily related to arithmetic, and these instructions aid that process. Instructions **std** and **cld** set and clear the Direction Flag DF; this flag is critical to the string manipulation instructions discussed below. Instructions **sti** and **cli** set and clear the Interrupt Flag, which is discussed in Section 6.5.

Figure 6.4.11, another extract from the PC/AT POST [20, p. 5-35], illustrates the use of several of these instructions. This routine tests all the registers and some register to register moves first by moving hex ffff through all registers, then hex 0000. The routine uses the Carry Flag CF as a switch, and halts the CPU if the test fails.

String manipulation instructions

The last category of 8086 family instructions provides fast manipulation of strings of up to 64 K bytes or words. There are five basic string instructions,

```
movs       cmps       scas       lods       stos
```

which *move, compare, scan, load,* and *store* strings. Each of these can be suffixed with the letter **b** or **w** to indicate a string of bytes or words. Actually, the assembler always encodes one of the basic instructions as the appropriate suffixed instruction, according to the definition of its operands as bytes or words.

```
;          read/write the x286 general and segmentation registers
;          with all one's and zeroes's {sic}
           mov  ax,0ffffh          ; set up one's pattern in ax
           stc                     ; set carry flag
           jnc  errol              ; go if no carry
c8:        mov  ds,ax              ; write pattern to all regs
           mov  bx,ds
           mov  es,bx
           mov  cx,es
           mov  ss,cx
           mov  dx,ss
           mov  sp,dx
           mov  bp,sp
           mov  si,bp
           mov  di,si
           jnc  c9
           xor  ax,di              ; pattern make it thru all regs
           jnc  errol              ; no - go to err routine
           clc                     ; clear carry flag
           jmp  c8
c9:                                ; tstla
           or   ax,di              ; zero pattern make it thru?
           jz   c10a               ; yes - go to next test
errol:     hlt                     ; halt system
```

Figure 6.4.11 PC/AT POST fragment*

*PC/AT Technical Reference manual [20 , p. 5-35].

After performing their respective operations, these instructions increment or decrement the index registers used for addressing the strings. They increment the indices just when the Direction Flag DF = 0. The amount of the increment or decrement is 1 or 2, the number of bytes in the string entries. You may provide these instructions with a *repeat prefix,* which causes the CPU to repeat them according to a countdown using the CX register like the loop instructions. Three types of repeat prefix are available: **rep, repe** alias **repz,** and **repne** alias **repnz.**

The direction specified by the flag DF is critical in cases where the source and destination of a string move overlap or where you are scanning for an entry of one string or comparing entries of two strings, searching for the first occurrence of some relation.

Note that the repeat prefix is *not required.* Occasionally, the exact operations of the basic instructions are useful without repetition. In particular, they work gracefully with loop instructions.

Move string The **movs** instructions move a source string, **s**, to a destination string, **d**. The segment:offset addresses of the string entries are normally as follows:

```
        source string   s:   DS:SI
destination string   d:   ES:DI
```

The entries of **s** and **d** must be both bytes or both words. You may override the source segment register designation but not the destination. The example in Figure 6.4.12 should clarify the string moving technique.

Compare string Instruction **cmps** compares the current entries of the destination and source strings like a **cmp** instruction, setting the Flags but not altering the strings, then it adjusts the index registers to refer to the next string entry. You could use the **rep** prefix, but that would be uninteresting, since it would merely compare the last two string entries. A more appropriate prefix is **repe**, also spelled **repz**, which stands for *repeat while equal to zero*. This prefix causes repetition until CX = 0 or ZF ≠ 0; that is, the repetition stops when a *mismatch* is found or the string is exhausted. The opposite effect is achieved with the prefix **repne**, also spelled **repnz**: repetition stops when a *match* is found or the string is exhausted.

Scan string Instruction **scas** works just like **cmps** except that the role of the source string is played by a constant in register AL or AX. AL is used when the entries of the destination string are bytes.

Load string The **lods** instruction is not normally repeated. It simply moves a source string entry into AL or AX, then adjusts the index register to refer to the next entry.

```
        segment sorcery
s    dw      10 dup(0)   ;s  is a string of  10 words  hex 0000 .
n    dw      10          ;n  tells how many words to move.
     ends
     segment destiny
d    dw      100 dup(1)  ;d  is a string of  100  hex 0001 's .
     ends
     lds     sorcery     ;Set up the segment registers,
     les     destiny
     assume  dds:sorcery ;and inform the assembler.
     assume  es:destiny
     cld                 ; Clear  DF  to increment index registers.
     lea     si,s        ; Load  s  offset relative to  DS .
     lea     di,es:d     ; It's necessary to override  DS  default.
     mov     cx,n        ; Initialize the repeat count.
rep movs     d,s         ; Replace the first  n  0001 's  in  d  by
                         ; zeros from  s .  This routine decrements
                         ; CX  by  1  each step until  CX = 0 , and
                         ; increments  si  and  di  by  2 .
```

The operands of the movs instruction tell the assembler nothing except that it should increment SI and DI by 2 (s and d are defined by dw statements). The assembler actually encodes the last instruction as rep movsw.

Figure 6.4.12 Example of string move instruction

Store string Instruction **stos** stores the byte or word in AL or AX in the current entry of the destination string, and adjusts the index register to refer to the next entry. Figure 6.4.13, another excerpt from the PC/AT POST [20, p. 5-76], illustrates the use of **lods** and **stos** within a loop. This routine must start with the Data Segment and Extra Segment Registers DS and ES equal to the segment address of a block of memory to be tested, and BX must contain the length of the block, in words. First the block is filled with a checkerboard bit pattern using **stosw** instructions in a loop; then the block is compared with the original pattern using another loop with **lodsw** instructions. Label **C13** is a general error exit; it's in a part of the POST that has not been published.

```
; ----- checker board test
c10:    sub   di,di                    ; point to start of block
        mov   cx,bx                    ; get the block count
        shr   cx,1                     ; divide by 2
c11:    mov   ax,0101010101010101b     ; first checker pattern
        stosw                          ; write it
        mov   ax,1010101010101010b     ; second checker pattern
        stosw                          ; write it
        loop  c11                      ; do it for cx count
        sub   si,si                    ; point to start of block
        mov   cx,bx                    ; get the block count
        shr   cx,1                     ; divide by 2
c12:    lodsw                          ; get the data
        xor   ax,0101010101010101b     ; check correct
        jnz   c13                      ; exit if not
        lodsw                          ; get next data
        xor   ax,1010101010101010b
        jnz   c13                      ; go if not correct
        loop  c12                      ; loop till done
```

Figure 6.4.13 PC/AT POST fragment*

*PC/AT Technical Reference manual [20 , p. 5-76].

6.5 Procedure calls and interrupts

Concepts

* Subprograms, procedures, and interrupt service routines   * Near and far procedure calls and returns   * Interrupts and interrupt vectors   * Overflow interrupt **into**   * Breakpoints, single stepping, and debuggers   * Hardware interrupts   * Nonmaskable interrupt NMI   * 8259A Interrupt Controller chip   * IRQ lines and maskable interrupt priorities   * Instructions **cli, sti**, and End of Interrupt signal   * PC/AT cascaded master and slave interrupt controllers

In Section 6.4 we considered in some detail the entire 8086 family instruction set except for several related instructions:

call	procedure call	int	interrupt
ret	return from procedure	iret	interrupt return
cli	clear IF	into	interrupt on overflow
sti	set IF		

These all have to do with subprogram execution, hence with different means of modularizing programs. Rather than looking at details of all these instructions at once, it is worthwhile to consider a general problem of program modularization and see how these instructions solve it. We can start with the simplest method, then progress to techniques that are more involved and more flexible.

Procedures

If you want to modularize a program but are using a language with no subprogram facility (for example, BASIC without the **gosub** command), then you can split your program into parts, but when you write each part, you must know precisely where the others are in order to transfer control among them—probably with jump instructions. This is difficult when the various parts are written independently, or when they are loaded in different parts of memory on different occasions. Moreover, such a program is hard to alter because most changes will result in some code relocation in memory.

The standard *procedure call* partially solves this problem. To illustrate the technique, let S be your main program or perhaps a subprogram, and suppose S needs to call upon another subprogram P to perform a task on some data. Then S sends P not only the data for the required computation, but also the address of your current position in S. Thus, when P is finished, it can transfer control back to the appropriate place in S. When this technique is used, S is called the *calling* subprogram and P is called a *procedure*.

When procedures call one another in succession, the return addresses are used in reverse order to return to the main program. Thus, the *stack* is a useful device for storing the return addresses. Moreover, if the variables local to each procedure (its scratchpad memory) are placed on the stack too, then the work of different invocations of the same procedure can be kept separate. This allows procedures to call each other in arbitrary ways. In particular, it permits use of *recursive* procedures, a very powerful technique in algorithm design.

Among a procedure's local variables are those that are used as *parameters:* its input data come from the calling subprogram and its results return via its parameters. These variables must be accessible to both routines. Execution of a procedure using a stack for parameters, return address, and other local variables is described briefly in Figure 6.5.1. Notice that calling subprogram S and procedure P must agree on the definition and order of the parameters, S must have access to its own address in order to push the return address in Step 2, and S must know where P is in order to perform the jump at Step 3.

The 8086 family CPUs implement this process with the procedure call and return instructions **call** and **ret**. In particular, **call** performs Step 2 and 3, and **ret** does Step 6 and (optionally) part of Step 7. The **call** instruction has two forms, *near* and *far*. The *near* form is used just when procedure P is in the same segment as the calling subprogram S. A near call only needs to push the offset part of the return address; but a far call must push the entire segment:offset address. Since the Instruction Pointer and Code Segment registers CS:IP always contain the address of the next instruction in the execution sequence, an instruction **call P** merely has to push IP or the full CS:IP. Then it replaces IP or the full CS:IP by the offset or segment:offset address of (the entry point of) procedure P, thus causing a jump to P.

Similarly, the **ret** instruction has near and far forms. It pops either one or two stack entries into IP or the full CS:IP, thus causing a jump back to the proper place in the calling subprogram S. This instruction has an optional parameter: **ret n** pops n bytes from the stack *after* jumping. (n must be even!) Thus, if you know that S won't refer to the n parameters stacked just below the return address, then you can use this feature to do some of S's Step 7 housecleaning.

How do you tell the assembler which form of the call and return instructions to use? This is done with the assembly language pseudo-operations **proc** and **endp**. The assembler knows that code lying between them constitutes a procedure. A label on the **proc** statement designates the procedure entry point. When you write procedure P, you decide whether you will ever need to call it from a subprogram in a different segment. In that case, you specify the attribute **far** after the **proc** pseudo-operation. The code is thus organized as in Figure 6.5.2.

If you decide that procedure P will always be called by subprograms in the same segment, you can omit the **far** attribute, or emphasize your decision by

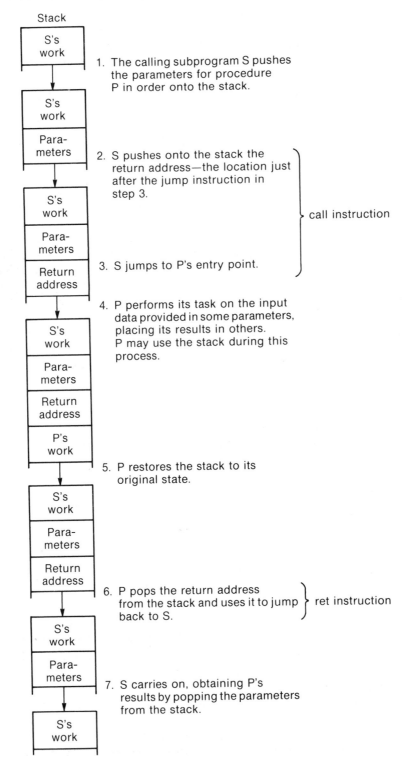

Stack

1. The calling subprogram S pushes the parameters for procedure P in order onto the stack.

2. S pushes onto the stack the return address—the location just after the jump instruction in step 3.

3. S jumps to P's entry point.

} call instruction

4. P performs its task on the input data provided in some parameters, placing its results in others. P may use the stack during this process.

5. P restores the stack to its original state.

6. P pops the return address from the stack and uses it to jump back to S.

} ret instruction

7. S carries on, obtaining P's results by popping the parameters from the stack.

Figure 6.5.1 Executing a procedure with call and ret instructions

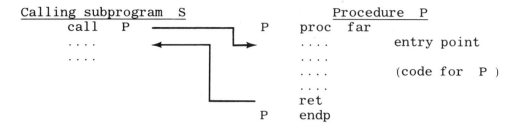

Figure 6.5.2 Assembly language procedure call

using the attribute **near**. A concrete example of a **near** procedure has already been included in Figure 6.4.5.

The example in Figure 6.5.2 used direct address mode for the call instruction. You can also use indirect addressing, referring to a memory location that contains the procedure address, or to a register that specifies a location that contains the address. The assembler can't foresee which procedure will be called in either situation, so you must specify a near or far call by using the **word ptr** or **dword ptr** attribute with the operand.

You now see how to specify the appropriate form of the call instruction. The same mechanism specifies a near or far return too since the **ret** instruction occurs between corresponding **proc** and **endp** pseudo-operations.

Interrupts

Procedure calls provide a major technique in modularizing program design. However, this device is still inadequate for many situations. The problem is that the calling subprogram S must somehow know where the procedure P is. P's address must be specified either when S is written or, at the latest, when the parts are loaded into memory. This may be very awkward if P is completely independent of the rest of the program. For example, if P is an operating system service routine, its memory location may need to change as the operating system evolves or is adapted to your needs. But such a routine is loaded independently of your program, and it would be very cumbersome for the loader to inform your program of the locations of all service routines every time it is executed.

The solution to this problem is the *interrupt*, a mechanism that permits one subprogram to call another even when neither one can know the location of the other ahead of time. This mechanism is named for another capability: it permits the hardware to interrupt whatever program is executing, call another routine to perform some service, and return to the original program when the service is complete. This is particularly useful when the hardware requires some attention that has little or nothing to do with the program currently running: for example, when you strike a key during some long computation. Thus, in describing this technique we will consider two types—both *software and hardware interrupts*. The main difference between them is simply that in the one, the subprogram call is initiated by software, and in the other by hardware. Hardware interrupts, however, involve further questions of priority that will be discussed later.

A subprogram that will be invoked via an interrupt is called an *interrupt service routine* (ISR). Setting up an ISR requires agreement in advance that whenever it is loaded its address will be stored in some fixed memory location called an *interrupt vector*. The 8086 family CPUs reserve the first 1024 bytes of RAM for storing 256 four byte segment:offset interrupt vectors.

The *interrupt* instruction **int** works rather like a call instruction. However, this instruction has no destination operand, but instead an *interrupt number* in the range 0..255. The interrupt number specifies which of the four-byte interrupt vectors contains the address of the desired service routine. For example, instruction **int 2** finds its destination address in the interrupt vector stored in bytes 0000:0008 through 0000:000b. There is one other difference. The interrupt instruction pushes the Flags register onto the stack just before it pushes the return address, and it turns off the Interrupt Enable bit in the Flags register itself. (On earlier 8086 family CPUs, an interrupt instruction would also turn off the Trap Flag TF. The PC/AT 80286 CPU does not. Further discussion of the Trap Flag is postponed until Chapter 9.) After these preparations, it jumps to the service routine just like a call instruction. This process is illustrated in Figure 6.5.3.

From Figure 6.5.3 you can see that returning to the interrupted program requires a **ret** instruction followed by **popf** to pop the Flags. The special *interrupt return* instruction **iret** performs exactly these two operations.

You will see later why the interrupt process treats the Flags specially.

Most of the ISRs that you will encounter while using the PC/AT provide BIOS and DOS services. IBM reserves many interrupt vectors for the addresses of the various service routines included in the BIOS and in DOS. These vectors are set appropriately every time you boot the machine. Chapters 7, 8, and 10 describe the BIOS and DOS services in detail.

The PC/AT POST fragment shown in Figure 6.5.4 is a near procedure, **prt_hex**, that contains an interrupt calling on the BIOS for a video output service. It is taken from the *PC/AT Technical Reference* manual, reference [20, p. 5-67]. This routine is called to display the character whose ASCII code is currently in register AL. The routine places the service code hex 14 in register AH, the current display page number 0 in BH, and then issues interrupt hex 10. By this time in the POST, the interrupt vectors have been initialized so that vector hex 10 points to the BIOS video service routine. That routine performs the designated service (display the character in AL) on the appropriate display page.

Interrupt service routines

Sometime you may want to substitute your own custom interrupt service routine (ISR) for a BIOS or DOS routine, or you may want to use one of the remaining interrupt vectors and provide your own routine to service a need

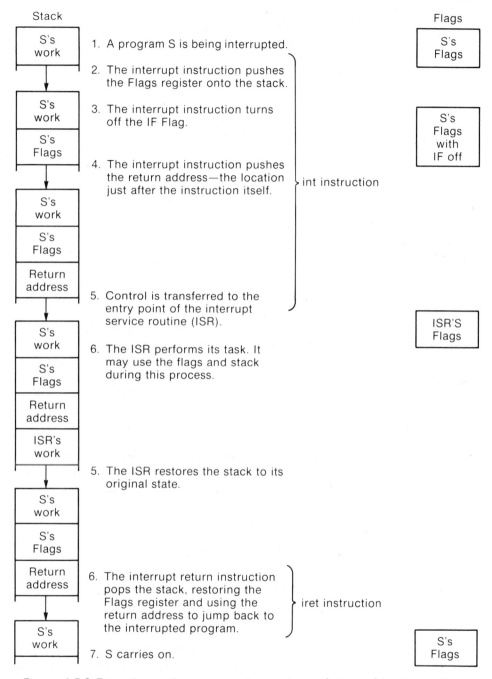

Figure 6.5.3 Executing an interrupt service routine with int and iret instructions

```
prt_hex proc near
        mov   ah,14   ; display character in  AL
        mov   bh,0
        int   10h
        ret
prt_hex endp
```

Figure 6.5.4 PC/AT POST fragment*

*PC/AT Technical Reference manual [20 , p. 5-67].

that IBM didn't anticipate. How do you write a program that operates as an ISR?

You can construct your custom service routine as a procedure **isr** in your application program. Such a routine must have three modes of operation. The best way to arrange that is to provide it two separate entry points (labels) besides its front entry (the one named **isr**). Let's call these two entry points **service** and **restore**. The code following the **service** entry must perform the appropriate service; when it is finished, the stack should be in the same state as when it started. This code is followed by an **iret** instruction. The code following the front entrance **isr** should first store someplace the current value of your chosen interrupt vector; then it should place in that vector the address of the **service** entrance. The code after the entrance point **restore** should merely restore the original value of the interrupt vector that you changed. These functions are depicted schematically in Figure 6.5.5.

When you wish to install your service routine, you call it from the application program by its name **isr**, thus entering by the front entry. This code just changes the interrupt vector to point to the **service** entrance. Now, whenever your application program (or any other program) issues the interrupt in question, control is transferred to the **service** entrance of **isr**, and your custom code takes over, returning to the interrupted program via your **iret** instruction. Finally, when you wish to restore the interrupt vector to its original status, you call it via the **restore** entry.

Restoring the interrupt vector is important because it may be used by some other software in memory that you need next (for example, DOS itself or some special utility that acts as an extension of DOS).

Overflow and breakpoint interrupts

A particularly useful custom ISR might handle error situations resulting from arithmetic overflow. A special *conditional* interrupt instruction **into** has been provided for this. This instruction behaves like **int 4** if the Overflow Flag OF is turned on; otherwise, **into** does nothing at all.

The **int 3** instruction has a special one byte machine code. Whereas the machine code for **int n** in general consists of two bytes—hex cd followed by **n**—the code for **int 3** is the single byte hex cc. This interrupt has no inherent special function, but its short code makes it easy for you to use **int 3** as a *breakpoint* instruction. If you wish to interrupt a program somewhere to execute some special code—for example, a "patch" to correct an error—or to stop and examine the contents of memory, you can put the patch or a memory inspection routine in an ISR for interrupt 3, then replace the first byte of the instruction code at the desired breakpoint with **int 3**. You must remember this replaced byte. As a first step in the ISR you should use the CS:IP values atop the stack to restore the byte to its former position. Then your ISR can execute the patch or inspect memory. An **iret** instruction will return to the instruction originally at the breakpoint, which is now in its original state.

Although breakpoint installation is delicate, it is routine, and common utilities called *debuggers* will install them for you. The **debug** utility supplied with DOS will let you install a breakpoint, then execute your program up to that point. As described in the last paragraph, the breakpoint disappears once used. The Microsoft debugger **symdeb**, an enhanced version of **debug** supplied with the Macro Assembler package, lets you install *sticky* breakpoints that don't disappear. You can rerun your program with the same breakpoints and different data.

The *single step* interrupt **int 1** is also a special case, designed for use by debugger utilities to step through a program one instruction at a time. Its operation depends on the use of the Trap Flag bit TF in the Flags register. Since the PC/AT 80286 CPU treats TF and the single step interrupt differently from the earlier 8086 family CPUs, discussion of single stepping is postponed until Chapter 9.

Hardware interrupts

Earlier, we noted that *hardware* interrupts involve questions of *priority*. A hardware interrupt consists of the same sequence of events as that described in Figure 6.5.3. However, it is initiated not by a software **int** instruction, but by the hardware itself. That is, your program S may suddenly be interrupted, and the entire sequence of Figure 6.5.3 may take place to service some special hardware need. Control may then be be transferred back to S, which may proceed as though nothing special had happened. Before we look at the priority problem, let's consider some examples of hardware interrupt situations.

Some device not necessarily controlled by your program needs service. For example, you may strike a key, which must then be processed, a byte of data may arrive over a serial communication line, or your printer may have completed a form feed operation and be ready to receive more output data.

Some instruction is in trouble—perhaps an operand is invalid, as in an attempt to divide by zero. If your program had to handle all possible problems of this sort, you would be overwhelmed with detail. Instead, the CPU issues an interrupt, and the BIOS or an operating system can provide ISRs, called *exception handlers*, to take care of such problems.

A hardware failure has occurred—perhaps a parity error or loss of power. A hardware interrupt in this situation can permit the BIOS or an operating system to diagnose the problem and prevent the worst catastrophes.

During debugging, you may want to single step through your program or to install a "breakpoint" that will stop it at a certain location so that you can inspect the contents of memory and registers.

From this list, you can see that various kinds of hardware interrupts should have different priorities. That is, certain interrupt services should not themselves be interrupted by lower priority requests. For example, a serial communication line should probably take priority over a printer, and hardware failure should probably have highest priority.

The CPU takes into account *some* priority questions in servicing hardware interrupts. These questions have to do with overall strategy and with interrupts generated by the CPU itself. Prioritization of interrupts generated by peripheral equipment is handled by another processor, an Interrupt Controller, that we will consider later.

The CPU takes care of one prioritization problem silently: hardware interrupts may occur only *between* instructions. For instance, this prevents call instructions from being interrupted while the stack and the CS:IP registers are in an inconsistent state. (There are some exceptions to this rule. First, interrupts are not allowed just after instructions that change segment registers. These are usually followed by instructions that change the corresponding offset addresses; this exception lets you ensure that two-word addresses are consistent before interrupts are enabled. On the other hand, **wait** instructions and instructions with **rep** prefixes may be interrupted because some of them take so long to execute that they might disrupt time dependent interrupt services.)

The interrupts with highest priority are software interrupts, including **into** and the breakpoint interrupt. These areexecuted whenever they are encountered in a program. One CPU-generated hardware interrupt has this same high priority: whenever a divide instruction attempts to divide by zero or produces a quotient that is too long for the destination operand, the CPU executes **int 0**. This is the only *exception interrupt* implemented on the earlier 8086 family members. The 80286 CPU has several others, that are discussed in Chapter 8.

Hardware interrupts that are not generated by the CPU are termed *external*. Among the external interrupts, a few are easily recognized as more urgent than others. Generally, they signal equipment failure, like a parity error or a drop in voltage. However, the earlier PC models classified in this group the interrupts originating from the 8087 Numeric Coprocessor chip. (That decision was awkward, but apparently dictated by potential conflicts with other hardware. It has been changed in the larger PC/AT.) These are called *nonmaskable* interrupts (NMI), because the CPU is not allowed to ignore them.

At times, particularly in ISRs, your software may be performing time-sensitive bookkeeping tasks that should not be interrupted. You may disable all external interrupts except the NMI by turning off the *Interrupt Enable* bit IF in the Flags register. This need is common enough that two special instructions are provided for handling IF:

The *clear IF* instruction **cli** turns IF off, disabling all maskable interrupts.

The *set IF* instruction **sti** turns IF on, enabling all maskable interrupts as soon as the *next* instruction has executed.

As you have seen, any interrupt automatically turns off IF. Otherwise, an ISR might be interrupted before it had a chance to execute a **cli**. This feature lies behind the design of the **int** and **iret** instructions. Since an interrupt must alter the Flags register, it pushes the old register value on the stack, for restoration by the **iret** instruction at the end of the ISR. Since other events might still be occurring that need interrupt service during your ISR, you should re-enable interrupts with the **sti** instruction as soon as possible.

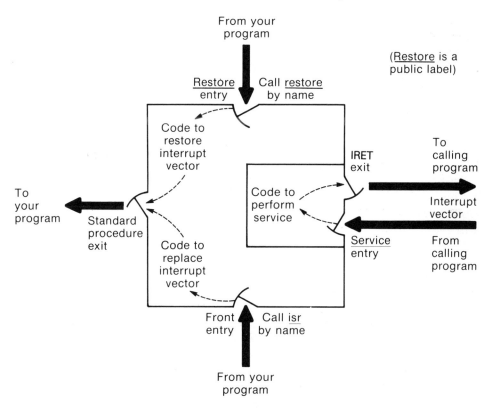

An interrupt service routine coded as a procedure in your program

Figure 6.5.5 Interrupt service routine

Intel 8259A Interrupt Controller

The CPU's interrupt prioritization capability is limited to distinguishing the NMI and CPU generated hardware interrupts, and making all-or-nothing-at-all decisions via the IF Flag. The possibilities for prioritization of maskable external interrupts vary so greatly over a range of applications that the CPU relegates this job to a separate processor. In the IBM PC family, this is an Intel 8259A Programmable Interrupt Controller chip. (Two of the 8086 family CPU chips, the 80186 and 80188, contain built in interrupt controllers equivalent to the 8259A.) This chip is programmable, and its full details lie beyond the scope of this book. However, you will find it useful to know generally how the 8259A is set up for use in the PC family and in the PC/AT in particular.

An 8259A has nine *interrupt request* input lines called NMI and IRQ0 to IRQ7. CPU components and peripheral devices request interrupt service by signalling the 8259A on these lines. A signal on the NMI line is never ignored. The POST programs the 8259A to assign decreasing priority to requests arriving on lines IRQ0.. IRQ7. When one of these interrupts is being serviced, no other request of equal or lower priority is granted. The 8259A uses an eight bit *mask register* to keep track of which IRQ lines are currently being serviced. When any mask bit is on, requests from lines with equal or lower priority are ignored. Remember, also, that no maskable interrupt will be serviced unless the CPU's IF Flag is on.

When the 8259A decides to honor an interrupt request, it sets the corresponding mask bit, then signals the CPU to execute the appropriate **int** instruction. The POST has already programmed the chip to associate the correct interrupt numbers with the NMI and IRQ lines. This hardware initiated **int** instruction interrupts whatever program is executing, then transfers control to the appropriate ISR. When the ISR is finished, it transfers control back to the interrupted program, which can then proceed as if nothing notable had happened.

This scheme provides no mechanism for turning off the 8259A mask register bit that indicated that this hardware interrupt was being serviced. Something must be done, else no further IRQ signals with equal or lower priority will ever be serviced! In the PC, a hardware ISR must send the 8259A a signal called *End of Interrupt* (EOI) to tell it to clear this bit. The same signal is used by all hardware ISRs, because the 8259A knows which bit to clear—the hardware ISR just completing is always the one corresponding to the NMI or else to the highest priority IRQ line being serviced!

How do you send an EOI signal to the 8259A? One of the CPU output ports is attached to an 8259A input port. Thus, an ISR sends an EOI signal by using an **out** instruction to send a particular EOI byte (hex 20) to that port.

In a PC/AT there are actually two 8259As handling an NMI line and fifteen IRQ lines. They are connected in a "cascaded" arrangement, that permits the CPU to communicate with one chip—the *master*—which in turn controls the other—its *slave*. Figure 6.5.6 shows how the IRQ lines are allocated to CPU

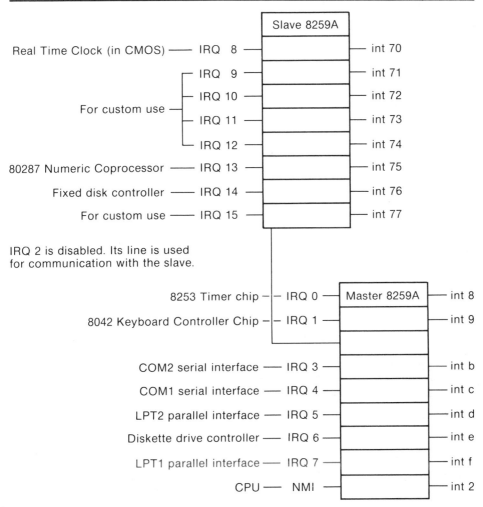

Figure 6.5.6 PC/AT IRQ line assignments

components and peripherals and indicates the corresponding interrupt numbers.

You should remember that the 8259A chip is programmable and carries out the prioritization scheme described earlier just because the PC POST routine programmed it to do so. How do you program this controller? It accepts program commands through its input ports, which are connected to certain CPU output ports. You can use **out** instructions to send it these commands. Thus, if you master the 8259A command language, you can reprogram it to handle maskable hardware interrupts differently. A full description of the 8259A functionality and command language is beyond the scope of this book. You can find more information in the *PC/AT Technical Reference* manual [20, Sec. 1], and references [7, pp. B-67 ff.], [8, pp. 2-89 ff.], [3, Ch. 9], and [26, Sec. 6.4].

7

DOS Structure II: BIOS and DOS Interrupt Services

Contents

In Chapter 5 you had a brief view of the overall "job description" for DOS, then considered in detail the services provided by the DOS commands and utilities. These included the organization and execution of program files. However, that chapter could not treat a major category of DOS services: those provided for use *by programs*. DOS offers a great variety of services to your programs, including

- access to the file system
- control of all input/output equipment, including
keyboard	disk drives	serial ports
screen	diskette drives	parallel ports
clock		
- memory allocation
- execution of DOS commands and other programs

Since the routines that perform these services were written independently of your programs and information about their details and location in memory is not generally available to you, the interrupt mechanism is appropriate for accessing them. This chapter considers first their overall organization as BIOS and DOS interrupt service routines. To obtain these services, your programs must be able to execute software interrupts. A method for using them with a higher level language, IBM Pascal, is described.

The chapter concludes with surveys of the interrupt services offered by the earlier members of the PC family via the BIOS and DOS 2.0. The new services offered by the PC/AT BIOS and DOS 3.0 are considered in more detail later in Chapters 8 and 10.

7.1 BIOS and DOS interrupts

Concepts

* Interrupt vectors   * Interrupt vector allocation to BIOS, DOS, BASIC, etc.   * Vectors available for commercial and custom software * Contention for interrupt vectors

---

In Chapter 6 you saw how the 8086 family CPUs reserve the first 1024 bytes in memory for 256 four-byte interrupt vectors. Each vector can store a segment:offset address of an interrupt service routine (ISR). A hardware or software interrupt instruction **int n** finds interrupt vector **n** at location 0000:4*n. As in all 8086 storage schemes, the vector is stored with the less significant bytes first:

location	byte of ISR address
4*n	low order byte of offset
4*n + 1	high order byte of offset
4*n + 2	low order byte of segment
4*n + 3	high order byte of segment

To use the interrupt mechanism for executing a service routine, the calling program and the software that loads the service routine must agree which interrupt vector will contain the routine's address. Thus, in the PC computers, IBM reserves a block of interrupt vectors (starting at vector 0) to point to specific service routines. Your programs obtain the services by placing parameters specifying in some standard place the details of the desired service, then executing the appropriate interrupt.

The interrupt vector allocation scheme is not as simple as you might think. First, the use of certain interrupts is specified by Intel's CPU design. (For example, the divide and overflow interrupt instructions on occasion execute specific hardware interrupts—0 and 4. Moreover, the breakpoint **int 3** instruction code is designed to facilitate invoking a particular type of ISR.) Next, a number of interrupt services are provided in the BIOS code, stored in the Read Only Memory of every PC, that is available for incorporation into any operating system. Certain vectors must be reserved for the BIOS services. Third, many more services are provided by the operating system itself, and vectors must be allocated for these. Both the BIOS and the operating system must also reserve vectors for use by future versions, to provide flexibility in evolution. Already, therefore, three different companies—Intel, IBM, and Microsoft—must agree on interrupt vector allocation. Finally, the remaining unassigned vectors form a combat arena for all commercial and custom software products that provide any services via interrupts. If two programs use the same vector, they cannot be installed simultaneously. The allocation scheme for BIOS and DOS interrupt vectors, particularly in the PC/AT, betrays some design errors that complicate your use of their services. Contention by other software for unassigned vectors is unrefereed and often leads to unfortunate results.

Figure 7.1.1 shows the interrupt vector allocation for the PC/AT. The scheme can be summarized numerically as follows:

no. of vectors	allocated to
40	BIOS
32	DOS
32	PC/AT peripherals
113	BASIC
39	Commercial or custom software
256	

The number of vectors allocated to BASIC seems excessive, while all commercial and custom software must vie for the remaining 39. However, this special software will often be installed only when BASIC is not in use, so it could use some of BASIC's vectors. The only way for software developers to ensure that two products do not attempt to use the same vectors simultaneously is to allow you to specify the vectors at installation. This tactic is not difficult to implement, but commercial packages rarely do. In fact, their documentation rarely indicates which vectors they selected. Of course, not many customers would know how to use such information!

Although there are fewer than one hundred BIOS and DOS interrupt vectors, perhaps twice that many distinct services are in fact offered. Often, you can request different services via the same interrupt by specifying a service code in one of the CPU registers before executing the interrupt instruction.

The next section shows you how to access these services from a high level language, IBM Pascal. The BIOS and DOS services available to earlier PC users under DOS 2.0 are sketched in Sections 3 and 4. New DOS 3.0 and PC/AT BIOS services are described in somewhat more detail in Chapters 8 and 10.

hex

0   These vectors were reserved by Intel in the 8086 design,
:   either for specific uses, or for future expansion. Most of
:   them have specific uses in the PC BIOS; all of them
1f   are used by the PC/AT BIOS*

20   These vectors are reserved for DOS, either for specific
:   uses, or for future expansion.
3f

40   These vectors are reserved for use by PC/AT peripheral
:   equipment. Several are in fact used by the PC/AT disk
5f   and diskette drive controller.

60
:   Not allocated. Available for commercial or custom use.
6f

70
:   Used by the PC/AT BIOS.
77

78
:   Not allocated. Available for commercial or custom use.
7f

80
:   Reserved for BASIC. (Available if BASIC is not in use.)
f0

f1
:   Not allocated. Available for commerical or custom use.
ff

*The original PC BIOS used most of these vectors, and was compatible with Intel's 8088 CPU design. However, for the 80286 CPU, Intel specified uses for several new vectors in this range, and conflicted with the PC BIOS. Since the PC/AT had to be compatible with the PC, these conflicts remain in the PC/AT design, and cause certain complications in BIOS usage. More details are given in Chapter 10.

Figure 7.1.1 PC/AT interrupt vector allocation

7.2 Interrupt services for high level languages

Concepts

∗ What are the principal steps necessary to execute an interrupt service routine (ISR)? ∗ How can a higher level language execute an
ISR possibly by using an assembly language procedure? ∗ What feature of IBM Pascal Version 2.0 facilitates invoking ISRs? ∗ How do
you use IBM Pascal units? ∗ Example Pascal program invoking an
ISR. ∗ Can you write an ISR in a higher level language?

In the previous section we noted that the BIOS and DOS provide many useful services for your programs by means of interrupt service routines (ISRs).
Moreover, if you need a service of this nature that is not provided, you can
write your own ISR for one of the the interrupt vectors set aside for your programs' use. Until now, ISRs have been discussed using assembly language
concepts, because the interrupt process involves manipulations at the CPU
register and instruction level. Specifically, execution of an ISR by your program involves

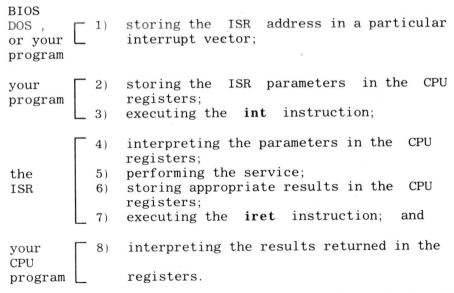

```
BIOS
DOS ,     ⌐ 1)  storing the  ISR  address in a particular
or your   └       interrupt vector;
program

your      ⌐ 2)  storing the  ISR  parameters  in the   CPU
program   │       registers;
          └ 3)  executing the  int  instruction;

          ⌐ 4)  interpreting the parameters in the   CPU
          │       registers;
the       │ 5)  performing the service;
ISR       │ 6)  storing appropriate results in the   CPU
          │       registers;
          └ 7)  executing the  iret  instruction;   and

your      ⌐ 8)  interpreting the results returned in the
CPU       │
program   └       registers.
```

It would be unfortunate if all programs using interrupts had to be written
entirely in assembly language. This would prevent systems programmers

from enjoying some of the benefits of higher level languages: the possiblity of making algorithm structure apparent in the code and making details concise and intelligible. Thus it is important to find a way to implement the interrupt process in a higher level language. (This of course contradicts one of the criteria which is sometimes used to distinguish a language as higher level: independence from machine level detail!)

Several higher level languages available for the PC family have implemented this feature at least partially, and some commercial software tools packages provide access. This book uses *IBM Pascal Version 2.0* to show how to invoke an ISR from a program written in a higher level language, and to give several example programs illustrating the use of various interrupt services. This implementation, using an IBM procedure called **intrp**, is about as general as possible. Implementations in some other languages restrict either the interrupts supported or the registers available for parameters and results. If your favorite language doesn't have a sufficiently general interrupt feature, you may be able to write for it an assembly language procedure functionally equivalent to **intrp**.

This feature of IBM Pascal uses the *unit* concept, an extension of standard Pascal developed by the Microsoft Corporation. (IBM Pascal Version 2.0 is a licensed adaptation of Microsoft Pascal Version 3.20.) We won't cover the unit concept in detail here, but must discuss it enough for you to understand how to use the **intrp** procedure.

A Pascal *unit* is a collection of data types, data structures, and routines that are compiled together for later use by various programs. A unit's source code consists of two files, its *interface* and *implementation* files. The interface file contains the information about the unit needed by programs that will use it. This includes the declarations of data types, data structures, and procedures that will actually appear *by name* in the programs, but not those involved only in the internal details of the implementation. The implementation file contains all other necessary declarations and the code for all the routines. You compile unit interface and implementation files together to get an object code file. You can either link this directly with your program's object code file, to produce the **.exe** file for your program, or you can put the unit's object code file into an object code library, which the linker will search when constructing the **.exe** file.

In IBM Pascal Version 2.0, the interrupt procedure **intrp** belongs to a predefined unit called **IBMintrp**. The interface file is **IBMintrp.int**, and the object code is contained with that of some other units in a library called **IBMpas.lib**.

An IBM Pascal program—call it **today** for example—that uses this unit should begin with the following lines:

```
{$include:'IBMintrp.int'}
program today(input,output);
uses IBMintrp;
```

The first line serves to include the interface file as a physical part of the program. The list following the program name identifies the files to which it will refer, in this case the standard input and output files. The program **today** may use all the identifiers provided for it in the interface file. If it mentions a procedure identifier provided by the interface, then the compiler will tell the linker, by a code in the program object file, to look for that procedure's code in an object file under the unit name **IBMintrp**.

IBMintrp is a small unit, consisting of just one data type and one procedure. Figure 7.2.1 lists its interface [17, Language reference, p. 2-177]. The list after the unit name contains the identifiers that the unit provides for programs using it. The **vars** parameter specification indicates that the full two word segment:offset parameter address will be sent to the procedure. Procedure **intrp** sets CPU registers AX through ES as specified by the components of record **inregs**, executes instruction **int intno**, then records in the components of record **outregs** the values returned by the ISR via CPU registers AX through Flags.

The program **today** mentioned earlier can refer to records of type **reglist** and to procedure **intrp** just as though they were declared in the program itself. After you have compiled the program, obtaining its object code file **today.obj**, you may link it to produce the executable file **today.exe**, telling the linker to search the library **IBMpas.lib** for additional object code. If this library and the file **today.obj** are in the current directory and DOS has a path leading to the linker program file **link.exe**, then you may invoke the linker by entering the DOS command

```
link today, , , IBMpas
```

Figure 7.2.2 is a sample program **today** that prints today's date, by using the BIOS Interrupt hex 1a Function 4 to read the PC/AT real time clock. The various functions performed by this ISR are specified by placing the function number in register AH before executing the interrupt. The ISR returns the date information encoded in registers CX and DX. (This ISR also includes functions that report the time, reset the date or time, and set or cancel an alarm.)

```
interface;
unit IBMintrp (reglist, intrp);
type
  reglist = record
              AX, BX, CX, DX, SI, DI, DS, ES, Flags:    word
            end;
procedure intrp(       intno : byte;
                vars  inregs: reglist;
                vars outregs: reglist);
end;
```

Figure 7.2.1 Interface for IBM Pascal unit IBMintrp*

Pascal compiler language reference manual [17 , p. 2-177]

(If you are using IBM Pascal Version 2.0 for the first time to follow this example, you may find that it balks at the **$include** line, claiming a file system error. To remedy this, insert a **files =** statement in your **config.sys** file to increase from the default of eight the number of simultaneous open files permitted. Then reboot.)

The IBM Pascal Version 2.0 manual [2, Language reference, p. 177] warns that an ISR invoked by the **intrp** procedure must return with the Pascal stack unchanged from its original state. This precludes using **intrp** for two DOS interrupts, hex 24 and 25. These have to do with error handling and reading from specific disk sectors; they are discussed in Section 4 and Chapter 8.

If your favorite higher level language has no feature like **intrp** and you want to use BIOS and DOS interrupts for services like **today**'s date, you may be able to write an assembly language routine, functionally equivalent to **intrp**, that can be invoked by your programs.

```
{$include:'IBMintrp.int'}
program today(input,output);
uses IBMintrp;

{Determine today's date by using BIOS real time clock Interrupt hex 1A Function 4:
invoke interrupt 1A with AH = 4. The ISR returns the year in CX and the month and
day in DH and DL. The BIOS listing says that these data are ''in BCD''. That means
that the registers consist of four concatenated four bit digit codes. On 5 January
1985 this program printed

                        Year:   1985
                        Month:  01
                        Day:    05  }

var
  registers: reglist;
  DH,DL:     byte;

begin {today}
  with registers do
    begin
      AX := byword(#4,#0);          ! Make a word from two bytes.
      intrp(#1A,registers,registers);
      DH := hibyte(DX);             ! Split a word into two bytes.
      DL := lobyte(DX);
      writeln('Year:   ',CX:4:16);  ! Write four hex digits.
      writeln('Month:  ',DH:2:16);  ! Write two hex  digits.
      writeln('Day:    ',DL:2:16)
    end
end. {today}
```

Figure 7.2.2 Pascal program using a BIOS ISR to determine today's date

You have seen how to invoke existing ISRs from programs written in a higher level language. We have not, however, discussed how to *write* an ISR in a higher order language. That is not possible in general, because an ISR must interpret parameters and return results in the CPU registers, and the very execution of higher level language statements usually perturbs the registers. Moreover, an ISR must execute an **iret** instruction. If you are writing a routine to service your own interrupts, you may decide to pass parameters and results some other way (for example, via some specific memory locations). In that case, you can in fact write an ISR in Microsoft Pascal Version 3.20, which has a type of procedure that returns to the calling program via an **iret** instead of the usual return instruction. Unfortunately, IBM Pascal Version 2.0 has no such feature, and Microsoft Pascal Version 3.2 provides no procedure like **intrp**! For general ISR capability, you may be able to write an assembly language procedure that interprets the registers, calls another procedure to perform the main service tasks, then executes the **iret**. That way, you can write the bulk of your ISR, the procedure that performs the main tasks, in a higher level language. The technique for setting an interrupt vector to point to your ISR is discussed briefly in Section 5, in the context of DOS Functions hex 25 and 35. Reference [2] is a commercial software tools package that helps you write ISRs in C or Pascal for the IBM PC family.

7.3 PC BIOS interrupt services

Concepts

* BIOS interrupt services supporting the screen, serial port, keyboard, and printer. * Which BIOS services have changed with the PC/AT?

In Section 1 you saw that the PC BIOS provides a number of services to your programs via software interrupts. Section 2 showed how a program in IBM Pascal can access these services, using the PC/AT calendar support function as an example. This section gives a brief survey of the BIOS services available in all PC models. Many of these services are covered in greater depth later in Chapter 10 when you will have more information about the details of the PC/AT. In particular, the new services offered by the PC/AT BIOS are described thoroughly there.

The interrupt vector allocation table in Figure 7.1.1 showed forty vectors reserved for BIOS use. Only ten of these actually provide direct services to your programs. The others are used internally by the BIOS and DOS, reserved for future BIOS use, or reserved for special functions for which your commercial or custom software can provide service routines. These ten service interrupts, however, provide more than fifty different functions; you specify which function you need by placing its number in the AH register before executing the interrupt. The ISRs use other registers to accept input and return output values. The program service interrupts are listed in Figure 7.3.1, then described rather briefly in turn, with examples of their use. For more detailed information, consult the BIOS listing in the *PC/AT Technical Reference* manual, reference [20, Sec. 5].

Print screen: Interrupt hex 5 This is a simple service for a first example. Executing **int 5** will print the screen, just like the **Shift-PrtSc** keystroke. When this ISR returns, the byte at 0050:0000 will be 0 if the function succeeded or hex ff if it failed. If the printer is not on, the ISR will wait a while, then give up and report failure. Figure 7.3.2 is an IBM Pascal function that implements this service.

Screen and light pen: Interrupt hex 10 You can obtain sixteen different functions via this interrupt. They are summarized as follows:

- Set or ascertain screen mode (for example, Color/Graphics 320x200 pixel or Monochrome text).
- Set or ascertain active page (for Color/Graphics text mode only).
- Set Color/Graphics palette.
- Set cursor size (top and bottom lines in dot matrix).
- Set or read cursor position.
- Read light pen position.
- Read or write a character and attribute at the cursor location.
- Write a character at the cursor location.
- Read or write a dot at a given location (graphics mode).
- Write a character in ASCII teletype mode.
- Scroll a screen window (text mode only).

More detail on using these functions is provided in Section 10.3. You will also find a description there of one new PC/AT BIOS screen service: write a string.

(hex)	Service
5	Print screen
10	Screen and light pen functions
11	What peripheral equipment is installed?
12	How much standard memory is installed?
13	Disk and diskette functions
14	Serial communications functions
15	Formerly cassette functions, now joystick, clock, and PC/AT extended memory
16	Keyboard functions
17	Printer functions
1a	Clock functions

Figure 7.3.1 BIOS program service interrupts

```
function PrtSc: Boolean;
```

{This function prints the screen, returning the value true if
it succeeded, and false otherwise.}

```
type
  adsbyte       = ads of byte;          ! segment:offset address
const
  status_byte   = adsbyte (#00,#50);             ! offset first
var
  registers     : reglist;
begin {PrtSc}
  intrp(5,registers,registers);             ! Register values
  PrtSc := (status_byte ^ = 0)    ! are irrelevant.
end; {PrtSc}
```

Figure 7.3.2 Pascal function to print the screen

Several of these functions refer to screen attributes. In text mode, each character on the screen has a one byte ASCII code and a one-byte attribute which can be set separately. The attribute byte determines foreground and background color, intensity, underline, and blinking. For example, the standard monochrome text attribute is 7. Refer to the descriptions of the Monochrome and Color/Graphics Adapters in the PC/AT Technical *Reference* manual for details.

Figure 7.3.3 is an IBM Pascal procedure that uses Interrupt hex 10 Function 6 to scroll a screen window upward. The effect of scrolling is depicted in Figure 7.3.4.

Equipment and standard memory installed: Interrupts hex 11 and 12 Because these interrupts report details of your PC/AT configuration, they are described in detail in Chapter 10.

Disk and diskette: Interrupt hex 13 Ordinary programmers rarely have to deal with disk and diskette operation at the low level of the BIOS. Some more detail is given in Section 10.3, but this area is really beyond the scope of this book. You will be using the DOS file system functions described in the next section instead.

Serial communication: Interrupt hex 14 The service routine for this interrupt provides four different functions:

- Set serial port parameters, like BAUD rate, parity checking method, etc.
- Transmit a byte.
- Receive a byte.
- Ascertain the port status.

You will find more details about these functions in Section 10.3. Here, though, in Figure 7.3.5, is an IBM Pascal function that uses Interrupt hex 14 Function 2 to receive a byte from a serial port. Function 2 always returns a status code in AH, which indicates abnormal conditions like parity error or break signal

```
procedure scrollup(top,left,bottom,right,rows,attribute:
byte);

{This procedure uses BIOS Interrupt hex 10 Function 6 to
scroll the window defined by the given corners upward the
indicated number of rows, setting the attribute for the new
blank rows as specified.}

var
  registers; reglist;

begin {scrollup}
  with registers do
    begin
      ax := byword(6,rows);                    ! Function 6
      bx := byword(attribute,0);
      cx := byword(top,left);
      dx := byword(bottom,right)
    end;
  intrp(10,registers,registers)
end;   {scrollup}
```

Figure 7.3.3 Pascal procedure to scroll a window

detected. If no byte arrives, the function waits a while, then gives up and re-ports a time out status in AH.

You should realize that the BIOS does not support one of the more sophisti-cated and useful features of the standard IBM serial ports: their ability to signal receipt of data and readiness to transmit by issuing hardware inter-rupts. To control a port with the BIOS functions, you must continually *poll* it,

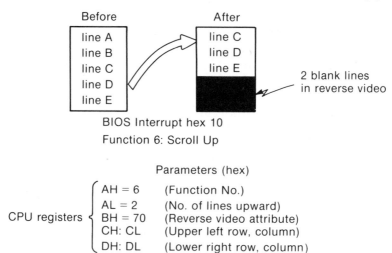

Figure 7.3.4 Scrolling

```
function rcv_byte(port,b: byte): byte;
```

{This function receives byte b from the indicated port. Only ports 1, 2 = COM1, COM2 are supported. It returns a status code whose bits contain the following information.

bit		bit	
7	Time out	2	Parity error
4	Break signal detected	1	Overrun error
3	Framing error }		

```
var
  registers: reglist;

begin {rcv_byte}
  with registers do
    begin
      ax        := byword(2,0);        ! Function  2
      dx        := byword(0,port);     ! Port number in  DL
      intrp(#14,registers,registers);
      b         := lobyte(ax);         ! Byte received in  AL
      rcv_byte  := hibyte(ax)          ! Status code in  AH
    end
end; {rcv_byte}
```

Figure 7.3.5 Pascal function to receive a byte from a serial port

inspecting the status information to determine if data have arrived or if it is ready to transmit. Polling generally prevents the CPU from doing other useful work between port services. To use hardware interrupts to control a port requires more sophisticated software. Some commercial packages are available. (See reference [1].)

Interrupt hex 15 service Originally Interrupt 15 provided four different cassette input/output services. Since later models of the PC have no cassette port, this ISR has been redesigned to provide several new services concerned with timing, joy stick control, PC/AT extended memory, and 80286 protected mode. These are described in Chapter 10.

Keyboard: Interrupt hex 16 You can obtain three keyboard functions with this interrupt:

- Wait for and read the next keystroke, removing it from the keyboard buffer.
- Inspect the keyboard buffer.
- Ascertain the current shift and toggle key status.

The keyboard buffer can hold codes corresponding to the last fifteen keystrokes: it allows you to type ahead. Keystroke codes are two bytes long. To use them you need to consult code tables in Sections 5 and 7 of the *PC/AT Technical Reference* manual and apply the following rules.

Construction of a keystroke code depends on whether it represents an ASCII character. In that case, the low order byte is the ASCII character code and the high order byte, called a *scan code,* identifies the key that was struck. For example, suppose you have have used the **Shift** key to place the keyboard in lower case, and strike key number hex 1e, labeled **A**. This keystroke represents lower case "a," which has ASCII code hex 61. Thus the keystroke code is hex 1e61.

On the other hand, if the keystroke has no ASCII code, the low order byte is zero and the high order byte is called an IBM *extended ASCII* code. For example, suppose you strike **Ctrl-PgUp**. This keystroke has IBM extended ASCII code hex 84, so the keystroke code is hex 8400.

Figure 7.3.6 is a Pascal procedure **read_key** that uses Interrupt hex 16 Function 0 to read a keystroke code from the keyboard buffer. It actually waits until you enter a keystroke (unless you have typed ahead), then returns two parameters. The first parameter indicates whether the second is an ASCII or extended ASCII code. Procedure **read_key** has many uses. For example,

- you can read the cursor control keys and move the cursor accordingly (using an Interrupt hex 10 service);
- you can detect keystrokes like backspace, **Ins**, and **Del**, that are used to edit keyboard input;
- you can let the user select actions by striking function keys **F1** to **F10**.

The PC's keyboard handling methods are complex, because our intuitive use of a typewriter is complex. The logic of this process is discussed in greater depth in Section 10.3.

Printer: Interrupt hex 17 This ISR provides three functions:

- To print a character.
- To initialize a printer port.
- To read the printer status.

Since a printer is such a slow device, it is frequently busy when you want to send it a character to print. When you request to print a character, the ISR will wait until the printer has signaled that it's ready. If this doesn't occur in a reasonable time, the ISR will give up and signal a time out error. Using this service is almost like using the serial communication interrupt, except that you don't have any choice over port parameters.

Clock: Interrupt hex 1a This ISR has been redesigned for the PC/AT to support its real time CMOS clock. The services are described in depth in Section 10.3.

```
procedure read_key(var ASCII: Boolean; var code; byte);

{This procedure uses BIOS Interrupt hex 16 Function 0 to read a keystroke code from
the keyboard buffer. It waits until you enter a keystroke, unless you have typed
ahead, then returns two parameters. If your keystroke represents a standard
character, then parameter ASCII is true and parameter code is its ASCII code.
Otherwise, ASCII is false and code is the IBM extended ASCII code for the
keystroke.}

var
  registers; reglist;

begin {read_key}
  with registers do
    begin
      ax := 0;                              ! Function code  0  in  AH
      intrp(#16,registers,registers);
      ASCII := (lobyte(ax) ‹ › 0);
      case ASCII of
          true : code := lobyte(ax);
          false: code := hibyte(ax)
        end
    end
end; {read_key}
```

Figure 7.3.6 Pascal procedure to read the keyboard.

7.4 DOS interrupt services

Concepts

* DOS interrupts and functions   * **Ctrl-Break, Crtl-C**, and critical
error handlers   * Asynchronous communication functions   * Clock
functions   * Directory manipulation functions   * Disk input/output
functions   * File control blocks   * File handles   * Memory management and program execution functions   * Printer output function
* Standard input/output functions

Earlier you saw how your programs can gain access to DOS services via
software interrupts. In the last section we discussed the interrupt services
provided for your use by the BIOS code stored in Read Only Memory (ROM).
These are the most fundamental services and can be incorporated into any PC

operating system. In the present section, we will consider the interrupt services provided specifically with DOS.

There are only a few DOS interrupts. However, you can access about one hundred different services, called DOS *functions*, by placing a *function number* in the AH register before executing DOS interrupt hex 21. The DOS interrupts and functions perform generally more complicated services than the BIOS interrupts. In fact, they usually call on BIOS interrupts to perform the basic components of their tasks. In this section we will consider first the various DOS interrupts, then go on to summarize the DOS functions provided through interrupt hex 21, giving examples of their use with IBM Pascal programs. This section considers only the services provided by DOS 2.0. The new DOS 3.0 interrupts and functions are described later in Chapter 8.

DOS interrupts

The following list summarizes the program services provided by the various DOS interrupts. All the commonly used services are provided as functions of Interrupt hex 21. You rarely encounter the others.

(hex)

20 Terminate your program. This ISR uses the data in the Program Segment Prefix to restore DOS interrupt vectors hex 23 and 24 to the values they had before entering your program. Then it transfers control back to the program that invoked yours (usually the DOS command processor). If your program is written in a high level language, it may execute this interrupt to terminate; the appropriate code is automatically inserted by the compiler.

21 About one hundred different DOS functions, discussed later in this section.

22 Not used. Its vector stores a copy of the address to which DOS will transfer control when your program is finished.

23 Executed when DOS senses a **Ctrl-C** keystroke. This service routine terminates your program and transfers control back to the program that invoked it (usually the DOS command processor). DOS also points BIOS interrupt vector hex 1b to this service routine, so that it will also be executed when the BIOS senses a **Ctrl-Break** keystroke. (Keyboard processing is described in more detail in Section 10.3.) If you don't want a user to be able to break out of your program this way, you must point vectors 23 and 1b to your own ISR.

24 Executed when DOS encounters a *critical error*—one it can't handle, like the printer running out of paper or certain drive failures, either mechanical or caused by a misfunctioning program. Handling many of these errors may require manual intervention or the operator's judgement. If you don't want this to happen, you must point vector 24 to your own critical error ISR.

25 Read from and write to specific sectors on a specified drive. Ordinary
26 programmers rarely need to handle disk or diskette drives at this low
     level. The DOS file system services provided as Interrupt 21 functions
     are much easier and safer to use.
2f This is a new DOS 3.0 interrupt that provides several printer services. It
     is described in Chapter 8.6.

Service 27 was commonly used in earlier versions of DOS, but has been super-
seded by DOS Function hex 31. Interrupt 28 is used internally by DOS but not
documented. Interrupts 29 .. 2e and 30 .. 3f are reserved for future DOS use.

DOS functions

About one hundred different useful program services, called *DOS Functions,* are provided through DOS interrupt hex 21. You specify which service
you want by placing its Function number in AH before executing the interrupt. There is no clear qualitative difference between the DOS interrupts discussed previously and the interrupt 21 functions. Since the number of
required services is growing rapidly as DOS and the 8086 family evolves but
the number of interrupt vectors remains constant, some device like this was
necessary.

The rest of this section is devoted to a summary of the DOS functions already available under DOS 2.0 and includes example Pascal programs illustrating their use. However, because there are so many different functions, a
complete discussion is impractical. You will find terse but reasonably complete descriptions of all of them in the *DOS 3.0 Technical Reference* manual,
reference [15, Sec. 5]. With DOS 3.0 some new functions have been added.
They are described in detail in Chapter 8.6 of the present book.

As you will see, there is some overlap between the areas where BIOS interrupts and DOS functions serve. This is understandable, because the BIOS interrupt services are simply those that IBM decided to put in ROM and make
available to all operating systems, while DOS is an operating system intended
for use on many different computers. The BIOS interrupt services are presented as a coherently organized package, but it is not clear why Microsoft
implemented exactly this set of functions, particularly those with the low
numbers. Probably the best answer is that these particular functions were
necessary for the rest of DOS, and Microsoft decided to make them available
to everyone.

Because the DOS function list is long and disorganized, it's best to divide
the functions into categories for discussion, as shown in Figure 7.4.1. All functions available with DOS 2.0 are listed in numerical order in Figure 7.4.2,
with short identifying phrases and category designations. Functions hex 0 to
2e were available with DOS 1.1; 2f to 57 were added with DOS 2.0. The new
DOS 3.0 functions hex 58 to 62 are described later in Section 8.6. We shall
describe each category now in more detail, with some examples illustrating
the use of the various functions.

Asynch   Asynchronous (serial port) input/output
Clock   CPU clock input/output

Drctory   Directory manipulation
FCB Dsk   Disk input/output with File Control Blocks
Gen Dsk   Disk input/output, general
Handles   Disk input/output with File Handles

Memory   Memory management and program execution
Misc   Miscellaneous
Printer   Printer output
Std I/O   Standard device input/output
   ?   Used by DOS but not documented

Figure 7.4.1 DOS function categories

Function (hex)	Category	Use	Function (hex)	Category	Use
0	Memory	Terminate	10	FCB dsk	Close
1	Std I/O	Input & echo	11	FCB dsk	Find first
2	Std I/O	Write char	12	FCB dsk	Find next
3	Asynch	Input	13	FCB dsk	Erase
4	Asynch	Output	14	FCB dsk	Sequential read
5	Printer	Output	15	FCB dsk	Sequential write
6	Std I/O	Input	16	FCB dsk	Create
7	Std I/O	Wait & input	17	FCB dsk	Rename
8	Std I/O	Wait & input	18	?	
9	Std I/O	Write string	19	Gen Dsk	Current drive?
a	Std I/O	Edited input	1a	Gen Dsk	Set DTA
b	Std I/O	Input ready?	1b	Gen Dsk	obsolete FAT info
c	Std I/O	Flush buffer	1c	Gen Dsk	obsolete FAT info
d	Gen Dsk	Reset	1d	?	
e	Gen Dsk	Select current	1e	?	
f	FCB dsk	Open	1f	?	
20	?		30	Misc	Version
21	FCB dsk	Random read	31	Memory	Stay resident
22	FCB dsk	Random write	32	?	
23	FCB dsk	File size	33	Misc	Break on?
24	FCB dsi	Sequential to random	34	?	
25	Misc	Set int vector	35	Misc	Int vector =?
26	Memory	(obsolete)	36	Gen Dsk	Free space =?
27	FCB dsk	Random block in	37	?	
28	FCB dsk	Random block out	38	Misc	Country format
29	FCB dsk	Parse file name	39	Drctory	Mkdir
2a	Clock	Get CPU date	3a	Drctory	Rmdir
2b	Clock	Set CPU date	3b	Drctory	Chdir
2c	Clock	Get CPU time	3c	Handles	Create

2d	Clock	Set CPU time	3d	Handles	Open
2e	Gen Dsk	Set verify	3e	Handles	Close
2f	Gen Dsk	Get DTA	3f	Handles	Read
40	Handles	Write	50	?	
41	Drctory	Erase	51	?	
42	Handles	Seek	52	?	
43	Drctory	File type	53	?	
44	Handles	Control	54	Gen Dsk	Verify on?
45	Handles	Duplicate	55	?	
46	Handles	Duplicate	56	Drctory	Rename
47	Drctory	Current dir ?	57	Drctory	Date stamp
48	Memory	Allocate			
49	Memory	Deallocate	58-	New DOS 3.0 functions	
4a	Memory	Set memory block	62	See Section 8.6	
4b	Memory	Execute program			
4c	Memory	Exit errorlevel			
4d	Memory	Read errorlevel			
4e	Drctory	Find first			
4f	Drctory	Find next			

Figure 7.4.2 DOS functions

Many of the DOS functions perform operations that could fail for various reasons (for example, an attempt to read from an unopened file, or to allocate more memory than is free for general use). Most of the functions use a standard error reporting system: the Carry Flag CF is turned on, and the function returns to your program with the AX register containing an error number. On the other hand, successful operation is indicated by CF = 0. DOS 3.0 has significantly elaborated this error reporting mechanism, so it will be discussed in detail in Section 8.6.

To use DOS directory or file handling functions, you must specify the file names. Actually, before executing Interrupt hex 21, you place in appropriate registers the addresses of strings in memory that contain the file names. The address of a string is the segment:offset address of its first byte, the first character of the file name. For these DOS function parameters, the file name must be followed by a zero byte. Strings like this are called *ASCIIZ strings*. The maximum number of characters permitted in a DOS file name is not documented. For the example Pascal programs that follow, this maximum length was assumed to be 128.

Asynchronous communication functions DOS functions hex 3 and 4 provide rudimentary input and output via **com1**, the first serial port. These services are less extensive and less robust than those offered via BIOS Interrupt hex 14.

Clock functions Functions hex 2a to 2d let you determine or reset the date or time on the DOS clock. This is a software clock; it must be be reset every time you start the PC. Once set, DOS uses a BIOS timer service to update the time approximately 18.2 times each second. The most convenient way to set or reset this clock is by inputting the date and time from a battery driven clock attached to a CPU port. The PC/AT has a battery driven clock on the CMOS chip. Earlier PC models had none; generally they were obtained as components of multifunction expansion boards. DOS does not directly support a battery driven clock. The PC/AT CMOS clock is supported by BIOS interrupt services discussed in Section 10.3. Clocks supplied with expansion boards come with their own software.

Figure 7.4.3 shows how these clock functions use the registers to display or set the time or date. Figure 7.4.4 is an IBM Pascal program that uses two of these functions to display the time and date. From the form of the **writeln** statements you can determine the way in which the functions store the data in the registers. (Note that this differs from the format used by the PC/AT BIOS Interrupt hex 1a service used earlier in Figure 7.2.2.

Directory manipulation DOS provides ten different directory manipulation functions. These include the following services (in several cases they coincide with familiar DOS commands).

- **mkdir**, **rmdir**, **cd**, **erase**, **rename** (Functions hex 39, 3a, 3b & 47, 41, 56)
- Find the first or next files in a directory that match a given file name with wildcards (Functions hex 4e, 4f).
- Set or determine the file type (standard, read only, hidden, system, and archive), and set or determine the file's date and time stamp (Functions hex 43, 57).

Files can have any combination of these attributes. Read only files cannot be altered or erased. Hidden and system files also have this property; moreover, they never appear in directory lists or in directory searches. The DOS program files **IBMBIO.com** and **IBMDOS.com** are hidden files. (There is no difference between the attributes "hidden" and "system.") The "archive" attri-

AH (hex)	Function	AL		CX	DH	DL
2a	Get date	Day 0 = Sun 6 = Sat		Year 1980..2099	Month 1..12	Day 1..31
2b	Set date	0 ff	Valid Invalid	Year 1980..2099	Month 1..12	Day 1..31

		AL	CH	CL	DH	DL
2c	Get time	Not used	Hr 0..23	Min 0..59	Sec 0..59	.01 sec 0..99
2d	Set time	0 Valid ff Invalid	Hr 0..23	Min 0..59	Sec 0..59	.01 sec 0..99

Figure 7.4.3 Registers used by DOS clock functions

```
{$include: 'IBMintrp.int'}
program datetime(input, output);
uses IBMintrp;

var
  registers: reglist;

begin {datetime}
  with registers do
    begin
      writeln('After the  DOS  date function  hex 2a ,');
      ax := byword(#2a, 0);
      intrp(#21, registers, registers);
      writeln('Weekday = AL = ', lobyte(ax):1);
      writeln('Year    = CX = ', cx:4);
      writeln('Month   = DH = ', hibyte(dx):2);
      writeln('Day     = DL = ', lobyte(dx):2);
      writeln;
      writeln('After the  DOS  time function  hex 2c ,');
      ax := byword(#2c, 0);
      intrp(#21, registers, registers);
      writeln('Hr      = CH = ', hibyte(cx):2);
      writeln('Min     = CL = ', lobyte(cx):2);
      writeln('Sec     = DH = ', hibyte(dx):2);
      writeln('.01 sec = DL = ', lobyte(dx):2)
    end
end. {datetime}
```

Figure 7.4.4 Pascal program to display date and time

bute is used to determine whether a file needs to be backed up. It is marked "archive" whenever it has been written to and closed; this attribute is canceled whenever the file is backed up with the DOS **backup** command.

For complete details on the register settings required to use these services, consult the *DOS 3.0 Technical Reference* manual.Here is a simple example: to rename a file, set up the CPU registers as follows.

DS:DX = the address of an ASCIIZ string containing the drive and full path name of the file to be renamed;

ES:DI = the address of an ASCIIZ string containing the new file name;

AH = the function number hex 56.

Then issue interrupt hex 21. If it cannot rename the file, this function sets the Carry Flag and returns an error code in AX. Function hex 56 is more general than the DOS **rename** command, because the new file name doesn't have to belong to the same directory as the old, as long as it's on the same drive. This function will move files between directories simply by manipulating directory information, without physically recopying the file. Figure 7.4.5 is an IBM Pascal routine that makes this function available to Pascal programs.

Disk input/output, general There are two methods for handling disk input/output: File Control Blocks and File Handles. (This includes input/output to other devices—virtual disks—that DOS handles just like disks.) Eight DOS functions support *both* methods. These include the following services.

```
function rename(const old_name: lstring;
                const new_name: lstring;
                    var status  : word)
        : Boolean;
```

```
{This routine uses DOS Function hex 56 to rename a file.
When it succeeds, it returns the value true and status = 0.
Otherwise, it returns false and stores in status the error
code placed in AX by the DOS function. The maximum permitted
length of DOS file names is not documented. This routine
assumes a maximum length of 128 characters.}
```

```
const                          ! The Carry Flag  CF  is bit
  CF = 1;                      ! 0  in the Flags register.
var
  s,d: lstring(129);           ! Needed for  ASCIIZ  strings.
  registers: reglist;

begin {rename}
  copylst(old_name,s);         ! Make  ASCIIZ  strings by
  copylst(new_name,d);         ! appending  null  characters.
  concat(s,chr(0));
  concat(d,chr(0));
  with registers do
    begin
      ax    := byword(#56,0);
      ds    := (ads s[1]).s;   ! Segment:offset addresses of
      dx    := (ads s[1]).r;   ! ASCIIZ  strings
      es    := (ads d[1]).s;
      di    := (ads d[1]).r;
      intrp(#21,registers,registers);
      rename := (flags and CF) = 0;   ! True when  CF  not set
      case result(rename) of
          true : status := 0;
          false: status := ax
        end
    end
end; {rename}
```

Figure 7.4.5 Pascal function to rename a file

- Reset the disk handling system (Function hex d).
- Set or determine the current drive (Functions hex e, 19).
- Set or determine the status of the software switch that causes disk output to be automatically verified (Functions hex 2e, 54).
- Find the Disk Transfer Area (DTA)—the memory buffer that DOS uses for blocks of data en route to and from disks (Function hex 2f).
- Define a larger DTA than the 128 byte buffer that DOS ordinarily uses (Function hex 1A).
- Determine how much free space is available on a disk (Function hex 36).

For details on these functions, consult the DOS 3.0 Technical *Reference* manual [15, Sec. 5].

Disk input/output with File Control Blocks Before DOS 2.0, file input/output required that a File Control Block (FCB) be assigned to each open file. This is a memory area, about 40 bytes, with a standard format that contains such information as file type, drive name, file name, file size, date stamp, file record size in bytes, current block number in the file (a block contains 128 records), and current record number within the block. The FCB does not provide space for full file path names. (If you want to use them with the DOS 2.0 file system, you must use current directory abbreviations.) Application programs were required to maintain these control blocks, and all requests for DOS disk input/output services (except the sector input/output interrupts hex 25 and 26) required the FCB address. This awkward method of file handling was supplanted in DOS 2.0 by the use of *file handles*. Fifteen DOS functions support FCB file handling. The following services are included.

- Create, open, rename, close, and erase files (Functions hex 16, f, 17, 10, 13).
- Determine file size (Function hex 23).
- Read and write records and blocks sequentially or in random order (Functions hex 14, 15, 21, 22, 27, 28).
- Find the first and next files in a directory that match a given file name with wildcards (Functions hex 11, 12).
- Parse a given file name (Function hex 29).

Some of these functions, like the rename function, overlap those in the directory manipulation category. When you use FCB file handling, you have to specify the FCB when performing those functions. Since the FCB file handling system has been supplanted, you will probably not need to use the functions just listed, unless you are maintaining or rewriting a program written before DOS 2.0. The recommended file input/output system uses file handles, described in the next paragraph.

Disk input/output with File Handles With the introduction of DOS 2.0, application programs were no longer required to manage their own FCBs. DOS will maintain up to eight FCBs internally, and you can even change this maximum by using the DOS **files** command. When you want a new FCB, you ask DOS for one by executing a DOS function, and DOS gives you a *handle*—just a number by which you identify this FCB when you need to.

DOS uses the first five file handles for special input/output files, as follows:

Handle	*Special file*
0	Standard input (redirectable; default is CON)
1	Standard output (redirectable; default is CON)
2	Standard error output (CON)
3	Standard auxiliary device (AUX = COM1)
4	Standard printer (PRN = LPT1)

Thus, the first handle assigned for your private use is generally handle 5.

Nine DOS functions support this more convenient method of file handling. The following services are included.

- Create, open, and close files (Functions hex 3c, 3d, 3e).
- Move the file pointer (Function hex 42).
- Read from or write to the file at the location indicated by the file pointer (Functions hex 3f, 40).
- Determine information about a device and its current status and send it control codes (Function hex 44).
- Duplicate a file handle (Functions hex 45, 46).

For complete details on these functions you must consult the DOS *3.0 Technical Reference* manual. A typical example that uses three of them is presented next, both from the assembly language point of view and as a Pascal program.

To read three bytes from file **c:\pascal\testdata** starting at byte number hex 20 you would use Functions hex 3d, 42, and 3f to open the file and obtain a handle, to move the file pointer seeking byte 20, and to read from the file. This process is depicted in Figure 7.4.6. The function requests are set up as follows.

First set up the registers so that

DS:DX = the address of an ASCIIZ string containing the file name **c:\pascal\testdata;**

AL = 0 indicating that the file is to be opened for reading;

AH = function number hex 3d for opening a file.

Execute Interrupt hex 21. When control is returned to your program, register AX contains the file handle or else the Carry Flag is set and AX contains an error code.

Next, set up

BX = the file handle;

AL = 0 indicating that bytes are to be counted relative to the beginning of the file;

Using DOS file handle functions
to read from a file

File name: c:\pascal\testdata

Location of data in file: 20 bytes from start

Number of bytes to read: 3

Address of destination in memory: given

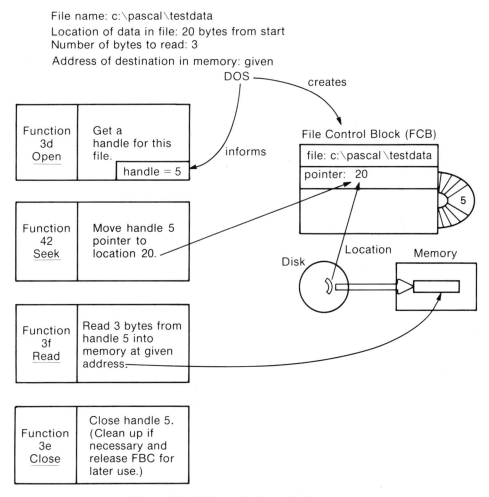

Figure 7.4.6 Using file handle functions

> CX,DX = 0,20, the desired file pointer location (two words are provided for this, to accommodate large files);
>
> AH = function number hex 42 for moving the file pointer.

Execute Interrupt hex 21. When control is returned to your program, either an error is indicated as before or else DX,AX contains the new pointer location (in this case 0,20).

Set up

> BX = the file handle;
>
> CX = 3, the number of bytes to read;

DS:DX = the address of the start of the memory area that will receive the data,

AH = function number hex 3f for file reading.

Execute Interrupt hex 21. When control is returned to your program, either an error is indicated as before or else AX contains the number of bytes actually read. (The file may have contained fewer than hex 23 bytes.)

You will probably want to use function hex 3e to close the file when you're done with it. This frees the handle and its FCB for later use.

Figure 7.4.7 is an IBM Pascal program that follows this example, but lets you input the file name, the location to seek, and the number of bytes to read. It outputs the file handle (5) and the number of bytes read and displays the bytes themselves as a character string. You should experiment with it on an ordinary text file. Be sure to try to read past the file's end and also to read a nonexistent file. In this last situation, the program will report an error.

```
{$include: 'IBMintrp.int'}
program fileread(input,output);
uses IBMintrp;

{This program asks you for a file name, then opens the file for
reading. It asks you for a byte number within that file, then
moves to that location. Finally, following your direction, it
reads and displays a number of bytes from the file. The program
aborts if it encounters an error while opening the file.}

const                              ! Carry Flag  CF  is bit
  CF = 1;                          ! 0  in Flags register.
var
  registers  : reglist;
  file name  : lstring(129);
  handle     : word;
  bytes_read : string(100);        ! You may read up to
                                   ! 100  bytes.

begin {fileread}
  with registers do
    begin
      write('File name: ');
      readln(file name);           !Name length < = 128 .
      concat(file_name,chr(0));    ! Make an  ASCIIZ string.
      ds := (ads file_name[1]).s;  ! Segment:offset address
      dx := (ads file name[1]).r;  ! in DS:DX
      ax := byword(#3d,0);         ! Function  #3d  to open;
      intrp(#21,registers,registers);  ! AL = 0  for reading.
      if (flags and CF) <> 0       ! An error sets  CF.
        them
          writeln('Error:  ax =',ax:1)
```

```
        else
          begin
            handle : = ax;
            writeln('Handle =
',handle:1);
            bx : = handle;
            cs : = 0;                    ! CX,DX  will con-
            write('Seek byte number;    ! tain a  32  bit
');
            readln(dx);                  ! byte count.
            ax : = byword(#42,0);        ! Function  #42  to
intrp(#21,registers,registers);          ! seek;  AL = 0 for
                                         ! forward direction.
                                         ! No error expected.
            bx : = handle;
            write('Read how many
bytes? ');
            readln(cx);
            ds : = (ads bytes_read).s;   ! Segment:offset ad-
            dx : = (ads bytes_read).r;   ! dress in  DS:DX .
            ax : = byword(#3f,0);        ! Function  #3f .
intrp(#21,registers,registers);          ! No error expected.
                                         ! AX = number read.
            writeln(ax:1,' bytes read:  ',bytes_read)
          end
    end
end. {fileread}
```

Figure 7.4.7 Pascal program to read from a file using file handles

Why might you want to use this file handling system instead of the standard Pascal procedures? First, the DOS functions provide greater flexibility. Second, it is easier for you to handle error situations. Third, your executable code can be smaller: if you use no Pascal file handling procedures, you can excise its entire file handling code from your **.exe** file.

A number of disk functions for the FCB protocol have no counterparts in the file handle category. These involve directory manipulation, not the files themselves, hence are included in that category. The user does not need to specify a file handle when requesting those services.

Memory management and program execution These may seem like two different types of function. However, the most common case when your program needs memory management services is when it wants to load and execute another program. Eight functions are provided, including the following services.

- Allocate memory to your program, adjust the size of an allocated memory block, or return allocated memory for general use (Functions hex 48, 4a, 49).

- Load a program into memory and execute it if you wish (Function hex 4b).
- Terminate your program, optionally setting the DOS **errorlevel** variable (Functions hex 0, 4c).
- Determine the value of the **errorlevel** variable (Function hex 4d).
- Terminate your program but stay resident (Function hex 31).

The memory management and program execution functions are among the most complicated provided by DOS. Using them requires thorough understanding of this area of the operating system, and of the memory allocation mechanisms used by the linker, the DOS loader, and your compiler. While the first two of these have been discussed to some extent earlier, the memory models of the various compilers are beyond the scope of this book. Commercial packages are available that implement these methods for several popular compilers. (See reference [2].) To illustrate the problems that arise in this area, a typical IBM Pascal example is discussed next. While some of the considerations are peculiar to Pascal, many do in fact apply as well to programs written in other languages.

Suppose you want to write an IBM Pascal *parent* program that lets the operator select from a menu one of several *child* programs to execute, then carries out the request and returns on completion to this menu to offer yet more choices. Unfortunately, when loading a Pascal program, DOS allocates to it *all* available memory. Although a DOS function is provided to load and execute the child program, there is nowhere to load it. The first step toward surmounting this problem is to determine how much memory the parent program actually uses. IBM Pascal does provide a way for the parent program to determine this information. Next, the parent program must execute Function hex 4a to release for general use all memory not actually required. Then it may use Function hex 4b to load and execute the child program. The parameters for this interrupt include addresses of ASCIIZ strings that contain the child program's file name and its command line parameters.

When the child program terminates, the DOS Function call Interrupt hex 21 service routine will regain control, reclaim all memory it had allocated to the child program, then return to the parent program. The child may send status information back to the parent by using Function hex 4c to set the DOS **errorlevel** variable. After regaining control, the parent can determine the **errorlevel** value by executing Function hex 4d. This is the same variable that is used by the DOS batch file command **if errorlevel**.

Let's pursue this parent-child example one step further. Suppose parent and child must both access a data array in memory. If the array lies within the area allocated to the parent, its segment:offset address could be ascertained by using the **ads** operator, then supplied to the child. There are at least two possibilities for this:

- parent and child could agree to use some otherwise unused interrupt vector to store the address; or
- the address could be encoded as a character string and supplied to the child as part of its command line or as an environment variable.

In many cases, the shared array is too large for the single 64 K data segment allowed IBM Pascal programs. The usual way of satisfying large memory requirements in IBM Pascal is to use the **ads** operator and address types or else a mechanism called the *long heap* to place arrays outside that 64 K segment. However, in this parent-child scenario the parent is allocated only its code segments and the 64 K data segment. You can in fact go ahead and use additional memory, but you will invariably confuse DOS' memory allocation bookkeeping, and DOS will be unable to load the child program. The solution is for the parent program to execute Function hex 48 to allocate to it the required memory; once allocated, this memory may be used freely.

The last function mentioned in this category, hex 31, is used to terminate execution of a program that must remain in memory to be executed later by some other program. Usually, the program being loaded is an interrupt service routine, and the code just before this function request is analogous to the code just after the front entry to an interrupt service routine, as described earlier in Section 7.2.

Printer output Function hex 5 sends one character to the standard parallel printer, **prn** = **lpt1**.

Standard device input/output DOS provides nine functions for input from the standard input device and output to the standard output device. Normally, these devices are the keyboard and screen (jointly named CON), but these input/output streams can be redirected to other devices, and the standard output can be piped to the standard input. The exact nature of the services provided seems not the result of planning but of accident—they are probably just those needed originally to implement the DOS command processor. Functions hex 1, 6, 7, and 8 permit keyboard input; they implement various combinations of the options to echo the input on the screen, to wait until a key is pressed, and to check for the **Ctrl-C** and **Ctrl-Break** keystrokes. Other services provide for

- writing a character or a string on the screen (Functions 2, 9);
- edited keyboard input—backspaces, etc., are handled automatically (Function hex a);
- determining if a key has been pressed (Function hex b);
- flushing the keyboard buffer (Function hex c).

The last function is often used to insure that the next keystroke read is a response to a screen directive.

How do you determine whether to use the DOS functions in this category, or the similar BIOS keyboard and screen services? Sometimes the DOS functions are handy because they combine several BIOS services; however, this feature also makes them less adaptable to your particular needs. The DOS functions apply to standard input/output even when directed to other devices; the BIOS services do not. Finally, programs that use the DOS services only are more readily adapted to run on other computers that use DOS but have incompatible BIOS code.

Miscellaneous functions The remaining five available DOS functions provide the following services.

- Determine the **break on** switch setting (Function hex 33).
- Set or inspect an interrupt vector (Functions hex 25, 35).
- Determine the DOS version, and determine its country specific information (Functions hex 30, 38).

The country specific information (date and time format, currency notation, and decimal separator) in DOS 2.0 was supplied when you purchased it, and you could not change it. With DOS 3.0 you can control it; this is discussed in detail in Section 8.6.

Used by DOS but not documented Functions hex 18 and 1d to 20 are not documented. Sometimes, sleuthing in the popular press or in DOS itself can uncover the specifications of these functions. However, since they are not documented, IBM or Microsoft could change them at any time. It's dangerous to use them.

8

DOS 3.0

Contents

Chapters 4, 5, and 7 contained a rather thorough introduction to the facilities provided by DOS, both from the viewpoint of the general user (DOS commands and utilities) and from the programmer's viewpoint. Because many programmers who will work on the PC/AT are already quite familiar with DOS 2.0, the material on DOS 3.0 has been gathered into the present chapter. Thus, you may skip whatever you want in the earlier chapters and still find here the DOS 3.0 information necessary to use the PC/AT effectively. Moreover, the new DOS 3.0 features are organized here into separate sections so that you can concentrate on the ones of particular interest to you. Section 1 gives an overview, while Sections 2 to 5 cover new DOS commands and utilities. The concluding Section 8.6 takes the programmer's viewpoint, and is devoted to the new and enhanced DOS interrupt services. One of these, the International Information Function hex 38, is illustrated by an IBM Pascal program using the same interrupt facilities already demonstrated in Chapter 7.

8.1 Overview

Concepts

* New features * Improved command syntax * More flexible **print** command

---

IBM introduced DOS 3.0 simultaneously with the PC/AT. An enhancement to the operating system was necessary to support the new diskette and fixed disk formats. DOS 3.0 provides this and many other new features and runs on the other PCs as well. This Chapter is based on the IBM Version of DOS 3.0. The operating system is owned and continually developed by Microsoft Corporation, who license it to IBM and other computer vendors. The licensees adapt it to their particular machines. When this Chapter was written about six months after IBM's introduction, IBM DOS 3.0 was the only version available. The new features can be grouped as follows.

- *Full pathnames* may be used for all DOS program execution commands.
- The **print** command is more elaborate and flexible.
- The **graphics** command supports more printers.
- *International conventions* for keyboards and date, time, and currency notation are supported.
- DOS supports the new PC/AT diskette and fixed disk formats.
- You now have more flexibility with *volume labels* and may use *read-only* files.
- DOS provides a *virtual disk* that may reside in the PC/AT memory above the one megabyte threshold.
- *Files may be shared* among several concurrent processes, and one process may control file access by others.
- Several enhanced or new DOS *interrupts and function calls* support the above features. Moreover, there is an extended and uniform *error handling protocol* for the function calls.

Some of these new features are discussed in more detail in this Section. Others require whole sections later in this Chapter. You should realize that this Chapter is really an outline. For full details, you may consult the *DOS 3.0 Reference* and *DOS 3.0 Technical Reference* manuals, references [14, Chaps.1,4,7] and [15, Chap. 5].

DOS 3.0 has removed an inconvenient restriction in the syntax of program execution commands. This was already described in Section 5.4; a program execution command consists of a line of the form

```
program name     program parameters
```

Programs are stored in **.bat, .com**, or **.exe** files. The program name is any form of the file name, without this extension. The full path name or any abbreviation using the current drive or directory is allowed. Moreover, the path to the file may be specified by a previous **path** command or any other means of setting the **PATH** variable in the DOS environment. (Under DOS 2.0, you were *required* to use a path command if the program was not in the current directory.)

The **print** command now lets you control technical parameters such as the maximum number of files in the queue waiting to be printed and the size of the buffer that stores characters en route from files to printer. Thus you can tune this command for efficiency. Note that the **print** command still provides just a method of printing *files*. It does not handle output going directly to the printer, like print *buffer* software. In fact, the **print** command interferes with any other printer output. Interrupt hex 2f, through which DOS executes the **print** command, is now available for your use in programs.

File sharing is implemented through DOS function hex 3d, by which your program opens a file. You can specify what access you wish (input or output), and you can deny others the privilege of reading or writing the file while it is still open. This is described under the heading **File handling functions** in Section 8.6. In order to use this feature, you must execute first the DOS utility program **share.com** that loads a part of DOS used only for this purpose. That requires about 5K bytes plus the area used to record the sharing information for all open files.

There is a new configuration command **lastdrive**, for optional inclusion in your **config.sys** file. It seems to have no effect other than evoking memories of Zane Gray novels.

8.2 Internationalism

Concepts

* Country dependent notational conventions * Determining and changing conventions * International keyboards

Realizing that a significant part of its PC business is outside the United States, IBM has made it possible for DOS to observe some foreign conventions in communicating with you. This does not extend so far as permitting command names and error messages in languages other than English, but it does include accommodating some potentially confusing differences in date and time notation. Thus German users will still have to enter English commands, but they can read the date in their own style—1.2.85 means 1 February 1985—instead of the confusing North American version 2-1-85.

Other DOS conventions that can be adjusted are

- the separators between hours, minutes, and seconds (15:46:02 in the United States, 15.46.02 in Germany);
- the decimal point (*pi* is about 3.1416 here, but 3,1416 there).

Moreover, DOS can provide your programs with some other data on notational conventions, so that you can input and output properly, provided users inform DOS of the conventions at their computer location. These other data include

- separators between list items (a,b,c is most common here, but a;b;c in Europe);
- currency symbols ($ or DM);
- usual accuracy in currency calculations ($0.01 is a significant amount here but Italians ignore 0.01 *lire*).

You can change DOS' conventions by two methods—including a **country** statement in your **config.sys** file or calling DOS Function hex 38 from a program. This function is described in more detail in Section 6. The conventions must be changed all at once; no method is given for changing one at a time. DOS organizes them by country, and provides data for fifteen countries, identified by their international telephone codes:

United States	001	Denmark	045
Netherlands	031	Sweden	046
Belgium	032	Norway	047
France	033	Germany (BRD)	049
Spain	034	Australia	061
Italy	039	Finland	358
Switzerland	041	Israel	972
United Kingdom	044		

The **config.sys** statement has the form **country = 049** for Germany. The default is, of course, **country = 1**. You don't have to set that. DOS function call hex 38 is described in detail in Section 8.6; it also lets your program determine what conventions are in effect at any time.

Another communication convention that differs between countries is the typewriter keyboard layout. Of course, there is probably no *real* standard in any one country, just as there is no standard IBM keyboard. However, DOS 3.0 now permits you to change its keyboard interpretation to come closer to a standard keyboard in any of six countries:

France	Spain
Germany (BRD)	United Kingdom
Italy	United States (the default).

Of course, it makes little sense to change the keyboard interpretation without changing the keytop labels. New keytops and, in fact, foreign keyboards are available for these countries. For example, the differences between the United States and German keyboards consist of reversal of the Y and Z keys and the interpretation of the top line and the symbol keys on the right side of the alphabetic keyboard. The details are shown in Figure 8.2.1.

There is only one way to change the keyboard interpretation from the default United States standard—execute one of the following programs provided with DOS 3.0:

keybfr.com   keybsp.com
keybgr.com   keybuk.com
keybit.com

For example, to change the keyboard interpretation to German, you must enter the command **keybgr** each time you boot your computer. DOS then loads program **keybgr**; this program will stay in memory and operate as an extension of DOS. More precisely, it is a service routine for the BIOS Keyboard Interrupt hex 9, as described later in Section 10.3. If you enter the **chkdsk** command before and after executing **keybgr**, you'll see that you have about 2200 bytes less memory to work with once **keybgr** is installed. Even though this routine processes your keystrokes *before* passing the interpreted information along to DOS, you won't notice any delay because you can't type fast enough for it to make any difference.

case	United States	Germany
upper	~!@#$%^&*()_+¦	>!"§$%&/()=?'^
lower	'1234567890-=\	≤1234567890β'#
upper	{}	Ü*
lower	[]	ü+
upper	:"	ÖÄ
lower	;'	öä
upper	<>?	;:_
lower	,./	.,-

Figure 8.2.1 Differences between U.S. and German keyboards

8.3 New disk drive support

Concepts

* What types of disk and diskette drives does DOS 3.0 support?
* New high capacity diskettes and 20 MB fixed disk   * Enhanced
DOS disk and diskette support commands   * DOS disk and diskette
space allocation   * File Allocation Table (FAT)

Since the PC/AT disk and diskette formats differ from those of previous PC models, DOS 3.0 must now support new formats. In all, it handles seven types:

- single-sided, 8-sector, 5.25-inch diskettes (the original DOS 1.0 format),
- double-sided 8-sector, 5.25-inch diskettes (introduced with DOS 1.1),
- single-sided 9-sector, 5.25-inch diskettes,
- double-sided 9-sector, 5.25-inch diskettes (the usual DOS 2.0 format— these are now called *standard diskettes*),
- high capacity 5.25-inch diskettes (new with the PC/AT),
- IBM 10-MB fixed disk drive (standard PC/XT equipment),
- IBM 20-MB fixed disk drive (new with the PC/AT).

The PC/AT BIOS partially supports several other drive types, but DOS works only with those listed above.

Disk and diskette surfaces are divided into concentric circular *tracks* and each track into *sectors* of 512 bytes, as in Figure 8.3.1. Standard diskettes have 40 tracks with nine sectors per track. The new high capacity diskettes have 80 tracks with 15 sectors. Since the diskettes are of the same physical-size, the recording density has doubled in terms of tracks per inch and nearly doubled in terms of bits per inch on a track. Thus, high capacity diskettes hold about four times as much information as standard diskettes. The high capacity diskette recording surfaces are made of a new material with finer magnetic resolution and are considerably more expensive than standard diskettes. Moreover, reading and writing them requires more sensitive equipment than the standard diskette drives. The new high capacity drive on the PC/AT is designed to read and write standard as well as high capacity diskettes; however, standard diskettes written by a high capacity drive cannot be read reliably by the less delicate standard drives. (In the author's experience, they can be read only if they contain just a small amount of data.)

Because of this incompatibility, the high capacity diskette drive is useful mainly as a backup device or as a medium for information interchange between PC/ATs. To transport data to or from other PCs, you need a standard drive or a telecommunication or network facility.

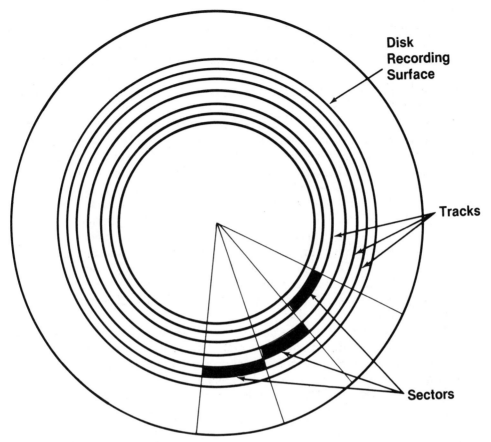

Figure 8.3.1 Disk tracks and sectors

The various DOS commands involving disk and diskette formats have been enhanced to support the high capacity diskette and 20-MB fixed disk drives. The **diskcomp, diskcopy, backup** and **restore** commands, for example, now work with any reasonable combination of source and target media. You will see an error message if the media are incompatible. *Caution:* if you use **diskcopy** to copy a standard diskette onto another standard diskette in a high capacity drive, the copy will probably be unreadable by a standard drive!

The **format** command has been enhanced, too. Normally, it determines the proper format by inspecting the drive and medium types. You can force it to format a standard diskette in the high capacity drive by using the parameter **/4**. (Maybe this means standard size = high capacity/4!) For example, the command

```
format a:/4/s/v
```

requests DOS to format a standard diskette in the high capacity drive **a:**, transfer to it the DOS 3.0 files

```
ibmbio.com    ibmdos.com    command.com
```

and to ask you for a volume name.

Formatting the fixed disk is not a routine operation; it was discussed briefly in Section 4.2. Other aspects of these commands remain the same as DOS 2.0; see the *DOS 3.0 Reference* manual, reference [14, Chap. 7], for details.

To understand how DOS allocates space on the new high capacity diskettes and the 20-MB fixed disk and how it organizes information flow, you will probably need to recall how it's done on the older media. Figure 8.3.2 shows the parameters for all supported formats. First, the number of sides is given. For diskettes, this is naturally 1 or 2. The fixed disk drives have two platters, hence four recording sides. Next, two more physical parameters are specified: numbers of tracks per side and sectors per track. A sector always contains 512 bytes. From this data you can calculate the total number of sectors on the medium. DOS always allocates space in sector units, even though most files will not fully occupy their last sectors. The next parameter is not physical, but specified by DOS: the maximum number of entries in the root directory. This is necessary because DOS handles root directories differently from other directories and allocates this space whether you use it or not. Directory entries always require 32 bytes, so you can calculate the number of sectors necessary for the root directory.

An additional sector is always used for the DOS *boot record*. This is a short program that is executed if you try to boot your system from this medium. It determines if the DOS system files are present and prompts you to change diskettes if necessary. A fixed disk also has one special sector to describe how it is partitioned between DOS and perhaps some other operating system.

The remaining space on the medium is devoted to data files and to the file allocation table (FAT) that tells where the files are located. For security, two copies of the FAT are stored. DOS' minimum file space allocation unit depends on the medium, but always consists of a small group of sectors, called a *cluster*. The criteria that determine the number of sectors per cluster are examined below. The FAT tells which clusters are allocated to each file; this requires for each cluster a table entry consisting of a cluster number. If there are few enough clusters to permit 12-bit (= 1.5-byte) cluster numbers, these are used. Otherwise, each FAT entry requires 2 bytes. Thus, from the number of FAT entries you can determine the number of sectors necessary for each of the two FAT copies.

The remaining sectors are available for file storage. Multiply this by 512 to get the data capacity in bytes. This is the figure reported by the **chkdsk** utility.

The FAT entries themselves are easy to understand: a file's directory entry points to the first allocated cluster; the FAT entry for that cluster points to the one for the next allocated cluster, and so on, until you reach the entry for the last allocated cluster, which contains an end of the line signal.

The DOS engineers consider two factors in determining the number of sectors per cluster—the proportion of space wasted when files do not fully occupy their last sectors and the efficiency and size of the FAT. Clearly, the smaller the cluster size, the less wasted space. This seems to be the governing crite-

Medium	Sides	Tracks /Side	Sectors /Track	Total Sectors	Root Direc- tory Entries	Root Direc- tory Sectors	FAT Sec- tors	Data Sec- tors	Data Capac- ity	Sec- tors/ Clus- ter	Data Clus- ters	FAT bytes /Clus- ter	FAT bytes
DOS 1.0 1 sided diskette	1	40	8	320	64	4	2	313	160K	1	313	1.5	470
DOS 2.0 1 sided diskette	1	40	9	360	64	4	4	351	180K	1	351	1.5	527
DOS 1.0 2 sided diskette	2	40	8	640	112	7	2	630	323K	2	315	1.5	473
DOS 2.0 2 sided diskette	1	40	9	720	112	7	4	708	362K	2	354	1.5	531
High ca- pacity diskette	2	80	15	2400	224	14	14	2371	1.21M	1	2371	1.5	3557
PC/XT fixed disk	4	305	17	20740	512	32	16	20691	10.6M	8	2586	1.5	3879
PC/AT fixed disk	4	614	17	41752	512	32	82	41636	21.3M	4	10409	2	20818

Figure 8.3.2 DOS diskette and disk space allocation

rion for the older diskette types (two sectors per cluster) and certainly for the high capacity diskette, which is intended principally for backup (one sector per cluster). On the other hand, as you see by comparing the tabulated data for the two fixed disks, the smaller the clusters, the larger the FAT. Large FATs require a lot of space on the medium, and time to search through. More importantly, though, they take up space in main memory. Since each file access requires prior access and inspection of the FAT, DOS cuts down the number of time consuming drive operations by making a copy of the FAT in main memory. To limit this memory requirement, the 10 MB PC/XT fixed disk uses eight sectors per cluster. (This means that, on the average, four sectors = 2K bytes are wasted per file. For 500 files, this amounts to 1 MB = 10% of disk capacity!) The DOS engineers have now decided that PC/AT main memory is cheap enough and its CPU fast enough to permit a 20-K fixed disk FAT. This is more than the *entire* main memory of some early examples of the PC!

8.4 New utilities attrib and label

Concepts

* File attributes   * **attrib** utility for setting and determining attribute   * **label** utility for setting and changing volume labels

---

There are several types of files that are handled differently by the basic DOS reading, writing, and directory operations. They are distinguished by their *file attributes*, six qualities that may be true or false for each file:

read-only	volume label
hidden	subdirectory
system	archive

These attributes are recorded as the values of six bits in the directory entry for each file. (You can find the details in the *DOS 3.0 Technical Reference* manual, reference [15, Chap. 4].)

DOS can't change or erase a file with the *read-only* attribute. This quality is exactly what you need when some files on a medium need protection but you can't write-protect the entire medium. While this attribute was available in DOS 2.0, you couldn't use it conveniently. With DOS 3.0, you can turn it on or off easily, as described below.

DOS treats *hidden* and *system* files similarly—they simply are not detected by directory searches. The *volume label* attribute may apply only to a file of at most eleven characters that is used for the volume label; this may exist only in a root directory. The *subdirectory* attribute merely identifies subdirectories. The *archive* attribute is used by the **backup** command to identify which files have changed since your last backup: it is turned on whenever you create or change a file and turned off only when the file is backed up.

You can encounter various combinations of attributes. For example, the DOS system files **ibmbio.com** and **ibmdos.com** are read-only hidden files: they never appear in directories and you can't change or erase them. This protects them against accidental damage. However, the DOS program file **command.com** is not hidden, because some sophisticated program execution control techniques, discussed earlier in Section 7.4, must be able to find it. It could be a read-only file, but it's not.

With DOS 3.0 you have the capacity to change some of these file attributes. Two of them, however, cannot be changed by any means: once a file is created as a volume label or a subdirectory, it cannot be used for any other purpose. The new DOS 3.0 **attrib** utility lets you change the read-only attribute directly. DOS function hex 43, described later in Section 6, lets your programs change all attributes except volume label and subdirectory.

Using **attrib** is simple: if you enter **attrib** followed by a file name, DOS will report the read-only attribute. Actually, it just lists the file name if it is not protected, but writes an **R** if it is a read-only file. To change the attribute, enter **attrib ±r** followed by the file name; **+r** makes it read-only, and **-r** returns it to unprotected status. In summary,

```
attrib a:b.c      reports the read-only attribute
attrib +r a:b.c   makes it read-only
attrib -r a:b.c   removes read-only protection
```

If you try to change or erase a read-only file, DOS will report an error. Unfortunately, it doesn't just say that the file is protected; rather, DOS writes a cryptic message,

Access denied or **File creation error**

Under DOS 2.0, you could give a medium a volume name when you formatted it, and you could determine the name by using the **vol** command. Moreover, DOS always reported the volume name in directory listings. However, you couldn't change or delete a label or create one for an unlabeled medium. The new DOS 3.0 **label** utility provides these features. If you enter **label** followed by a drive name, DOS will delete the label of the medium on that drive. If you enter **label** followed by a drive name and a label, DOS will create or change the medium label accordingly. (Of course, you can always omit the drive name if you want the current drive.) A label consists of a string of up to eleven characters; any characters are allowed except those expressly forbidden in filenames. In short,

```
label a:        removes the label from the medium in
                    drive a:
label a:recipes changes the label to recipes
```

8.5 Virtual disk vdisk

Concepts

* Virtual disks * Examples of virtual disk usage * **vdisk** configuration * Incompatibility with **diskcopy**

With DOS 3.0, IBM supplies a virtual disk device driver called **vdisk.sys**. In fact, DOS 2.0 supported this type of software; although IBM did not supply one, virtual disks became so popular that most vendors of expansion memory for the PC provided them free or at nominal cost. IBM's driver displays most of the capabilities generally demanded of this type of software, so it will probably become standard.

A *virtual disk* is a part of main memory set up for use like a disk. It has a drive name, may have a volume name (even though the medium is not removable), and stores files in the familiar DOS tree structure, with directories and file allocation tables. You can store files, read them, copy them, inspect directories, etc., just as though you were using a diskette or fixed disk. There are three important differences to keep in mind. First, you lose general use of memory that you allocate to a virtual disk. Second, information stored in a virtual disk is lost every time you lose power or reboot. Third, a virtual disk operates *much faster* than a diskette drive or even a fixed disk. Input/output with a diskette or fixed disk requires positioning the read head over the proper track, then waiting for the proper sector to rotate into position by the head. Input/output operations on a virtual disk are done at main memory access speed; there is no mechanical delay.

Since PCs don't all have the same amount of main memory and most have nowhere near the amount that is becoming common with the PC/AT, software designers minimize the amount of data that absolutely *must* reside in main memory. Information that is used relatively infrequently is put on files that can be stored on a diskette, fixed disk, or virtual disk and accessed when needed. Since these devices appear identical to software developers—they are just different drives—only one software routine is necessary to control them. The software user may specify which drive to use, and select whatever kind of drive is most efficient for the installation and application at hand.

For example, the word processor used to prepare this text stores its main program and the text itself in main memory to insure maximum speed for most text manipulation. It stores all its text format specifications, messages, and screen designs on auxiliary files that are accessed only when needed. This happens *relatively* infrequently, but often enough to cause tedious delays, especially when editing corrections or handling many small text files. Therefore, when the PC's capacity allows, it is most efficient to store all these word processor files on a virtual disk. Then the only delays noticeable are those caused by the operation of writing on the screen.

Some additional examples of virtual disk usage are given later, after **vdisk.sys** is described in more detail.

With DOS 3.0, you can set up one or more virtual disks by including in your **config.sys** file lines of the form

```
device=c:vdisk.sys bbb sss ddd
```

perhaps followed by the the symbol /**e**. Each such line will install a virtual disk. The **vdisk** drive names start after the names of the diskette and fixed disk drives already known to DOS. For the PC/AT, this usually means that **vdisk** drives will be named **d:, e:**, etc. The drive name **c:** in the line displayed above is merely an example path name for the DOS file **vdisk.sys**, that must be available to DOS when you boot your system. The parameters **bbb, sss, ddd**, and /**e** specify certain characteristics of your virtual disk, as follows:

bbb   is the number of kilobytes of memory that you want to allocate to this disk;
sss   is the sector size, in bytes (128, 256, or 512);
ddd   is the maximum number of directory entries for the disk (maximum 512).

The *sector size* is the smallest unit of memory in the virtual disk that DOS will allocate to a file; DOS manipulates these sectors as single units for input/output. Thus, if the sector size is 512, then a 600-byte file will be allocated $1024 = 2*512$ bytes. The smaller the sector size, the less memory will be wasted when files don't completely fill their last sectors. The larger the sector size, the fewer individual operations DOS must make to access a given file. If you think that most of the files on your virtual disk will be small, you should use a small sector size; with large files, large sectors will improve efficiency.

If you know that you will only need a few directory entries, you can save memory space by specifying a small directory size, because the directory space is reserved whether you use it or not.

There are some restrictions concerning the relative sizes of the parameters **bbb, sss, ddd** and the main memory of your PC. The details are specified in the *DOS 3.0 Reference* manual, reference [14, Chap. 4].

The optional /**e** parameter is for use only on a PC/AT with more than one megabyte of main memory. If you qualify, specifying /**e** will cause DOS to locate your virtual disk entirely in memory above the one megabyte barrier. This is in fact the only *direct* way that DOS 3.0 can use this memory!

(Of course, programs like **vdisk** can use this memory via BIOS Interrupt hex 15, described in Section 8.6. IBM supplies with DOS the entire assembly language source code of **vdisk.sys** as a model of a device driver and of the use of the PC/AT's high address memory.)

Let's look at virtual disk setups for several applications, starting with the first example above, word processor files. If you think that you will *always* want your word processor installed, then you might specify a virtual disk **d:** specifically for this purpose. You could restrict its size and directory to exactly what you need (plus a little room for maneuvering, should you need to change it later). Moreover, you will avoid confusing your word processor files (which probably have unfamiliar names) with others in daily use. To do this, just gather them into some directory available at boot time, for example **c:wp_files**. Then include in your autoexec file the command

```
copy c:wp_files d: )nul.
```

(Redirecting standard output to the **nul** file avoids cluttering your screen with the report from the copy command.) Another nice autoexec touch would be to label the virtual disk appropriately—for example, **label d:wp_vdisk**; if you don't label it, it will just be called **vdisk**.

Some common application programs, like word processors and compilers, produce temporary files when the material being processed might exceed main memory capacity. These may be ideal for storage on virtual disks. For one thing, they are sometimes read (too) frequently, like scrolling back and forth between word processing text in main memory and in a spill file. More-over, some programs have gained bad reputations for leaving such files in disarray if they crash unexpectedly. This could scramble the entire contents of a volume. You definitely don't want that to happen to your twenty megabyte PC/AT fixed disk! One solution is to direct those temporary files to a virtual disk; that way a disaster can be confined. A general purpose virtual disk for this kind of application would probably have large sectors and a small direc-tory; its overall size would have to be tailored to your individual situation.

Another example is storage of procedure libraries while linking large pro-grams. (Compilers produce separate object code files for each part of a large program. These must be linked together with sometimes hundreds of object files in libraries of routines that handle common tasks like arithmetic, text manipulation, input/output, etc. Linking produces the **.exe** file that DOS will load and execute.) In a large, complex program, many routines refer to others, so that the linker must make a number of passes through the libraries, in-specting hundreds of entries on each pass before it finds all the required rou-tines. These libraries are too large to fit in the main memory of many PCs. But thousands of library accesses take a long time when libraries are stored on a slow rotating medium. This is especially intolerable during debugging, which often requires relinking after each of many changes before your pro-gram finally operates correctly. You can save time by loading the libraries into a virtual disk before linking.

A final example of virtual disk usage is program overlays. To allow their programs to run on smaller machines, software designers often split them into parts called *overlays* that never need to be in main memory simultaneously. When one overlay is finished and another is needed, the new one is read from a file into the same main memory area that the old one used. Frequent read-ing of overlays from a rotating medium can slow a program considerably. This problem is avoided if the overlays are kept on a virtual disk.

There is one situation that **vdisk** will *not* accommodate, even though it is a common application of some other vendors' virtual disk software. Repeated diskette copying or comparison is very tedious when you don't have two diskette drives of the same type. On the PC/XT and PC/AT, the **diskcopy** command reads part of the source diskette into memory, prompts you to replace it with the target diskette, copies data from memory to the target, and repeats this process several times. Some brands of virtual disks can be configured exactly like a diskette, so that you can use **diskcopy** to copy the entire source diskette to a virtual disk, then switch diskettes *once* and copy the virtual disk to the target diskette. This is *not possible* with **vdisk**: the **diskcopy** and **diskcomp** commands simply do not accept its format.

8.6 New and enhanced DOS interrupts and functions

Concepts

* Printer control interrupt * International information function
* New and enhanced file handling functions * File sharing
* Finding the Program Segment Prefix * New systematic error handling methods

DOS 3.0 has added a number of new features to its repertoire of interrupts and function calls. These are summarized in Figure 8.6.1, which uses the DOS function categories of Section 7.4. (Remember, you invoke the DOS functions by putting the function number in the AH register, setting the other CPU registers appropriately, then executing interrupt hex 21.)

The functions in the **?** category are undocumented, hence not available for use. Some others are straightforward and will be described immediately below. The most important new feature is an enhanced error handling procedure that is now uniform for all DOS function calls. It will be described last in this section. The information contained in this section is just an outline. For complete details, consult the *DOS 3.0 Technical Reference* manual, reference [15, Chap. 5].

Printer control interrupt hex 2f

This new interrupt provides a means of invoking the DOS printer driver, or any printer driver that you might want to substitute for it. You may set the AL register to request the following services:

DOS   Interrupts

hex	New/ Enhanced	Description
21 } 24 }	Enhanced	New, uniform methods for handling errors (hex 24) in all DOS function calls (hex 21).
2f	New	Printer control

DOS   functions (Interrupt   hex 21)

hex	Category	New/ Enhanced	Description
38	Misc	Enhanced	International information
3d	Handles	Enhanced	Open a file. Now you can share.
44	Handles	Enhanced	Input/output control
58	?	New	
59	Misc	New	Get error information.
5a	Handles	New	Create a temporary file.
5b	Handles	New	Create a new file.
5c	Handles	New	Lock/unlock part of a file.
5d	?	New	
5e	?	New	
5f	?	New	
60	?	New	
61	?	New	
62	Memory	New	Get Program Segment Prefix.

Figure 8.6.1 New and enhanced DOS 3.0 interrupts and functions

AL	Service
0	Determine if the driver is installed or installable.
1	Submit a file to the printer queue.
2	Cancel a file from the printer queue.
3	Cancel all files in the printer queue.
4	Suspend printing in order to inspect the status of the queue.
5	Resume printing after a queue status check.

The other CPU registers are used to point to strings in memory that contain the indicated files. The structure of the queue of file names is specified clearly, but the method of returning error information for queued files is not. However, since this interrupt is apparently used to drive the DOS **print** command, you should be able to figure out these details with some sleuthing.

International information function hex 38

This function can be used to determine the country dependent information for the current country or any specified country that DOS supports. This information, consisting of date, time, currency, and alphabet conventions, was described earlier in Section 8.1. The countries are indicated by their international telephone codes, with code 0 representing the current country. Figure 8.6.2 shows an example IBM Pascal procedure **get_notation** that accesses this information via the software interrupt facility described earlier in Section 7.2. Function hex 38 actually sends the information to a 32-byte buffer, whose address you provide in CPU registers DS:DX. The buffer format is specified in the *DOS 3.0 Technical Reference* manual, Chapter 5. Since this buffer is not very easy to access, **get_notation** moves the notation information into a convenient Pascal record structure. Data structures are also provided to permit the procedure to determine the country name from its code.

```
{Several data types and constants are defined to enable IBM
Pascal programs to use the country dependent notation convestions
conveniently.}
type
  country     = 1..15;
  name_type   = lstring(15);
  name_array  = array [country] of name_type;
  code_array  = array [country] of word;
const
  country_name = name_array ('United States', 'Netherlands'   ,
                             'Belgium'      , 'France'         ,
                             'Spain'        , 'Italy'          ,
                             'Switzerland'  , 'United Kingdom',
                             'Denmark'      , 'Sweden'         ,
                             'Norway'       , 'Germany (BRD)'  ,
                             'Australia'    , 'Finland'        ,
                             'Israel'       );

  country_code = code_array (1, 31, 32, 33, 34, 39, 41, 44, 45, 46, 47, 49,
                             61, 358, 972);

type
  notation_record =
    record
        name             : name type;
        currency_symbol: lstring(4);
        currency_1st   : Boolean;   ! Currency symbol comes first?
        currency_space : Boolean;   ! Space between symbol, amount?
        currency_places: byte;      ! Accuracy in currency amounts
        date_format    : byte;           ! 0, 1, 2 = mdy, day, ymd
        date_separator : char;
        clock_24 hours : Boolean;
        time_separator : char;
        thousands_separator: char;
        decimal_separator  : char;
        list_separator     : char;
        case_map_address   : adsmem      ! Explained in text
    end;
```

{The following procedure uses DOS Function hex 38 to read the notation conventions for any country supported by DOS 3.0. Its parameter code is a country code or else zero, indicating the current country. In parameter status the procedure returns 0 if the operation is successful, or else the error code returned by the DOS function in AX. If successful, the procedure sets up a notation record including all the conventions, the country name, and the case map address.}

```
procedure get_notation(    code    : word;
                       var notation: notation_record;
                       var status  : word);

const                                   ! Carry Flag CF is
  CF = 1;                               ! bit 0 in Flags.
var
  registers: reglist;
  ah,al     : byte;
  buffer    : array [1..32] of byte;
  k         : country;
  i,j       : integer;

begin (get_notation)
  with registers,notation do
    begin
      ah := #38;                        ! Function number in AH.
      if code < 255
        then
          al := code                    ! Country code in AL.
        else
          begin                         ! This is how DOS
            al := #ff;                  ! wants to get long
            bx := code                  ! country codes.
          end;
      ax := byword(ah,al);              ! Make a word
      ds := (ads buffer).s;             ! Segment:offset address
      dx := (ads buffer).r;             ! of buffer in DS:DX.
      intrp(#21,registers,registers);   ! Execute DOS function.
      if (Flags and CF) = 0             ! If CF is not set ...
        then
          status := 0                   ! Successful operation.
        else
          begin
            status :- ax;
            return
          end;
```

{ BX now contains the country code, even if originally al = 0 , signifying the current country. Find its name.}

```
for k := lower(country code) to upper(country_code) do
```

```
      if bx = country_code[k] then break;
    name : = country_name[k];

    {The country dependent information is now in the buffer.
    Look at each byte and build the notation record. The first
    byte is the date format;   the second is always zero.}

    date_format : = buffer[1];

    {Next comes the currency symbol;  1  to  4  characters left
    justified in a five byte field, filled with  #ff  bytes.}

    i : = 0;
    j : = 3;
    while j <= 7 and then buffer[j] <> #ff do
      begin
        i : = i+1;
        currency_symbol[i] : = chr(buffer[j]);
        j : = j+1
      end;
    currency_symbol.len : = wrd(i);

    {Read the separators, ignoring the following #ff bytes.}

    thousands_separator : = chr(buffer[8]);
    decimal_separator   : = chr(buffer[10]);
    date_separator      : = chr(buffer[12]);
    time_separator      : = chr(buffer[14]);
    list_separator      : = chr(buffer[23]);

    {Finally, read the rest of the information.}

    currency_space      : = (buffer[16] and 2) <> 0;
    currency_1st        : = not odd(buffer[16]);
    currency_places     : = buffer[17];
    clock_24_hours      : = odd(buffer[18]);
    case_map_address.r  : = byword(buffer[20],buffer[19]);
    case_map_address.s  : = byword(buffer[22],buffer[21])
  end
end; {get_notation}
```

Figure 8.6.2 Pascal procedure to read country dependent information

The last item in the notation buffer is the segment:offset address of a procedure that will facilitate lower- to uppercase character conversion for the country concerned. (This conversion is not trivial for letters with accent marks, etc.) Instructions for using the procedure are found in the *MS-DOS Programmer's Reference Manual* [24, Chap. 1].

You can also change the current country by setting DX = hex ffff before executing the interrupt.

File handling functions hex 3d, 44, and 5a to 5c

The DOS 3.0 changes to file handling procedures are principally directed toward implementing file sharing for networks, to be featured in DOS 3.1. The changes affect only the more recent functions that use *file handles*. The older functions that directly manipulate file control blocks will evidently not be enhanced for file sharing.

Functions hex 5a to 5c are useful even in non-sharing situations. With function 5a, you can create in a given directory a file whose name is guaranteed to be different from any others present; the function will return the new name to you. Function hex 5b is almost like 3c—create a new file with a given name. However, function 5b will fail and issue an error message if the specified file already exists. (Function 3c will destroy it!) Function hex 5c allows you to lock or unlock specific ranges of bytes in a file. This is intended to prevent another program from accessing that information while you are updating it, because its contents may not be consistent during that period. Function 5c is not intended for general read and write protection.

File sharing involves three concepts:

Access mode: What do *you* want to do to the file that you are opening?

Sharing mode: What do you want to prevent *others* from doing? (This seems like a rather negative concept of sharing!)

Inheritance: Do you want your child processes to have the same access to and control of the file that you enjoy?

When you open a file with function hex 3d, you can specify whether you want to access it for input, output, or both. You can deny others the ability to read it, write it, or both, until you close it. And you can give your children equal access and control or treat them the same as other processes. (A child process is one that you invoke through Function hex 4b.) A table showing how other processes may open a shared file once you have established its access and sharing parameters is included in the discussion of this function in the *DOS 3.0 Technical Reference* manual, Chapter 5. If you wish to use this file sharing capability, you must first execute the DOS utility program **share.exe**. This loads a part of the operating system, about 5K bytes, that is used for no other purpose.

The input/output control function hex 44 has been enhanced to report information about removable media.

Determining the Program Segment Prefix (PSP)

The new DOS function hex 62 simply returns in the BX register the PSP segment address of the currently executing process. For details about the PSP, see Section 5.4. Since the process itself generally starts at offset hex 100 in this segment, the new function provides an easy way to find the current addresses of data and instructions relevant to your own program.

New error handling conventions

Interrupt hex 24 is executed when DOS encounters a critical error, i.e., one it can't handle, like the printer running out of paper or certain drive failures, either mechanical or caused by a malfunctioning program. Handling many of these errors may require manual intervention or the operator's judgement. The service routine writes the familiar **Abort, Retry, Ignore?** message and handles your reponse. Under 3.0, more information is available when the interrupt occurs, and more support is provided for an interrupt service routine that you might substitute for the DOS routine. In particular, three bits in the AH register indicate the propriety of the responses **retry** and **ignore** and of one new response, **fail**. DOS' own service routine doesn't let you specify **fail** in response to the fateful question; however, this course is taken in some instances when your response is inappropriate.

If you substitute your own service routine, you can inspect the information that DOS provides concerning the error, then specify **abort, retry, ignore**, or **fail** by setting the AL register before you return. DOS' response to the **fail** option is to cause the new uniform error handling system for DOS functions, described below, to report failure of whatever DOS function encountered the critical error. You can take advantage of this new option by substituting your own service routine that always returns the **fail** response. If that is inappropriate, then DOS will abort. Otherwise, the DOS function that you requested, which encountered the critical error, will report its failure back to you. This allows you to handle DOS error situations individually, in the routines where you request DOS services, instead of using one general Interrupt hex 24 service routine that must figure out not only what error occurred but what you were doing at the time.

In earlier versions of DOS, the various functions reported errors in several different ways. To handle them all, you had to provide different kinds of error routines. With DOS 3.0, the old ways are still valid (so that error routines written for DOS 2.0, for instance, will still work). However, a new uniform error handling system has been implemented. Many DOS functions report errors by setting the Carry Flag (CF) or by setting AL = hex ff and reporting further information in various other registers. With DOS 3.0, they will, in addition, set up some error information in tables that you can access by requesting the new DOS function hex 59 service immediately after you perceive the error indication. For example, you could use function hex 3d to open file **b:\ab.cd\ef.gh by setting**

```
DS:DX = the address of a string containing the file name
          b:\ab.cd\ef.gh,
   AL = 0  indicating that the file is to be opened for
          reading,
   AH = function number  hex 3d,
```

and executing interrupt hex 21, the general DOS function call. If the function succeeds, it will return to your program with CF off and the file handle number in register AX. Otherwise, CF will signal the error, and AX will contain an error code. Now your program can test CF; if it is on, the program can set

```
AH  =   function number   hex 59,
```

and execute interrupt hex 21 again. DOS will now return with error information in a format that is standard over a very broad range of DOS functions.

The new *error information format* uses several CPU registers:

```
AX  =   error code,
BH  =   error class,
BL  =   suggested act,
CH  =   error location.
```

The *error codes* consist of all the error codes used in previous versions of DOS for interrupts or function calls, plus some codes for new DOS 3.0 functions. There are about forty of these, plus that many more reserved for future use. For details, consult the *DOS 3.0 Technical Reference* manual, Chapter 5. Thirteen *error classes* are distinguished:

1. Out of resource
2. Temporary situation
3. Authorization
4. Internal (probably a DOS bug)
5. Hardware failure
6. System failure
7. Application program error
8. Not found
9. Bad format
10. Locked
11. Media
12. Already exists
13. Unknown

For example, a request to allocate more memory than is available would result in a Class 1 error; a request to print when the printer is busy would result in Class 2. Class 4 and 5 errors are situations beyond user control, whereas Class 7 would result if your requests were inconsistent. If you intend to use this classification to direct your error handling, you should perform extensive experiments to see how DOS classifies various situations that might arise in your application.

Via register BL, DOS can indicate seven different error *response suggestions*:

1. Retry (several times before giving up).
2. Delay retry (wait a while, then retry).
3. Ask user to reenter information like drive name or file name.
4. Abort (in an orderly way, closing files, etc.).
5. Exit immediately (because attempting to do any cleanup can inflict further damage to your data).
6. Ignore.
7. Ask the user to do something (like turn on the printer) then retry.

Remember that these are only suggestions. If you exercise this facility, you will surely find situations where the suggestions are inappropriate, and perhaps hilarious. Nevertheless, this kind of information can make it much easier for you to write error handling programs.

Finally, the *error locations* indicated in the CH register include

1. Unknown
2. Block device (some sort of drive)
3. Reserved for future use
4. Serial device
5. Memory

9

INTEL 80286

Contents

This Chapter describes the features that distinguish the PC/AT's Intel 80286 CPU from the 8088 CPU of the earlier PCs. The 80286 is really two computers in one. In *real mode* it is really an enhanced 8086. It runs faster and has a few more instructions; beyond that, there are only very minor differences. Section 9.1 considers in detail the differences between the 8088 and the 80286 in real mode. Some of these are features that you may want to use right away. Others are more obscure, to be shelved and recalled if you ever have the need.

Section 9.2 is devoted to the virtual memory system implemented in the 80286 in protected mode. First, virtual memory is considered in general. The

80286 protected mode physical addresses are described—it can address a Gigabyte, $2^{24} = 10^9$ bytes. Finally, the 80286 virtual addressing scheme is considered, with its method of mapping virtual addresses to physical ones using segment selectors and descriptors. Familiarity with this material is required for understanding how you can use the PC/AT extended memory, even if you don't intend to run your programs in protected mode.

The 80286 task management and memory protection systems are described in Sections 9.3 and 9.4. Even though those sections are long and detailed, they give only an overview of these features, concentrating on the logic of their design. A thorough treatment, with examples sufficient to give you a really good idea how these systems are used and to guide you in writing programs for them, would require an entire book in itself. That is beyond the scope of the present text. References are given to lead you to more complete information on this subject.

9.1 Real mode: an enhanced 8086

Concepts

* Differences between the 8088 and the 80286 in real mode   * How much faster is the 80286? Why?   * New string input/output instructions   * Using the **bound** instruction to check for valid array indices   * Intel stack frames   * **enter** and **leave** instructions   * Minor changes to push, shift, rotate, and divide instructions   * New interrupts reserved for handling exceptions   * Change in single step interrupt   * New interrupt priorities

In real mode, the 80286 CPU operates like an enhanced 8086 or 8088. The main differences are

- its speed,
- a few new instructions, and
- some newly assigned interrupt vectors.

In addition, some 8086 design mistakes are corrected, some CPU behavior under error conditions is different, and the protocol that the 80286 uses to handle an 80287 mathematics coprocessor is different from that used by the earlier CPUs with the 8087 coprocessor. These differences are discussed in turn below, except for the last two. If you need to transport to an 80286 a program written for the earlier CPUs whose operation depended on the details of CPU behavior under certain error conditions, you may need to consult the *iAPX286 Programmer's Reference Manual,* reference [5, App. D]. If you are transporting a program that uses the mathematics coprocessor, you may need to consult the Numeric Supplement of the same manual.

Speed

The first major difference you encounter in switching from an older IBM PC to a PC/AT is the increase in speed. The actual time saved depends on several factors and thus varies between programs. Two of these factors have nothing to do with the CPU: decreased average access time for the hard disk, and the ability to trade off increased memory usage for increased speed. A program whose speed is not limited by that of external devices like disk drives or video controllers and which uses memory in a way independent of the total amount available will run faster on the PC/AT because the 80286 is faster than the 8088 on earlier PC models. This increased speed is due basically to three 80286 design features.

- The fundamental clock frequency of the 8088 in the earlier PC models is 4.77 Mhz. The 80286 in the PC/AT runs at 6 Mhz.
- A number of 80286 operations are pipelined and executed in parallel.
- The 80286 transmits data internally and to and from main memory, sixteen bits at a time. The 8088 is an eight bit machine.

The fundamental clock frequency is half the frequency of the clock crystal chip connected to the PC/AT CPU. The PC/AT uses a 12-Mhz crystal, so its CPU runs at 6 Mhz. The speed of a program is, of course, directly proportional to this frequency, so on this count alone, the PC/AT is about 25% faster than earlier PC models. The 80286 was in fact designed to operate at frequencies up to 10 Mhz. Several authors have reported in the technical literature that their PC/ATs work properly when the 12-Mhz crystal is replaced by a compatible 16-Mhz component. That surgery increases the 80286 frequency to eight Mhz, nearly twice that of the earlier PCs. However, when questioned on this point, IBM engineers merely repeat that the PC/AT runs at six Mhz. Evidently, some components of the system are not reliable at the higher speed, but further details are not yet public.

By pipelining internal CPU operations, the 80286 is able to execute most instructions with fewer clock cycles than earlier CPUs. While the 80286 is executing one instruction, it is decoding another and fetching yet others from memory. Figure 9.1.1 shows clock cycle comparisons for some common instructions. According to Intel, the actual speed increase due to pipelining is not quite so dramatic, because an instruction may finish executing before the parallel fetching operation is completed. Obviously the effect of this efficiency on program speed is considerable, but depends on the mixture of instruction types in a program. Intel claims that pipelining accounts for an average 100% increase in program speed.

Finally, since the data bus width of the 80286 is sixteen bits, twice that of the 8088, data transfer to and from memory can proceed at twice the rate of the older CPU. To take advantage of this advance, you should avoid moving

instruction	explanation	8086 cycles required	80286 cycles required
inc ax	increment AX	2	2
pushf	push Flags	10	3
mov ax,mem	move to AX from memory	10	5
mul bl	multiply AL by BL	70-77	13

Figure 9.1.1 8086 and 80286 clock cycles required for certain instructions

data only one byte at a time, arrange that data words being moved begin at even addresses, and use the string move instruction whenever possible.

Because the 80286 runs faster than the 8088, peripheral devices may not be able to handle two successive **in** or **out** instructions even if they were executed correctly by an 8086 or 8088. IBM recommends inserting the instruction

```
jmp short $+2
```

between two adjacent input/output instructions and in fact uses that tactic often in the PC/AT BIOS. This instruction does nothing but jump to the next one, wasting a few cycles on the way.

In summary, according to the above considerations, the 80286 PC/AT CPU accounts for an increase in program speed by a factor of about

  1.25 due to 6 Mhz clock frequency
  x2.0 due to instruction pipelining (underestimate?)
  x2.0 due to doubling data bus width (overestimate?)
  5.0 calculated overall improvement factor

This factor is *not* observed in practice. A factor around three for programs that do not involve input-output is often mentioned in the technical literature, and the author confirmed this factor. Perhaps the two 2.0 factors are too large, because most PC software does not take advantage of the 80286 design.

Note, however, that the improvement figures for some programs may be quite different because their speed is not really dependent on the CPU. Some may gain considerably more speed with a PC/AT because they benefit by using more memory or by using the faster disk drive. On the other hand, some may show little improvement because their speed is really restricted by the slow Color/Graphics Adapter.

New 80286 real mode instructions

The 80286 supports a number of instructions beyond the basic 8086 family instructions set described in Section 6.4. Some of these are involved only with its operation in protected mode. However, several have been provided for the real mode as well; in fact, the new real mode instructions are also available on the 80186 CPU. These instructions will be discussed in turn below:

```
ins     pusha     enter     bound
outs    popa      leave
```

The remaining new instructions are involved with memory management and protection and are discussed later in Section 9.3 and 9.4. Several 8086 family instructions have been modified slightly for the 80286. The modifications are discussed at the end of the current section.

String input and output instructions Instructions **ins** and **outs** fill a gap in the category of string manipulation instructions. They are used like the string move instruction **movs**, but the source operand for **ins**—and the destination for **outs**—is a CPU port whose number is in register DX. Figure 9.1.2 shows code that sends ten zeros to an output port; it is patterned after an example of the **movs** instruction in Chapter 6.4. In this program, you may use **outs s** in place of **outsw** and let the assembler determine that **outsw** is appropriate because **s** was defined as a word array. You may also use **outsb** to specify byte output, and use **ins, insb**, and **insw** the same way. While the repeat prefixes are legal as far as the 80286 is concerned and have their usual meaning, they result in back to back input or output commands, which the PC/AT manuals caution against. Therefore, the delay command **jmp short $ + 2** was included, necessitating a **loop** structure instead of just a **rep outsw** instruction.

Range checking The **bound** instruction provides an easy way to check whether a value x lies in an interval a..b, i.e., whether a $\le$ x $\le$ b. The first operand specifies a general register in which x is found. The second, with which you can use any appropriate addressing mode, refers to a; the very next memory word must contain b. If x fails to lie in the interval, the instruction issues a hardware **int 5** instruction. (Unfortunately, in the PC/AT, this interrupt is used for the Print Screen service. To use the **bound** instruction on a PC/AT, you must first point interrupt vector 5 to your own service routine. This disables the Print Screen service.) For example, here is some code which

```
           segment sorcery
s          dw      10 dup(0)     ;s  is a string of  10  zeros.
n          dw      10            ;n  tells how many words to output.
           ends

           lds     sorcery       ;Set up segment register.
           assume  ds:sorcery    ;Inform the assembler.

           mov     dx,port_no    ;Put the port number in  DX .
           cld                   ;Clear  DF  to increment  SI .
           lea     si,s          ;Initialize the source address.
           mov     cx,n          ;Initialize the count in  CX .
inloop:    outsw                 ;Output  DS:SI  and decrement  CX.
           jmp     short $+2     ;Delay.
           loop    inloop        ;loop while  CX ≠ 0.
```

Figure 9.1.2 Program using outsw instruction

checks whether an index in register DI is in the interval 5..10 before it stores the value in AX in an array entry.

```
a       dw      5              ; If you store the bounds
b .     dw      10             ; just below the array,
array   dw      100 dup ()     ; you can use its name to
                               ; refer to them.
bound   di, array-4
mov     array [di] , aw
```

Push and pop all The new instruction **pusha** pushes onto the the stack the contents of all eight general registers in this order: AX, BX, CX, DX, original value of SP, BP, SI, and DI. Its companion instruction **popa** pops eight words from the stack and stores them in the same registers in the proper order, except that it does not replace the Stack Pointer SP value with a value from the stack. Figure 9.1.3 illustrates the effect of these instructions. They provide a convenient means for saving and restoring the registers when entering or leaving a procedure.

Enter and leave instructions Another pair of instructions **enter** and **leave**, provides a convenient way to set up and dispose of some rather complicated stack structures of the type commonly used to implement procedure calls in higher level languages.

Nesting of procedure definitions in a structured language can be described using a tree structure. Nesting level is the same as depth in the tree structure. Figure 9.1.4 shows an example of nested procedures in Pascal, and two equivalent ways of viewing the nesting. A program p is shown, and procedures a, b, c, and d with nesting levels 1, 2, 3, 4, and 3, respectively. (Main programs always have nesting level 1.) Each procedure knows its own name and its offsprings': the main program p knows a, a knows b and d, and b knows c. Moreover, each procedure inherits the identifiers known to its ancestors. For a procedure x to invoke another procedure, it is only necessary for x to know its name. Thus the procedures that x can call are just the direct offspring of its ancestors. In the example, procedure c can call procedure d but not vice versa, since d does not know about c. When a procedure x invokes another procedure y, certain data structures must be set up to give y access to all the information it's entitled to (and no more):

- x must give y its return address;
- x must send y its parameters (or at least their addresses);
- y must set up a work space in memory for its local data;
- y must be provided access to the workspaces of the current invocations of all its ancestors in the procedure nesting tree.

It's important to keep separate the notions of a procedure and its invocations; since most structured languages permit *recursive* procedures that call themselves or procedures that call each other, it's common to have more than one invocation of the same procedure active at the same time. Each invocation has a separate workspace and separately transmitted pa-

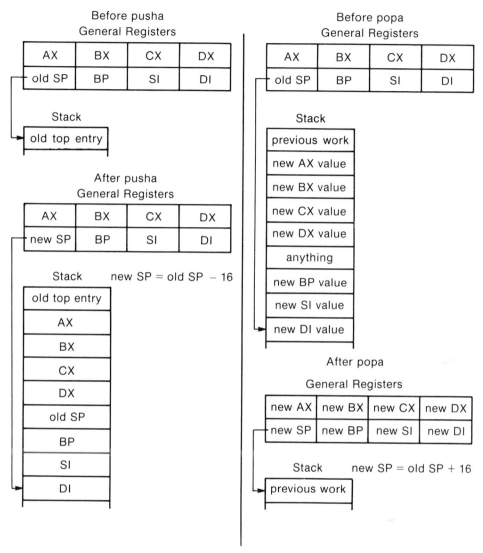

Figure 9.1.3 Instructions pusha and popa

rameters. Note that the nesting level is an attribute of the procedure, not the invocation. A procedure with a given nesting level may be called recursively; later invocations have greater *recursion depth* but the same nesting level.

The stack provides a convenient way to keep track of all this information. When x calls y, x pushes its return address and the parameters onto the stack following a given protocol, and y sets up its workspace on the stack. When y is ready to return to x, it can pop the workspace and parameters (just discarding them); at that point the return address is atop the stack, ready to lead the way back.

Pascal Example:

Equivalent
Visualization:

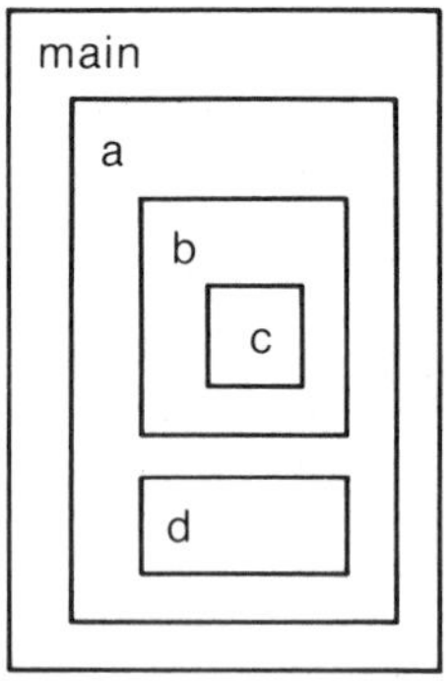

```
program p;
var (n_a words of data);

    procedure a(m_a words of parameters);
    var (na words of data);

        procedure b(m_b words of parameters);
        var (n_b words of parameters);
            procedure c(m_c words of parameters);
            var (n_c words of data);
            begin {c}
            end; {c}
        begin {b}
        end; {b}

        procedure d(m_d words of parameters);
        var (n_d words of data);
        begin {d}
        end;{d}

    begin {a}
    end;{a}

begin {main}
end. {main}
```

Equivalent Tree Structure

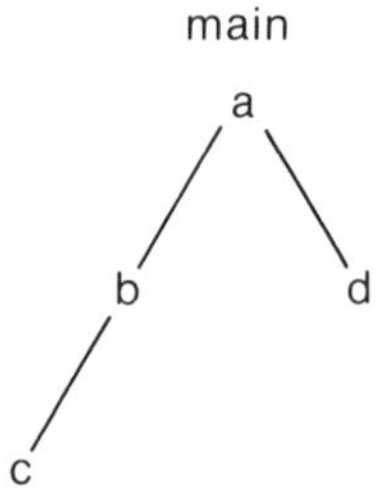

Note that c can call d because d
is an offspring of an ancestor of c.

Figure 9.1.4 Example of procedure nesting

How does y gain access to the workspaces of its ancestors' current invocations? Several methods are used by various compilers, generally involving a data structure on the stack known as a *stack frame*. Intel's 80286 engineers decided to implement one such method in hardware to provide ultrafast procedure calls that are moreover easy to program and to remember. Their method, implemented in the **enter** and **leave** instructions, makes use of the notion of nesting level, but is independent of the exact way that this might be related to procedure definitions in the higher level language. Thus it might be used with languages whose procedure definitions are interrelated in ways different from Pascal's.

The **enter** statement is complicated, and most easily described by the Pascal-like program in Figure 9.1.5 that involves simpler 80286 instructions. In this figure, the notation **push [bp]** means push the word whose address is in BP. You may think of **FP** as a temporary storage location private to the **enter** instruction. Actually, it will be very useful for us to have a notation for the address stored here while **enter** is executing, so below we will think of **FP** as a public variable whose name includes that of the procedure in question. That is, instead of having every execution of the **enter** instruction use that same private variable, let's imagine that the **enter** instruction uses a variable called **y**'s **FP** to set up the stack frame for procedure y. Then, when we trace the execution of several **enters**, we can think of the various **FP**s as variables containing offsets of important locations on the stack.

The first parameter of the **enter** instruction can be **level** = 0, to provide for a less elaborate *non-nested* frame pointer. You may consult the *iAPX 286 Programmer's Reference Manual* [5, Chap. 4] for detail about that. Here, we consider using **enter** for nested procedures only, so that **level** ⟩ 0. Consider first the instruction **enter 1,n** that would be used by a main program—for example p in Figure 9.1.4—to set up an n word stack work space. For this special case, the definition of **enter** is

```
push bp;
FP : = sp;
push FP
bp : = FP;
sp : = sp-n
```

This has the following effect on the stack. (Remember, in this example, we're regarding **FP** as a variable **p**'s **FP** to which we have access.)

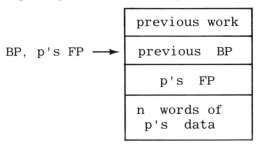

```
level : = level mod 32;
push bp;
FP : = sp;
if level ⟩ 0
   then
     begin
       for i : = 1 to level-1 do
         begin
           bp : = bp-2;
           push [bp]
         end;
       push FP
     end
bp : = FP;
sp : = sp-n
```

Figure 9.1.5 Definition of instruction enter n,level

Note that the new value of the Base Pointer is the same as that of the newly created FP. It points to an entry on the stack that can lead you back to previous work. After this entry comes one FP—this reflects the fact that p's nesting level is one. Then come all of p's local data. These entries stacked by the **enter** instruction constitute p's *stack frame*; a compiler knows enough about p to assign offsets of all these entries relative to p's FP, and the **enter** instruction insures that at execution time the BP register contains the value of p's FP. So far, you've seen this work just for level one. Now look at Figure 9.1.6, which shows the stack frames created by **enter** instructions corresponding to a typical sequence of invocations of the procedures in the program of Figure 9.1.4. You will see that each procedure's FP points back to previous work and is preceded by a return address and its parameters and followed by the FPs of the current invocations of its ancestors, then by the procedure's local variables. A compiler knows enough about the procedure to assign offsets of all these entries relative to the FP, and after the **enter** instruction, the BP register contains the value of the FP. Thus the compiler, by using stack frames set up by **enter** instructions, can provide each procedure access to exactly the right information in its workspace and those of its ancestor's current invocations.

A **leave** instruction simply undoes an **enter** instruction. When your procedure has finished its task, it should restore the stack and the BP register to their states just after the **enter** instruction. Executing a **leave** instruction then performs two steps:

```
mov sp, bp
pop bp
```

The first of these, in effect, pops all your procedure's local data. The second pops its FP into register BP. From Figure 9.1.6 you notice that this puts its parent's FP into BP. Then you should execute a **ret k** instruction corresponding to the **call** that invoked your procedure; **k** is the number of bytes of parameters for your procedure. This instruction pops all the parameters and the return address, then returns to your procedure's parent.

Clearly, the **enter** and **leave** instructions provide an ingenious and efficient way for compilers and humans to implement procedure calls. However, you should note that there are other possible designs for stack frames. In particular, IBM Pascal uses a different setup, in which a stack frame contains pointers not to all ancestral frames but just to its parent's and the main program's. This saves a little space and perhaps is quicker to set up, but more time is spent tracing pointers back to ancestral frames.

80286 real mode instruction changes

A few familiar 8086 family instructions operate slightly differently on the 80286; these are considered in turn below. In addition, there are a number of technical changes in the treatment of interrupts; for these consult the *iAPX 286 Programmer's Reference Manual* [5, App. D].

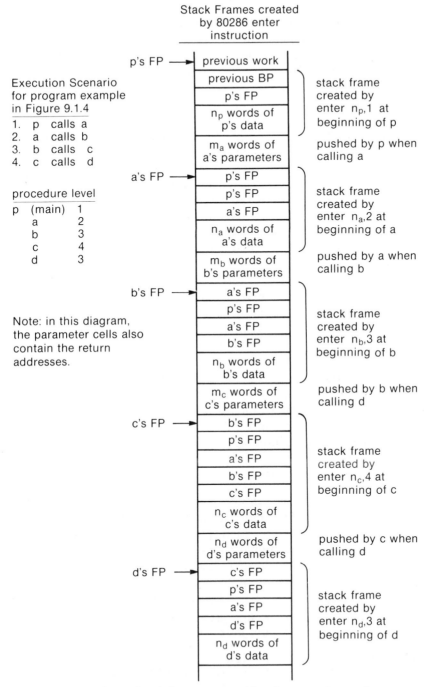

Figure 9.1.6 Stack frame created by the enter instruction

Changes in push instruction There are two changes to the **push** instruction. First, you can push an immediate operand. This always pushes a *word*. If you specify only a byte, it becomes the low order byte of a word; its high order bit is replicated to form the rest of the word. For example,

push e0h   pushes   hex 00e0,
push f0h   pushes   hex fffh.

On the 8086 or 8088, instruction **push sp** decremented the stack pointer SP by 2, then moved it to the top of the stack. As a result, the top stack entry contained its own offset address relative to SP. The 80286, on the other hand, records the value of register SP, then decrements SP and moves the recorded value to the top of the stack. This results in the top entry pointing to the word immediately below it on the stack (i.e., immediately above it in memory). It's not clear how useful this instruction is, but an 8086 or 8088 program that uses it will probably misfunction on an 80286.

Changes in shift and rotate instructions You may use immediate mode for the second operand of a shift or rotate instruction on the 80286. For example, to rotate the AX register leftward seven bits requires on the 80286 only one instruction, **rol ax,7**, whereas on the 8086 or 8088 it required two:

```
mov cl,7
shl ax,cl
```

Also on the 80286, the shift bit count (7 in the above example) is always interpreted modulo 32. (This change could conceivably affect some timing details.)

Change in divide instructions The byte and word quotients -128 and -32768 are attainable by the signed division **idiv** instruction, whereas they caused the divide exception interrupt **int 0** on the 8086 and 8088.

New reserved interrupts

You saw earlier that by reserving Interrupt 5 for the **bound** instruction exception handler, the 80286 comes into conflict with the PC/AT's use of that interrupt for the Print Screen function. The same situation occurs with three other interrupts. Here is a summary of their use by the 80286; the conflicts with the PC/AT BIOS are discussed in Section 10.3.

Interrupt	80286 function
5	**bound** instruction exception
8	**lidt** instruction exception
9	80287 instruction segment overrun
d	80286 instruction segment overrun

Instruction **lidt** is used only in preparing to enter protected mode, and it causes Interrupt 8 only if a certain error occurs. The segment overrun exceptions occur when an instruction attempts to access a word whose address has offset ffff. (Should the high order byte come from offset 0000 in the current segment or in the next?) More details on these exceptions are given in the *iAPX 286 Programmer's Reference Manual* [5, Chap. 5 and App. D]. The resulting conflicts with the PC/AT BIOS are discussed in Section 10.3.

Single step interrupt

The so-called *single step* Interrupt 1 was available in the earlier 8086 family CPUs. However, its operation is different in the 80286, so its discussion was postponed to this point.

Interrupt 1 is reserved for use by debugging software to produce the effect of stepping through your program one instruction at a time. Its execution is controlled by the Trap Flag (TF), a bit in the Flags register. When TF is set, exactly one instruction will complete execution, then the CPU hardware orginates an **int** 1 instruction. This interrupt behaves like any other, except that it *clears* TF. The Interrupt 1 service routine (ISR) is to be supplied by the debugging software (for example, the DOS **debug** utility).

This idea is clever. To single step your program, the debugger sets TF and transfers control to your program. Your first instruction executes, then **int 1**. This interrupt clears TF and invokes the debugger's ISR. The ISR takes over, operating now at normal speed, perhaps displaying register values and asking what to do next. If it is to continue single stepping, it simply sets TF again and returns. The **iret** instruction goes back to your program, your next instruction executes, then the **int 1** process repeats.

Unfortunately, this elegant design does not provide for handling other hardware interrupts that may occur during debugging. For example, you may have a time- or communications-dependent process going on at the same time. What happens if an external interrupt occurs during execution of one of your instructions when TF is set for single stepping? When your instruction finishes, the external interrupt and **int 1** are vying for attention. The 80286 solution is to give **int 1** priority. It executes, turns off TF, and transfers control to the debugger's ISR. Before the debugger can execute even one instruction, however, it is interrupted by the pending external interrupt. That urgent service request is handled (at normal speed), and eventually control is returned to the debugger, which proceeds as described earlier.

The earlier 8086 family CPUs solved this problem differently. Like the 80286, they avoided single stepping critical external interrupt servicing. However, to do so, they made it impossible to single-step *any* interrupt service routine. On the 80286, you can single step a communications service routine by invoking it via a software interrupt; but whenever it is invoked externally via the Interrupt Controller chip, it works at normal speed.

Interrupt priorities

The contention between external and single step interrupts brings up a general question: when two interrupts vie for attention, which is served? Here is the 80286 prioritization:

Priority	Interrupt
Highest = 0	All software interrupts and 80286 exceptions
1	Single step (hardware originated **int 1**)
2	Non-maskable (hardware originated **int 2**)
3	80287 segment overrun exception
4	Other hardware interrupts

In the older 8086 family CPUs, the single step interrupt had the lowest priority.

9.2 Protected mode addressing

Concepts

* Virtual memory * Transparent memory management * Protected mode virtual memory organization * Mapping virtual addresses into physical addresses * Segment selectors and descriptor tables * Local and Global Descriptor Table Registers * Instructions for loading and storing these registers * Insuring that descriptor table indices and segment offsets stay within bounds

Aside from its increased speed, the main features of the Intel 80286 that distinguish it from the earlier members of the 8086 family are its implementation of virtual memory and memory protection. These features characterize its operation in *protected mode*, whereas in real mode, as described in the previous section, the 80286 is organized like the 8086. Except via the **vdisk** virtual disk device driver, DOS 3.0 does not support use of virtual memory. In fact, you cannot even use BIOS services in protected mode. However, with some operating system that supports these new capabilities, applications programmers will be able to write programs that manipulate very large amounts of data independent of their storage in main memory or on external devices. Moreover, they will be able to write programs that share memory and CPU resources in a multitasking environment without referring to other programs that may be running concurrently. The operating system will manage the memory and program execution so that the right data are available at the right time, and it will prevent concurrent tasks from improperly accessing or interfering with each other's data or code.

In this section, you will see how virtual addressing techniques can be used in general to free programmers from address limitations imposed by main memory size and to keep separate the data belonging to different tasks in a multitasking system. Then the 80286 protected mode virtual memory management system is discussed in detail. The protected mode scheme is quite different from the familiar 80286 real mode segment:offset addressing technique. An attempt is made to distinguish *management* from *protection* considerations in order to consider the latter in Section 9.4. Since some features of the memory management system are designed to implement its protection scheme, you will encounter some forward references to that section.

Virtual memory

It is important to understand two opposite qualities, *virtual* and *transparent*:

Something is *virtual* if it is not really there but seems to be.

Something is *transparent* if it is really there but seems not to be.

You have already encountered the DOS 3.0 virtual disk **vdisk**. When you use it, it seems that you are storing data on a fixed disk. However, you really are not. You are just using part of main memory to imitate a disk. The **vdisk** device driver software, which translates your disk storage commands into instructions appropriate for main memory storage, is transparent to you. You don't seem to be using it, but you really are.

A *virtual memory* system allows you to write programs that appear to use more main memory than may actually be present. The memory seems to be there, but the data may in fact be stored on an external device. This type of programming is made possible by a *memory management* system, which should be *transparent* to you. Your programs actually use the memory management services, but these operate so smoothly that they seem not to be there.

Why is virtual memory an important concept? Consider how a programmer uses the addresses of data in main memory. Addresses generally serve two functions:

1. locating data physically in memory, and
2. organizing the memory, distinguishing data of different type, and relating similar data.

While locating data physically in memory is important at execution time, programmers rarely are concerned with this level of detail. However, using different address schemes for different types of data—for example, executable program code, data belonging to different users or operating system information—is an important component of efficient programming. Allowing programmers to use addresses entirely for organizing memory and to ignore considerations of physical location enhances their efficiency. Such an addressing technique is called *virtual addressing*.

Virtual addressing is particularly appropriate when many different data areas must be kept separate but more or less equally accessible, and not all need be accessible at once. This situation might arise with a single program that must operate sequentially with many large tables. On the other hand, several programs, as in a network, might need to timeshare, keeping their executable code and data areas entirely private from each other.

In cases like these, programs can use different virtual addresses to keep the data separate. The memory management system should

determine which virtual addresses refer to data currently in main memory and find their physical location;

load data from an external device when the virtual address does not refer to main memory;

store data on an external device when more room in main memory is needed.

If it can perform these services without becoming apparent to the programmer, the memory management system may properly be termed *transparent*.

Protected mode physical addresses

You will remember that the real mode segment:offset address of a byte in main memory consists of two 16-bit words, the segment s and offset r. The physical address of this byte is $16 s + r$; to compute it you merely shift s leftward four bits and add r. This physical address is 20 bits long, so you can address at most 2^{20} bytes—one megabyte—of main memory. In real mode, you may consider main memory as consisting of overlapping 64K byte segments whose physical base addresses are multiples of $16 = $ hex 10. While different physical addresses always refer to different memory locations, segment overlapping permits different segment:offset addresses, for example hex 0000:0010 and 0001:0000, to refer to the same memory location.

In protected mode, the 80286 handles addresses quite differently. A physical address is 24 bits long, so you can address up to 2^{24} bytes—sixteen megabytes—of main memory. The real mode segment:offset addresses are not used at all in protected mode.

Memory mapping

In a virtual memory system, virtual addresses are assigned to data without regard to the physical arrangement of memory. Programmers are free to use addressing systems that reflect only the logical relationships among their data. The memory management component of the operating system must determine whether a given virtual address refers to data currently in main memory and, if it does, determine its physical address. If the required data is not currently in main memory, then it must be retrieved from an external device. If main memory is currently full, the operating system will have to move some low priority data to an external device in order to bring in the needed data. Translation from virtual to physical addresses is called *memory mapping*.

The 80286 implements protected mode memory mapping and some other aspects of memory management and protection in hardware to permit very efficient operating system implementations. With DOS 3.0, you have almost no access to these features, but later operating systems will provide it as they include multitasking and multiuser capabilities. (Even in real addressing mode, the 80286 does a kind of memory mapping: the formula 16 s + r determines the real address of the byte with segment:offset address s:r).

Virtual addressing in protected mode is entirely different from the familiar real mode segment:offset addressing scheme, though a few similarities are highlighted by common terminology. In protected mode, virtual memory is organized as a collection of segments, which may have *any convenient length* up to 64K. Segments are *disjoint:* they may not overlap. In protected mode, a virtual address consists of two 16 bit words: a segment *selector* and an *offset*. It will be called a *selector:offset* address. The concept of offset is similar to that in real mode: a quantity to be added to a segment's physical base address to obtain the physical address of the byte addressed. The memory mapping is an algorithm that inspects a virtual address to determine if the segment selector refers to a segment in real memory, and if so, to calculate its physical base address.

Two bits in the segment selector are used by the 80286 for memory protection and do not play any role in the mapping. Thus a program can have access to at most $2^{16-2} = 2^{14}$ segments of virtual memory. If each of these contained the full $2^{16} = 64K$ bytes, the virtual memory would contain $2^{14}*2^{16} = 2^{30} =$ one Gigabyte, or approximately 10^9 bytes. Of course, utilization of this total amount of storage would be very rare, because it would need an enormous external storage system. Nevertheless, the *ability* to use it provides programmers great flexibility.

How is the memory mapping implemented? In designing it, the 80286 architects considered how the processor would be used. They assumed that at any given time a single *task* would be running, one which has its own private segments—but which also uses system programs and other information that serve all tasks. Thus it would need access to its own *local* segments, and to the system or *global* segments. One bit in a segment selector distinguishes the two types of segments.

The 80286 has two special registers, not present in earlier members of the 8086 family, that help it perform the memory mapping. These are called the *local and global descriptor table registers* LDTR and GDTR. At all times in protected mode operation, they contain information that enables the 80286 to locate two tables which actually contain the segment base addresses that are added to the offsets to determine the physical addresses. These two tables are called the *local and global descriptor tables* LDT and GDT. It is the responsibility of the memory management component of the operating system (not the 80286 itself) to keep these registers updated. The local table must be replaced as each new task begins execution and the local register updated to locate the table properly. The global table is task independent. The first step in mapping a selector:offset virtual address to a physical address is to examine the segment selector Table Indicator bit (TI), which distinguishes local from global segments. Then the 80286 uses the LDTR or GDTR to find the local or global descriptor table.

You now have enough information to visualize a segment selector, depicted in Figure 9.2.1. The Index specifies which entry of the appropriate descriptor table contains the mapping information for the segment. Since it's 13 bits long, a descriptor table may have at most $2^{13} = 8192$ entries. The RPL is a privilege level in the range 0..3 used by the memory protection scheme. It indicates the privilege level of the program that originated this selector and is compared with the privilege level (recorded in the descriptor table) required to access the segment. By keeping this information in the selector, the 80286 can prevent a highly privileged system routine from providing an untrusted application routine—the selector's originator—access to sensitive data. (Most details of the protection system are discussed in the next section.)

The descriptor tables contain entires for all the local and global segments in use and certain other system descriptors. Each task needs its own LDT, and the operating system needs access to all the LDTs in order to switch between tasks. The 80286 has a systematic way of keeping track of the various LDTs: they are set up like global segments with descriptors in the GDT.

The various descriptors in a descriptor table are all eight bytes long, as shown in the first panel of Figure 9.2.2. One byte, the Access Rights Byte, indicates the type of descriptor. The remaining format details for all *segment* descriptors are similar, shown in the second panel. Note that 24 bits are provided for the physical base address of a segment and 16 bits for the segment length, which may not exceed $2^{16} = 64K$ bytes. The bytes that are labeled "Reserved for future use by Intel" must be filled with zeroes to insure that an 80286 program will also run on the Intel 80386 CPU. For certain kinds of *system* descriptors the format is different. These descriptors have to do with memory protection and are discussed in the next section.

The Access Rights byte of a descriptor table entry is shown in Figure 9.2.3. One bit distinguishes first between segment and other system descriptors. The only system descriptors of concern here are the LDT descriptors. Their type code is shown in the first panel of the Figure. For the segment descriptors, a second bit distinguishes between code and data segments. Two further bits tell whether a code segment may be read and whether it is conformant. (The latter notion has to do with memory protection and is discussed in the next section.) These same two bits are used to tell whether a data segment is writeable and whether it should be expanded downward or upward. (If you exhaust a temporary storage segment, the operating system might want to extend it upward, or perhaps downward like a stack.) Three more bits have the same meaning for all three types. Bit P is turned on if the segment is present in main memory. Bit A is turned on whenever the segment is accessed. (If it's off, an operating system might place the segment on an external device if more main memory is needed.) Finally, the two DPL bits, the Descriptor Privilege

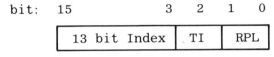

bit: 15   3   2   1   0

| 13 bit Index | TI | RPL |

TI = Table Indicator bit
    = 0 for Global Segment, 1 for Local
RPL = 2 bit Requested Privilege Level

Figure 9.2.1 Segment selector

Level, indicate how privileged a task must be to access the segment. You will see in the next section how the DPL is compared with the RPL bits in a segment selector to determine if a task has access to a segment.

To map a selector:offset virtual address into a physical address, the 80286 first uses the TI bit in the selector to determine whether to use the Local or Global Descriptor Table Register. (See Figure 9.2.4.) Then it uses the selector Index bits to find the proper entry of the Descriptor Table. (It must multiply the Index by eight, the length of a Table entry.) From Bit P of this descriptor the 80286 determines whether the segment is present in main memory. If not, it issues an interrupt, relying on an interrupt service routine in operating system software to find the appropriate segment in external storage, make room for it in main memory, load it, and update the descriptor. With the descriptor now referring to a segment present in main memory, the 80286

Byte 7	Byte 6
Access Rights Byte	Byte 4
Byte 3	Byte 2
Byte 1	Byte 0

Format for all entries of a descriptor table

Reserved for future use by Intel	
Access Rights Byte	High order address
Low order bytes of physical base address	
Segment length	

Format for all segment descriptors

Figure 9.2.2 Descriptor formats

Access Rights Byte for a Local Descriptor Table Descriptor

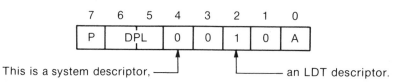

This is a system descriptor, ———⌐   ⌐——— an LDT descriptor.

Access Rights Byte for a Code Segment Descriptor

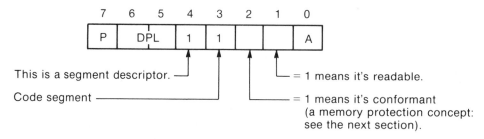

This is a segment descriptor. ———⌐   ⌐—— = 1 means it's readable.

Code segment ——————————————⌐   ⌐—— = 1 means it's conformant
(a memory protection concept:
see the next section).

Access Rights Byte for a data segment descriptor

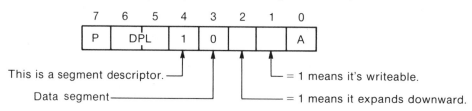

This is a segment descriptor. ———⌐   ⌐—— = 1 means it's writeable.

Data segment——————————————⌐   ⌐—— = 1 means it expands downward.

*P = 1 means the segment is present.

*DPL is the Descriptor Privilege Level (a memory protection device: see the next section).

*A = 1 means that the segment has been accessed (can be used by the operating system to establish segment priorities).

Figure 9.2.3 Descriptor Access Rights Byte

extracts its 24-bit base address. Finally, it adds the offset to obtain the physical address.

Since most programs must access many data from the same few segments, memory mapping might require repeatedly fetching the same few descriptors from the same tables in memory. The 80286 avoids this inefficiency by extending to protected mode the technique of using the segment registers for addressing code and data. As in real mode, instructions can only address memory via one of the four segment registers CS, SS, DS, and ES. However, in protected mode, these registers are each eight bytes long. A segment register consists of a *visible part* that holds a two byte segment selector and a *hidden part* that holds all of the appropriate segment descriptor except the two unused high order bytes. When you load a selector into a segment register, the

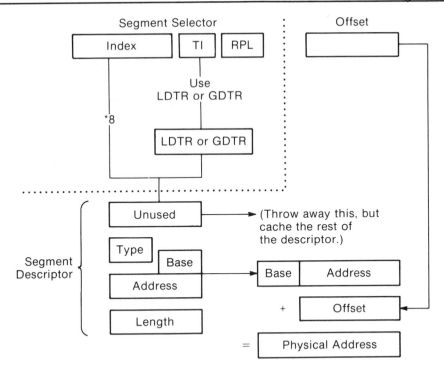

The part of the process above the dotted line is carried out when the segment register is loaded. The segment descriptor is cached in the hidden part of the segment register, and used later to map the offset to the physical address.

Figure 9.2.4 Mapping a selector: offset address to a physical address

first part of the mapping process is performed, involving the selector Index and the Local or Global Descriptor Table, and the relevant portion of the appropriate segment descriptor is cached in the hidden part of the segment register. This makes readily available the physical base address to which offsets will be added every time an instruction refers to memory via this segment register. Because that base address is in the hidden part of the segment register, your program has no direct access to it.

Two steps in the memory mapping process are subject to out-of-bounds errors. The selector Index could refer to a supposed descriptor beyond the end of the appropriate descriptor table, or the offset could refer to a memory location beyond the end of the segment. Besides merely constituting errors, such situations could result in one task gaining improper access to another's code or data. Our description above shows how the 80286 can avoid the second of these problems. Since the segment length is a descriptor entry cached in the hidden part of the segment register, the 80286 can easily check whether the offset is within bounds while computing the physical address. It issues an interrupt if an out-of-bounds error occurs. To see how the other out-of-bounds situation is avoided, you need to know how the Local and Global Descriptor Table Registers LDTR and GDTR are arranged.

As noted above, an LDT is merely a global segment with a descriptor in the GDT like an ordinary global segment except for the code in its Access Rights Byte. Thus the structure of the LDTR can be exactly the same as that of any segment register, and the 80286 can use exactly the same mechanism as described in the last paragraph to keep the LDTR from referring to a supposed LDT that is actually beyond the end of the GDT. The GDTR is a five byte register that contains the three-byte base address of the GDT and two bytes indicating its length. Thus the 80286 can easily check whether a global segment selector Index is within bounds before using it to find a global segment descriptor in the GDT.

Four instructions are provided for operating systems to manipulate the LDTR and GDTR:

```
lldt    sldt    lgdt    sgdt
```

The *load local descriptor table register* instruction **lldt** has one source operand. This is used as a global segment selector to load an LDT descriptor from the GDTR to the LDT. The *store local descriptor table register* instruction **sldt** is just the reverse: it copies the value of the LDTR to a descriptor in the GDT. The *load global descriptor table* instruction **lgdt** has one source operand that points to a byte in memory. This byte and the next are loaded into the GDTR field that indicates the length of the GDT. The following three bytes are loaded into the field that indicates its base address. The *store global descriptor register* instruction **sgdt** is just the reverse, storing in five bytes of memory the contents of the GDT. Instructions **lldt** and **sldt** may be executed only in protected mode, **lldt** and **lgdt** only by tasks at the most privileged level in protected mode. Instructions **lgdt** and **sgdt** are available in real mode to facilitate transfer to and from protected mode.

9.3 Task management

Concepts

* Task segregation through memory management and protection * Setting up descriptor tables and their registers * *Alias* descriptors * Are tasks re-entrant? * Switching tasks using the Task State Segment and Task Register * How are gates used in switching tasks? * Protected mode interrupts via gates * Interrupt Descriptor Table (IDT) and its register * Protected mode CPU interrupts and exceptions

---

This section and the next outline the main features of the 80286 CPU that are devoted to task management and protection. They provide only an introductory sketch, emphasizing the underlying logic. You will find the principal aspects of these topics covered, certainly enough to explain the PC/AT BIOS. However, lack of time and space make it impossible to give here details and examples sufficient to guide you in any substantial systems programming task involving these 80286 capabilities. For further information, you should consult the *iAPX 286 Programmer's Reference Manual* and *iAPX 286 Operating Systems Writer's Guide*, references [5] and [6]. *The PC/AT Technical Reference* manual unfortunately gives almost no detail on these topics.

The 80286 protected mode configuration is designed to permit several tasks to reside in main memory simultaneously, with a software system allocating CPU and memory resources among them as appropriate. While the 80286 hardware facilitates switching between tasks, the software system must decide *when* to do so. A resource scheduling algorithm would be based partly on on static aspects of the software system design (two necessary operations might simply be assigned to different tasks) or on priorities of certain events (one task's demands for memory might always take priority over another's, for example).

The 80286 task management and protection features are closely intertwined. One of the major goals of the protection system is to prevent unauthorized interaction between tasks. The other is to prevent a program from running astray in a way that's hard to trace, perhaps destroying valuable information belonging to its own task. This section will introduce you to the main task management features, leaving the protection system to Section 9.4. This order of topics is based on the fact that the task management system uses virtual memory segments as its main organizational device, but could it function with minimal protection. On the other hand, much of the complexity of the protection system is due to its provisions for accommodating task switching and other interactions between virtual memory segments. While it is possible to consider the main aspects of task management without going into detail about protection, it will be necessary occasionally to refer to a discussion in Section 9.4 to make sense of some aspect of task management.

Descriptor table setup

Task segregation in the 80286 is based on the virtual memory addressing scheme described in the previous section. Figure 9.3.1 depicts a very simple segregation model that uses only these addressing concepts; this model will be elaborated on later. Half of virtual memory is reserved for global segments, accessible to all tasks. Each global segment has a descriptor in the GDT, and the GDT Register points to the GDT. Each task has its own private segments with descriptors in its own Local Descriptor Table (LDT). The LDTs themselves are global system control segments, hence have descriptors in the GDT. The LDT register contains a selector pointing to the descriptor of the LDT of the current task.

It is anticipated that some system-type data and programs will reside for convenience in segments belonging to individual tasks, rather than in global segments. Concepts of protection and privilege will be developed to afford such valuable data protection against untrusted programs. When Figure 9.3.1 is altered to include these concepts, the more protected data and privileged code segments will be depicted near its center.

Every virtual memory segment must have a descriptor in the GDT or some LDT. In particular, the GDT must contain descriptors for every global segment, including

- ordinary data and code segment descriptors,
- one for itself,
- descriptors for all LDTs,
- descriptors containing other information about tasks and system organization,
- a dummy first descriptor to serve as a target for selectors with the value zero.

(If you forget to initialize a selector, its value will probably be zero, hence it will point to the first GDT descriptor. The Access Rights Byte of the dummy first descriptor is set equal to zero, which the 80286 recognizes as invalid.)

How do you set up the descriptor tables and their registers for protected mode operation? To build the tables the first time, you may use ordinary move instructions. To inspect and set the registers, the 80286 has four instructions:

sgdt   lgdt   sldt   lldt

The *store GDTR* instruction **sgdt** has a destination operand for which you must use direct mode addressing. You may execute it at any time to store the GDT Register: its limit field is transferred to the word at the destination address and its base address field to the next three bytes; the sixth byte of the destination is (perhaps) destroyed in this process. You may use the comple-

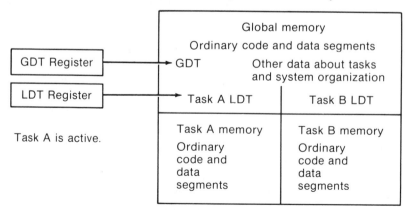

Figure 9.3.1 Simple model of task segregation

mentary *load GDTR* instruction **lgdt** to set the GDT Register after you have constructed a GDT. Instruction **lgdt** is normally used in real mode before switching to protected. Its use in protected mode is restricted to the most privileged programs.

The *store LDTR* instruction **sldt** moves the selector in the LDT Register to its destination operand, a word for which you may use any addressing mode. The source operand of the complementary *load LDTR* instruction **lldt** is a selector pointing to a descriptor in the GDT. You may use any addressing mode for this operand. Instruction **lldt** copies this descriptor into the LDT Register. The two LDT Register instructions may be used only in protected mode and only by the most privileged programs.

You can find several examples of the use of the four descriptor table instructions in the PC/AT BIOS, particularly where the Power On Self Test (POST) must verify that various protected mode features are working and in the Interrupt hex 15 function hex 89 service routine in the section whose pages are labeled "BIOS 1". This routine is provided specifically to put the CPU in protected mode. In each case, the code near the instruction is nearly unintelligible because it was evidently assembled with an assembler that recognized only the standard 8086 instructions. IBM used an artifice to fool the assembler into creating the correct binary instruction code. You can read that in the leftmost columns, referring to the binary codes defined in the *iAPX Programmer's Reference Manual* [5, App. B].

In order for the 80286 to detect an invalid source operand for instruction **lldt**, an LDT descriptor must have an Access Rights Byte that distinguishes it from other kinds of descriptors. This code was already indicated in the previous section. (In protected mode, the 80286 can detect many types of invalid instructions or operands and issue an *exception* interrupt with a code identifying the error. The operating system's exception interrupt service routine can then take appropriate action. Exception interrupts will be described later.) This consideration does not apply to instruction **lgdt**, whose source operand is just a memory location.

Once the descriptor tables and their registers have been set up, how can you change them? Consider the GDT. You want to use a move instruction with an offset corresponding to an entry in a certain descriptor; you would have loaded the appropriate segment selector into the DS or ES register. The memory management system allows you to store only data segments in these registers. Therefore, the GDT must be a data segment. One of the descriptors in the GDT refers to the GDT itself; its Access Rights Byte must indicate that it refers to a data segment.

This solution won't work for changing an LDT: as you saw above, the Access Rights Byte of an LDT descriptor must distinguish it as *different* from a data segment! In this situation you must construct and use an *alias* descriptor, identical to the LDT descriptor in question, but identified as a writeable data segment. In general, alias descriptors refer to the same segment, perhaps differing in some details, and occurring in different descriptor tables. Another example of their use is to allow two tasks to share a non-global segment. Using them is risky and requires great care, because they serve mainly to contravene some of the rules of the task management or protection systems.

You will see below that you can set protection codes in the GDT and LDT descriptors so that only the most privileged programs can alter the descriptor tables.

Task state segments

Once a set of tasks is set up in memory and a particular task is running, the software system may need to switch tasks, perhaps for one of these reasons:

- an interrupt has occurred, and its service routine belongs to another task,
- the current task is waiting for some event that might not occur for a while,
- the time interval allocated the current task has expired,
- the current task is completed.

The 80286 includes features that facilitate task switching. These are not separate instructions, but consist of the mechanisms built into the call, interrupt, return, and jump instructions for transferring program control between segments. You may use a call instruction to switch to a subtask or an interrupt instruction to switch to an interrupt service task, indicating that you wish to return and resume the original task when the subtask or service task is completed. (You must use an interrupt return instruction to return after either a call or an interrupt.) A jump instruction imposes no such return requirement.

The call, interrupt, return, and jump instructions may also be used to transfer program control within a segment or to another segment within the same task. In the former case, they work like the standard 8086 instructions. On the other hand, the protection system scrutinizes an intersegment transfer even if it causes no task switch; that process is discussed later.

To understand the logic of task switching, you must realize that tasks are not re-entrant. If you start one and then suspend it, you may not restart it on new data but only resume its operation on its original data exactly where it was suspended. This means that if a task is currently executing, has called a subtask, or has been interrupted, you may not switch to it again except on the return from the subtask or the interrupt service task.

Before turning to details of intertask transfers, consider this question: what information must you retain about tasks so that you can suspend a task, switch to another, and resume the original one later? From the above discussion you can construct a list containing most of the necessary information:

- a flag to indicate whetherthe task is currently busy or expects a return and therefore may not be entered any other way,
- a flag that indicates whether the task must return to some other task once it is completed,
- the contents of all registers at the time the task was last suspended,
- a means of finding its local descriptor table,
- the address of the instruction at which it will resume operation.

Actually, the last two items are redundant, because they are contained in registers LDTR, CS, and IP. Presumably, the task's code and data will be retained intact, because it lies in memory segments segregated and protected from other tasks.

When a call or interrupt instruction switches tasks, you must set the new task's flag to indicate that it must return somewhere, and you must give it a pointer back to the old task. Note that these two items pertain to the *incoming* task, whereas all the others pertain to the *outgoing* one.

To permit fast task switches, the 80286 uses a special data structure to hold all the task information listed above and a few additional items concerned with protection. This is called a *task state segment* (TSS); its format is described in Figure 9.3.2. It must be at least 22 words = 44 bytes long, and the first 22 must adhere to the format shown. You may lengthen it to store more information should that facilitate task switching in your system.

One word of a task state segment stores the Flags register. Not all bits of that register are actually used for flags, so the 80286 devotes the previously unassigned bit 14 to the flag that indicates whether it is required to return somewhere when the task is completed. Bit 14 in the Flags register is called NT, the *Nested Task Bit*. The first word in a task state segment, the *return selector,* is used only when the NT bit is set; it points to the state segment for

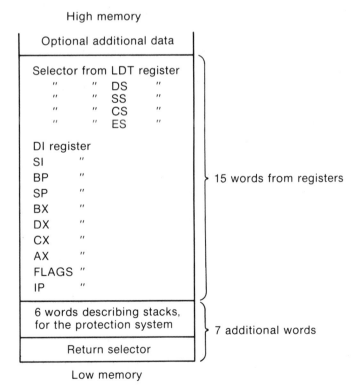

Figure 9.3.2 Task status segment

the task to which it must return when it is completed. Note that a task switching call or interrupt instruction requires that the NT bit and return selector of the *incoming* state segment be updated, whereas all other updates pertain to the *outgoing* state segment.

The state segments of all tasks are global control segments, hence they have descriptors in the Global Descriptor Table, called TSS descriptors. These have the same format as other segment descriptors shown earlier in Figures 9.2.2 and 9.2.3. The Access Rights Byte of a TSS descriptor is shown in Figure 9.3.3.

There is no provision in a task state segment for the flag that indicates whether the task is currently busy or expects a return and hence cannot be entered any other way. The flag is placed instead in the TSS descriptor for this segment, so that a multitasking scheduler can quickly determine which tasks are busy. This *Busy Bit* is Bit 1 in the TSS descriptor Access Rights byte, called Bit B in Figure 9.2.3. It is also set whenever this task is being executed.

How can the CPU find the TSS of the current task? Another new register is involved: the *Task Register* TR. This register has the same structure as the extended segment registers and the LDTR: a visible selector pointing to the current TSS descriptor in the GDT, and a hidden cache of the limit and base address fields of that descriptor. Figure 9.3.4 shows the relations between the descriptor tables, descriptor table registers, task state segments, and Task Register for the scenario of Figure 9.3.1.

The task switching process may be outlined as follows: a call, interrupt, interrupt return, or jump instruction provides (perhaps indirectly) a selector pointing to the incoming TSS. Then the CPU executes the instruction by

(1) storing the appropriate registers in the outgoing TSS;
(2) adjusting the Busy bit, the NT bit, and the return selector of the outgoing and incoming tasks;
(3) loading the incoming TSS selector into the Task Register;
(4) loading the appropriate registers from the incoming TSS.

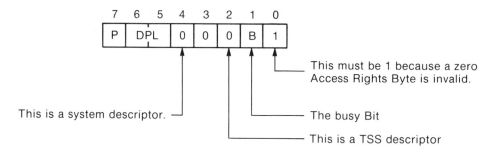

*P = 1 means the segment is present.

*DPL is the Descriptor Privilege Level (a memory protection device: see the next section).

*B = 1 means that the task is busy or expects a return, hence cannot be entered any other way.

Figure 9.3.3 TSS descriptor Access Rights Byte

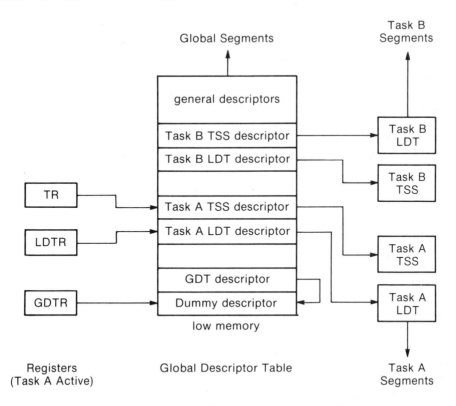

Figure 9.3.4 Descriptor tables, task state segments, and associated registers

Since (4) loads the Code Segment and Instruction Pointer registers CS:IP from the incoming TSS, the next instruction executed is the one with which the incoming task is supposed to resume. The interrupt return instruction causes this sequence of steps only when the NT flag of the outgoing TSS is set. (Otherwise, the CPU interprets it as a return from an interrupt that did not involve a task switch.) Figure 9.3.5 summarizes step (2) in a very succinct and effective manner; it is adapted from the *iAPX 286 Programmer's Reference Manual* [5, Table 8-2].

How can you create or change a task state segment? The problem is exactly the same as that with a local descriptor. A TSS can be created with ordinary move instructions as long as its descriptor is identified as a data segment descriptor. Once its Access Rights Byte identifies it as a system control descriptor, you'll need an alias data segment descriptor to access it.

How can you inspect or modify the Task Register TR? It is modified by any task switching instruction. To manipulate it directly, the 80286 provides two instructions, **str** and **ltr**. The *store TR* instruction **str** moves the selector in the Task Register to the destination operand. The complementary *load TR* instruction **ltr** loads the TR from the source operand and sets the Busy Bit in the corresponding task state segment. You may use any addressing mode with

Adjusted field	call or interrupt	interrupt return	jump
Incoming Busy Bit	Change 0 to 1.	Leave it = 1.	Change 0 to 1.
Outgoing Busy Bit	Leave it = 1.	Change 1 to 0.	Change 1 to 0.
Incoming NT Bit	Set it = 1.	Leave it as is.	Set it = 0.
Outgoing NT Bit	Leave it as is.	Change 1 to 0.	Leave it as is.
Incoming return selector	Set it from TR.	Leave it as is.	Irrelevant
Outgoing return selector	Leave it as is.	Irrelevant	Leave it as is.

Figure 9.3.5 Adjustment of TSS and TSS descriptor fields during task switching

the operands. These instructions may be executed only in protected mode, and **ltr** only by the most privileged programs.

It was noted above that task switches can be effected by call, interrupt, interrupt return, or jump instructions; then you saw how task state segments are used to keep track of the necessary information. Just how do the task switches look in assembly language? A return is just an **iret** instruction, executed when the NT bit in the current TSS is set. A call or jump is almost as simple: its target operand, for which you can use any appropriate mode, is a selector:offset address whose selector points to the target task state segment descriptor. The offset part of the operand address is ignored. Remember that by using a call instruction, you are anticipating a return. Intertask calls unfortunately cannot pass parameters, although tasks can share data by (carefully) using alias descriptors. Interrupts don't fit into this scheme, since they don't have target operands, but specify interrupt numbers. Another method, described below, is used for interrupts.

Using task state segments as targets for call and jump instructions has a disadvantage. They are global segments, hence accessible to all tasks. The protection system tends to make them accessible either to all programs, including many untrusted ones, or to only a few highly privileged programs. A more flexible task switching mechanism, the task gate, is introduced below. It works with interrupts as well.

Gates

A *gate* is a mechanism for transferring control between programs so that each is independent of the location of the other. The outgoing program needs access to the gate, and the gate needs to know the location of the incoming program. Gates can be assigned relatively fixed locations, and then initialized with the addresses of their target programs only when the latter are loaded. A gate serves much the same purpose as an interrupt vector, but is more elaborate in order to serve the needs of the task management and protection systems.

Formally, gates are certain system descriptors and may be placed in any descriptor table. There are four kinds of gates: *call gates, task gates, interrupt gates, and trap gates*. Though they are eight bytes long like all other descriptors, they differ in format from segment descriptors. Their formats are shown in Figure 9.3.6.

The target operand of an intertask call or jump instruction can also be a task gate located in the Global or Local Descriptor Table. Its destination selector merely points to the target task state segment descriptor. By providing an extra level of indirection, task gates give added flexibility. You can control calls or jumps to a task by protecting its TSS (in the GDT) and placing copies of its task gate only in appropriate LDTs.

Gates provide a general method of transferring control between segments— not just for the intertask transfers mentioned above, but also for interrupts and for transfers between privilege levels. These are discussed below.

Interrupts

An interrupt service routine will almost certainly be in a different segment, at a different privilege level, or even in a different task from the program interrupted. Therefore, controlling interrupts in protected mode requires a

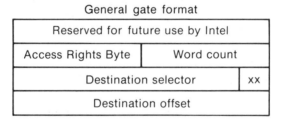

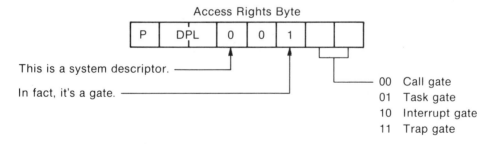

P = 1 means the gate is valid. Setting P = 0 is an easy way to temporarily disable a gate.

DPL (Descriptor Privilege Level) is used for protection.

The low order two bits of the selector are not used.

The reserved area must be zero for Intel 80386 compatibility.

The Word Count field is used only by call gates. Its value, which must lie in 0..31, indicates the number of words of parameters to place on the called program's stack.

The destination offset field is not used by a task gate.

Figure 9.3.6 Descriptor formats

more elaborate mechanism than the real mode Interrupt Vector Table. In protected mode, that table is replaced by an *Interrupt Descriptor Table* (IDT) whose entries are task gates, interrupt gates, or trap gates. IDTs are global segments. There may be only one IDT in effect at any time. Since there are 256 possible interrupts, the IDT contains at most 256 gates. The 80286 reserves for its own use interrupts 0..31, so gates for these *must* be present. When an interrupt occurs, control is transferred to a service routine via whatever gate appears at the appropriate place in the IDT. An **iret** instruction is anticipated to return control to the interrupted program.

When an interrupt service routine is entered via a task gate in the IDT, a task switch occurs as described above. Note that the routine is a *task*, not a procedure. That is, it is always *resumed* with the instruction whose address is given by the CS:IP values saved in the incoming TSS; it is not restarted from the beginning. Interrupt service routines accessed via task gates are protected from interference by programs in other tasks.

Interrupt service routines using interrupt or trap gates reside in global segments. They are *procedures*, always started from the beginning. The two types differ only in one detail: when an interrupt service routine is entered via an interrupt gate, the Interrupt Flag IF is cleared, disabling further interrupts. With trap gate access, IF is unchanged. This latter type of interrupt is used for less critical services that can themselves be interrupted.

interrupt	function
0	Attempted division by zero, or quotient too large
1	Single step
2	NMI
3	Breakpoint
4	Instruction **into** detected overflow
5	Instruction **bound** operand out of range
6	Attempted to execute invalid instruction code
7	80287 or other coprocessor not available
8	Double fault
9	80287 or other coprocessor attempted to access data beyond end of segment
10	Invalid task state segment
11	Segment not present
12	Stack overflow
13	General protection fault

Interrupts 0..7, 9 have similar functions in real mode.

Interrupts 10..13 place on the interrupt service routine's stack a code identifying the error more precisely.

Interrupt 11 is used to notify a memory management system that it needs to bring into main memory a virtual segment that is not currently present.

Figure 9.3.7 Special protected mode interrupts

How does the CPU find the current IDT ? It uses another register, the *Interrupt Descriptor Table Register* IDTR, that is structured and manipulated exactly like the Global Descriptor Table Register GDTR. It contains the physical address of the IDT and its length. To execute an interrupt, the 80286 first uses this table to find the IDT, then uses the interrupt number as an index to find the appropriate gate in the table. Two instructions are provided to inspect and set this register:

sidt *store IDT*
lidt *load   IDT*

They work exactly like **sgdt** and **lgdt**.

The IDT itself can be built and modified by ordinary move instructions, since it is just a global data segment.

While the 80286 reserves interrupts 0..31 for its own use, it actually uses only interrupts 0..13. Figure 9.3.7 summarizes their functions.

9.4 Protection

Concepts

* Entering protected mode * Can you return? * Preventing unauthorized task interaction by controlling access to critical segments and registers * Data protection, program privilege, and risk * Protecting input/output and interrupt control instructions * Controlling access to data and stack segments * Monitoring the risk involved in intersegment jumps

This section outlines the main aspects of the 80286 protection system, complementing the discussion of the task management system in the previous section. It is only an introductory sketch, emphasizing the underlying logic. Lack of time and space make it impossible to give here details and examples sufficient to guide you in any substantial systems programming task involving protected mode. For further information, you should consult the *iAPX 286 Programmer's Reference Manual* and *iAPX 286 Operating Systems Writer's Guide*, references [5] and [6]. The *PC/AT Technical Reference* manual unfortunately gives almost no detail on these topics.

Entering protected mode

The 80286 protected mode addressing scheme was described in Section 9.2 and basic to the discussion in 9.3. However, we have never considered how you *enter* protected mode. Of course, when you turn on the machine, it starts in real mode. You switch mode by using a CPU register that hasn't been mentioned yet: the *Machine Status Word* (MSW). Although this is a sixteen bit register, only the low order four bits are used. Three of these help control the 80287 Numeric Coprocessor, or some other coprocessor should it be present. Setting Bit Zero equal to 1, however, puts the CPU in protected mode.

Two 80286 instructions are provided for manipulating this register: **lmsw** and **smsw**. The *store MSW* instruction **smsw** has a destination operand that can be addressed in any appropriate mode and can be executed at any time to store the MSW somewhere for safekeeping or inspection. You can then set Bit Zero and execute the complementary load *MSW* instruction **lmsw** to put the word back in the register. At that point you will be in protected mode. The **lmsw** instruction must always be followed by a jump (perhaps only a jump to the next instruction) in order to flush the 80286 instruction fetching queue, because some upcoming instructions may have been partially interpreted already in real mode.

You can find examples of the use of the **lmsw** instruction in the PC/AT BIOS, near the examples mentioned in Section 9.3 of the instructions for loading and storing the descriptor table registers. However, to understand their details, you may have to disassemble the hex machine code in the leftmost columns.

Switching from real to protected mode involves more steps. In protected mode, many instructions use segment registers in addressing, so you have to set up the Global Descriptor Table (GDT) and the GDT Register before you switch modes. Moreover, as you saw earlier, interrupts are handled differently in protected mode, so you will have to initialize the interrupt system, too. These steps are considered in next chapter's discussion of the BIOS Interrupt hex 15 service routine.

Once in protected mode, **lmsw** is regarded as a very risky instruction, and can be executed only at the most privileged level. In fact, it is *so* risky that it may *not* be used to switch *back* to real mode! How do you get back? There is *no way* to switch back without resetting the CPU. This happens, for instance, when you type **Ctrl-Alt-Del** to reboot. However, rebooting includes a memory purge and test as well. This can be viewed as reasonable, since a program that could switch from protected to real mode could gain access to all information in the system. But there is a mystery here: the PC/AT BIOS is able to switch to and from protected mode in order to test its features during the POST and in order to move data to and from the extended memory (Interrupt hex 15 function hex 87). How does it do that? The solution is discussed in the next chapter. Hint: it resets the CPU!

Protection system

As mentioned in the previous section, the two main goals of the 80286 protection system are to prevent programs from running astray and perhaps destroying valuable data and to prevent unauthorized interaction between tasks. The 80286 has many mechanisms for detecting errors that lead programs astray; these go a long way toward achieving the first goal. For example, it can detect

- invalid operation codes (binary codes that correspond to no instruction);
- invalid operand formats (e.g., an attempt to jump via a data segment descriptor instead of a TSS descriptor, or an attempt to load the DS register with a code segment or TSS descriptor);
- invalid operands (e.g., division by zero);
- references to entries beyond the bounds of the appropriate segments (by using the limit fields in descriptors).

The CPU reacts to errors of this sort by executing hardware interrupts called *exceptions*. Many of the reserved interrupts in Figure 9.3.7 are of this type. In some cases, while executing such an interrupt, the CPU places on the service routine's stack an error code describing the circumstances that led to the exception. There are too many different exception conditions to give details here. You should refer to the *iAPX 80286 Programmer's Reference Manual*; the description of each instruction there includes a list of possible exceptions. An operating system that provides service routines to handle and clearly identify all exception conditions provides a great service to programmers.

You have already seen how the 80286 memory management system can segregate different tasks' memory allocations from each other. The only way a task can access data in memory is through a data segment register. A selector in one of these registers always specifies a descriptor table register, hence refers to a data segment described in the global or local descriptor table. Global segments are accessible to all tasks; local segments are intended to be private to the current task. An operating system maintains the currency and integrity of these tables as it moves segments in and out of main memory. Privacy of a task's local data segments can thus be assured by preventing unauthorized access to its Local Descriptor Table and the Local Descriptor Table Register.

Similarly, the use of gates or TSS descriptors as targets for all intersegment transfer of control instructions reduces the problem of preventing unauthorized execution of a task's local code segments to that of controlling access to its gates and TSS descriptor.

Thus, the 80286 can prevent unauthorized interaction between tasks by protecting a few critical segments and descriptors from unauthorized access. The overall design of the protection system is based on general principles for determining when access is authorized.

A task can be viewed as a succession of activities—of program actions on data. The protection system must monitor the risk involved in these activities and inhibit or forbid activities whenever they become too risky. Note that risk is dynamic: a particular activity may be risky at one time but not at another.

For example, consider a program that alters index records in a data base; its action may not be risky at all if it has been ordered by a data base management task, but is probably unacceptably risky if ordered by some ordinary data base user task.

The fact that risk is dynamic—that it varies with time—complicates protection system design because the algorithms that monitor risk must provide for this variability. The design can be simplified by removing some of the time dependence.

You have already seen some of the mechanisms by which the 80286 simply forbids certain activities that are *always* too risky. For example, you cannot load into the Code Segment register a selector for a non-executable segment. This prevents you from trying to execute ordinary data as though they were instruction codes. Similarly, you are inhibited from moving *to* a read-only data segment and *from* an execute-only code segment.

Apparently, the risk involved in an activity is somehow dependent on the value of the data affected. We give highly valued data heavy protection. Similarly, it must be dependent on the reliability of the program involved. We regard some programs —especially system routines—as more trusted than others, and we award great privilege to highly trusted ones. An activity's risk can be regarded as a relation between the protection afforded the data and the privilege granted the program. The greatest risk results when an untrusted, nonprivileged program gains access to heavily protected, highly valued data.

The 80286 protection system enables you to assign to data and programs appropriate *levels* of protection and privilege. There are four possible levels. This number is not important: you could implement an effective but rather inflexible protection scheme with only two levels. Protection and privilege levels are closely related: data afforded a certain protection level are shielded from access by programs that enjoy less privilege. In the 80286 literature, the concepts of protection and privilege levels are confused; the letters PL designate both. Unfortunately, the numbers 0..3 assigned these levels fall in the order opposite their meaning. The most heavily protected data and highly privileged programs have PL = 0. As PL increases, protection and privilege decrease; PL = 3 identifies the least protected data and least privileged programs.

Remember that protection and privilege level together are dynamic: their difference is the level of risk, which may vary with time. However, the 80286 design simplifies risk monitoring by assuming that a data segment can be given an almost static protection level. This is assigned when the segment is created and changed only by deliberate programming steps. The protection level is encoded in the two-bit Descriptor Protection Level (DPL) field of a data segment descriptor. In particular, by setting DPL = 0 in a segment descriptor, you can shield it from access by all but the most trusted programs. How can you keep an unauthorized program from changing a DPL ? All the descriptors are in the descriptor tables, which are themselves global segments with descriptors in the GDT, so you merely set DPL = 0 in the descriptors that refer to the tables themselves.

How does the CPU insure that a program has access only to data segments to which its privilege level entitles it? A program can access a data segment only through a data segment register. The CPU will not load a data segment register with a selector that points to a descriptor whose DPL indicates that the privilege currently enjoyed by the program is insufficient. If this condition is violated, the CPU will execute a General Protection Exception Interrupt hex D, placing on that service routine's stack a code identifying the violation. The CPU algorithm for determining the privilege level currently in effect is discussed next.

The simplest protection system design would merely assign to each code segment a privilege level encoded in the Descriptor Privilege Level (DPL) field of its segment descriptor. The DPL would indicate which data segments the program in this segment could access. These two bits would then appear in the Current Privilege Level (CPL) field of the Code Segment register whenever this program is executing, and the CPU could monitor the risk of the program's activity by comparing that field with the DPL of the affected data segment.

This simple scheme, however, is not dynamic. The risk of an activity would be dependent only on the protection and privilege levels assigned when the relevant data and code segments were created. In particular, this scheme could not deal with the data base protection problem sketched earlier in the box. In that situation the index maintenance program in question is highly trusted but is acting only at the behest of another program, which might be part of a privileged data base management task or of an untrusted user task. An untrusted task can't access the heavily protected index segment itself, but could call the privileged maintenance program to do so, passing the index segment selector as a parameter on the maintenance program's stack. The 80286 does not automatically prevent this situation, but does provide a mechanism for a privileged program to prevent its being misused in this way.

First, recall that selectors have two-bit Requested Privilege Level (RPL) fields. The 80286 *adjust RPL* instruction **arpl** allows a privileged program to adjust this field, as follows. The destination operand is assumed to be a selector, stored in memory or in a register; the source operand is a selector in a register. The instruction performs this adjustment:

destination RPL ⟵ max (destination RPL, source RPL),

setting the Zero Flag ZF = 1 if it changes the destination RPL. This will *lower* the privilege level of the destination selector, if necessary, to match that of the source. A privileged program can use this to decrease the privilege level requested by a selector passed it by some perhaps untrusted calling program. In such a situation, the caller's code segment selector is available as a return address for the privileged program's stack and is used as the source operand for **arpl**.

When a program, preparing to access a data segment, loads a data segment register, the 80286 uses three parameters to assess the risk involved:

- the DPL in the segment descriptor in a descriptor table—this reflects the protection level afforded the data;
- the CPL in the code segment register—this reflects the privilege level of the programm currently running;
- the RPL in the data segment register—this reflects the privilege level of the program that requested the service, *provided* the current program used the **arpl** instruction appropriately.

Given this data, the risk monitoring algorithm is straightforward. At this instant, the CPU assigns to the program the least privilege that the CPL and RPL warrant. That is, the CPU will load the selector into a data segment register only when CPL $\leq$ DPL and RPL $\leq$ DPL.

If this condition fails, the CPU will execute a General Protection Exception Interrupt.

A much more restrictive risk monitoring algorithm is provided for accessing stack segments: The CPU will load a selector into the stack segment register only when CPL = DPL.

This means that each privilege level must have its own stack. You saw this restriction earlier while considering 80286 task management mechanisms. It applies even when there's only one task.

By using the CPL, the 80286 can control execution of certain instructions that are *always* risky. You have already seen a number of instructions—for example, **lgdt** and **lldt** —that can be executed only by the most privileged programs. If the CPU encounters such an instruction when CPL $\rangle$ 0, then it executes a General Protection Exception interrupt.

In some contexts, you may want to restrict use of input/output instructions—barring their execution by programs of insufficient privilege. Because input/output control commonly involves enabling and disabling interrupts, these two activities are handled together. This is the function of the *Input/Output Protection Level Flag* IOPL (two bits in the Flags register). The CPU will execute the following instructions only when CPL $\leq$ IOPL:

```
cli    in     ins    insb    insw
sti    out    outs   outsb   outsw
```

The **popf** instruction will alter the Interrupt Flag IF only when CPL $\leq$ IOPL. This instruction will alter the IOPL Flag itself only when CPL = 0. (This is how you set IOPL.)

The condition displayed above for monitoring risk when a program accesses a data segment is only half of the risk monitoring algorithm, because it only accounts for the risk involved when a program accesses a data segment. Programs can also access code segments through jump, call, interrupt, and return instructions, so the algorithm must be expanded to monitor the risk involved in transfer of control instructions. This is more complicated for several reasons:

- call and interrupt instructions use stacks to transfer parameters and return addresses;
- there are several different transfer instructions, and the target of a transfer can be a selector:offset address, a TSS selector, or one of the four types of gate;
- transfer of control may entail switching tasks.

Fortunately, the mechanisms for intertask transfers are nearly independent of the protection system; they have already been outlined. Below, you will find a discussion of the principles underlying the protection system's treatment of transfer of control instructions, and a single example explained in detail. You will see that the steps involved in monitoring the risk can be deduced from the principles. For the details in the other cases, consult the *iAPX 286 Programmer's Reference Manual*.

When a program uses a call instruction to invoke another, it places parameters and the return address on a stack. If the two programs have different privilege levels but use the same stack, this could give the less privileged program access to data to which it is not entitled. Therefore, it is necessary to use different stacks. In fact, each task maintains four stacks, one for each privilege level. The Task State Segment (TSS), shown in Figure 9.3.2, includes six words describing these stacks, the selector:offset addresses of the bottoms of the stacks for privilege levels 0..2. When the TSS is created, the selector:offset address of the bottom of the level 3 stack is placed in the TSS entries for the current SS:SP.

A moment's reflection will convince you that this is enough information to keep track of all four stacks. For example, if a level 3 program calls a level 2 program, then the current level 3 SS:SP is pushed onto the level 2 stack (whose address is found in the TSS). When the level 2 program returns to level 3, it pops the level 3 SS:SP and empties its stack.

The principles for monitoring transfer of control instructions can be summarized as follows:

- Jump instructions may transfer control only to equally privileged programs.
- Call and interrupt instructions may not transfer control to less trusted programs.
- Calls and interrupts may transfer control to more trusted programs only via gates.
- Gates are protected like data segments. That is, to transfer control via a gate, a program must have enough privilege to access the gate. Then it may transfer control according to the rules already stated.

The above transfer of control principles can be illustrated by the steps necessary to execute a call instruction that invokes via a call gate a more privileged program in the same task. Other transfer instructions within the same task are simpler. For intertask transfers, the task switching steps described previously must be added. The list of steps is taken directly from the *iAPX 286 Programmer's Reference Manual* [5, App. B: description of the **call** instruction] and displayed in Figure 9.4.1. You will note that each of the 32 steps can be explained in terms of the principles already described. Given this example, you should be able to follow similar descriptions of the other transfer of control instructions easily. It is remarkable that this extremely complex instruction requires only ninety clock cycles plus four for each parameter transferred.

Step	Manual Description	Interpretation
	CALL FAR:	
1	If indirect then check access of EA doubleword #GP (0) if limit violation	General Protection (GP) Exception Interrupt if indirect addressing is used and the two words that are supposed to contain the
	[Note: # means ''Exception Interrupt'' and the expression in parentheses signifies the error message on the stack.]	effective address (EA) --i.e. the selector: offset address of the gate--lie outside the limits of the current segment.
2	New CS selector must not be null else #GP (0)	GP exception if the gate selector points at the dummy first descriptor in the GDT.
3	Check that new CS selector index is within its descriptor table limits; else #GP (new CS selector)	GP exception if the gate selector points beyond the limit of the descriptor table.
4	Examine AR byte of selected descriptor for various legal values:	AR byte = Access Rights Byte.
	CALL TO CALL GATE:	The descriptor is recognized as a call gate.
5	Call gate DPL must be ≥ CPL else #GP (call gate selector)	The current program must have sufficient privilege to access the call gate.
6	Call gate DPL must be ≥ RPL else #GP (call gate selector)	The selector's RPL must not indicate that it came from an insufficiently privileged program.

7	Call gate must be PRESENT else #NP	If the call gate indicates that the target code segment is not present in main memory, then execute a Not Present Exception Interrupt so that the operating system can load it from external storage.
8	Examine code segment selector in call gate descriptor:	This selector is supposed to point to the target code segment descriptor.
9	Selector must not be null else #GP (0)	The selector must not point to the dummy first descriptor in the GDT.
10	Selector must be within its descriptor table limits else #GP (code segment selector)	The selector must not point beyond the limit of the descriptor table.
11	AR byte of selected descriptor must indicate code segment else #GP (code segment descriptor)	The selector must point to a code segment descriptor
12	DPL of selected descriptor must be ≤ CPL else #GP (code segment selector)	You may not call a less privileged program.
13	If non-conforming code segment and DPL ‹ CPL then	If this is a call to a more privileged ordinary (nonconforming) program then

CALL GATE TO MORE PRIVILEGE:

14	Get new SS selector for new privilege level from TSS	The new level can't be level 3, so the TSS contains the SS:SP address of the bottom of the new stack. The stack is now empty.
15	Check selector and descriptor for new SS:	Don't trust this information to be valid.
16	Selector must not be null else #TS (0)	Execute an Invalid Task State Segment (TS) Exception Interrupt if the new stack selector points to the dummy first descriptor in the GDT.

17	Selector index must be within its descriptor table limits else #TS (SS selector)	The new stack selector must not point outside the limits of its descriptor table.
18	Selector's RPL must equal DPL of code segment else #TS (SS selector)	This is supposed to be a stack for the current privilege level.
19	Stack segment DPL must equal DPL of code segment else #TS (SS selector)	Ditto. This DPL is in the new stack segment descriptor.
20	Descriptor must indicate writable data segment else #TS (SS selector)	A stack is no good if you can't write on it.
21	Segment PRESENT else #SS (SS selector)	If the new stack segment is not present in main memory, execute a Stack Fault (SS) Exception Interrupt so that the operating system can bring it in from external memory or create it. (Note: it's now empty.)
22	New stack must have room for parameters plus 8 bytes else #SS (0)	8 bytes = 4 for SS:SP of old stack, plus 4 for return address.
23	IP must be in code segment limit else #GP (0)	The next instruction in the current program may not take you beyond the limit of the current code segment.
23.5	Save SS:SP for use in Step 28	The Intel manual forgot this.
24	Load new SS:SP value from TSS	That's the one that was checked out above.
24.5	Save CS:IP for use in Step 31	The Intel manual forgot this.
25	Load new CS:IP value from gate	Set CS:IP to the entry point of the new program, as given by the gate. This does not load the RPL field of CS.
26	Load CS descriptor	Load the CS cache from the new code segment descriptor.
27	Load SS descriptor	Load the SS cache from the new stack segment descriptor.

28	Push long pointer of old stack onto new stack	We saved the old SS:SP in Step 23.5. Put on the new stack, so that we can resume using the old stack when we return.
29	Get word count from call gate, mask to 5 bits	The word count tells how many words of parameters are to be copied from the old stack to the new. At most 32 words are permitted.
30	Copy parameters from old stack onto new stack	These are *copied*, not popped and pushed. The old stack remains unaltered.
31	Push return address onto new stack	The return address is the old CS:IP saved in Step 24.5. (IP always points at the next instruction.)
31	Set CPL to stack segment DPL	In Step 19, we insured that this DPL is the same as the new code segment's. This step is necessary because in Step 25, CS was loaded from the gate, which has no CPL field.
32	Set RPL of CS to CPL	? This seems redundant, since CPL is defined to be the RPL of the CS.

Figure 9.4.1 Steps involved in executing a *call* instruction to transfer control to a more privileged program within the same task

The protection system admits another type of code segment called *conforming*, identified by one bit in the Access Rights Byte of their descriptor (see Figure 9.2.2). When a routine in a conforming segment is invoked through a call or interrupt by a less privileged program, the CPL is not set to match the DPL of the called routine, as in the last steps of Figure 9.4.1, but rather to match the CPL of the calling program. Thus, the called routine inherits the privilege level of the calling program. Conforming segments are sometimes used for interrupt service routines that should not be trusted more than the programs they happen to be serving.

The 80286 provides four protected mode instructions that permit you to determine whether a reference to a selector will succeed without actually making the reference and perhaps causing an exception interrupt. This gives you a chance to fix up or detour around an invalid reference. The four instructions are

lar   *Load Access Rights Byte*
lsl   *Load segment limit*
verr   *Verify a segment for reading*
verw   *Verify a segment for writing*

For details, consult the *iAPX 286 Programmer's Reference Manual.*

10

PC/AT BIOS

Contents

The best way to introduce yourself to low level PC/AT programming methods is to become familiar with the BIOS. Most of the techniques you'll need appear there and are documented in extreme, if sometimes cryptic, detail. Moreover, even if you will not be programming in assembly language yourself, you will need to use the BIOS services. You may need to incorporate even in high-level language programs some of the input/output operations used by the BIOS to control various pieces of equipment (for example, to turn the display off and on). Finally, the BIOS code can help you interpret the sometimes inadequate or misleading documentation for this equipment: after all, the BIOS is an example of code that works. Thus, in the end you'll become familiar with it, so why not begin there?

This chapter takes you on a tour of the PC/AT BIOS. First, it follows the Power On Self Test through the entire booting process, watching how it tests and initializes the various system components. Particular attention is given the trickery involved in entering and leaving protected mode. Then the many BIOS interrupt services are surveyed. More detail is given here than earlier in Chapter 7, because you have more background. Particular emphasis is afforded the new PC/AT BIOS services, especially the timer and extended memory services. Pascal programs are provided to demonstrate the use of the CMOS alarm function and to move data to or from extended memory.

Because the PC/AT is a more complicated system than the older PCs, its BIOS is more complex and harder to read. Familiarity with an older BIOS will help you understand this one, but will not substitute. In particular, the PC/AT Power on Self Test (POST) includes test routines for nearly all features of the 80286 that do not occur on the older 8088 CPU. Exactly why IBM chose to test these features so thoroughly each time you boot while not testing certain others is not clear.

Contributing to the difficulty of reading the PC/AT BIOS is its poor index, the absence of an easy correlation between lines in the assembly language code and the corresponding locations in ROM, and the presence of three different place numbering systems in the POST.

The BIOS code is contained in twenty files named

Test 1	Test 6	Diskette	Video
Test 2	Test 7	Disk	BIOS
Test 3	SysInit	Keyboard	BIOS 1
Test 4	GDT_BLD	Printer	BIOS 2
Test 5	SIDT_BLD	RS232	ORGS

They are listed in this order in the *PC/AT Technical Reference* manual, reference [20, pp. 5-27..5-175]. There is little system to these names, and some of them are misleading. However, since they are used as page footers, the names will be used in this text to help you locate various BIOS routines. When you read this chapter, you will find it useful to have a copy of that manual handy for quick reference.

The only index is the two lists of public BIOS labels on the pages labeled "ROS Map": 5-23 to 5-25. The order of the labels in the second list coincides with their order in the following 150 pages of assembly language code. You should indicate the appropriate pages on the second list. If you need to find the definition of a particular symbol, see if you can find it in the list of external symbols near the beginning of the code in the listing file you are looking at. If not, its definition is somewhere in that file. If it is listed as external, find it in the alphabetical first list in the ROS Map file. Use the address given there to find it in the second list, then follow your indicated page number to the definition.

The addresses in the ROS Map are useful. If you add hex F000 to the segment address you will get the actual segment:offset address in ROM of the corresponding line of assembly code.

The POST testing and initialization routines are found in the first seven listing files; they are discussed in detail in Sections 10.1 and 10.2. The BIOS service routine codes are found in the last ten or so listing files; they are described in Sections 10.3 and 10.4. Several files contain code used by both the POST and the BIOS services.

10.1 Power on self test

Concepts

∗ What can you learn from the POST ?   ∗ The main POST functions
∗ Determining the PC model and BIOS version   ∗ Which PC/AT
features are tested during the POST ?   ∗ Messages and signals that
you observe during the POST   ∗ Testing custom ROM modules
∗ When do the necessary initializations take place?   ∗ How do warm
and cold boots differ?   ∗ Operating system bootstrap

Much of the PC/AT BIOS code is devoted to the Power On Self Test (POST)
that is executed whenever you boot the computer. Knowledge of the POST
code is certainly not *required* of every PC/AT programmer. However, familiarity with it can help you for several reasons:

- The POST is a complete program, whereas the rest of the BIOS is devoted
  to services for other programs.
- The POST sets up all hardware and software subsystems that are independent of the operating system, so you can learn how these are organized
  and initialized.
- Nearly all 80286 instructions are used somewhere in the POST.

This section follows the POST from the instant you turn the power on or
type **Ctrl-Alt-Del** through loading the operating system boot record. It explains the sequence of events and delays that you observe and describes the
various equipment tests and initializations that take place during that time.
Since some of these tests run in protected mode, you will see how the PC/AT
enters and leaves this mode.

The POST contains routines labeled TEST 1 through TEST 22, performed in
roughly that order. Their codes are found in listing files Test 1 through Test 3.
There is no real distinction between test and initialization routines; the latter
are generally interspersed unlabeled among the tests. The test and initialization routines use various procedures whose code is scattered throughout the
other files.

POST overview

Because of the length and complexity of the POST, you may find an overview helpful before considering its functions in detail. Here is a list of its main
tasks, not necessarily in the order performed.

Test the most essential operations. If these fail, you can't trust any other tests. For example, verify the check sum of the BIOS ROM.

Test the CMOS battery and verify the CMOS check sum. Check the mechanism required to enter and leave protected mode.

Thoroughly test and then clear the first 64K segment of main memory.

Initialize the two 8259A Interrupt Controller chips and the BIOS interrupt vectors. Test that chip and the 8253 Timer chip.

Determine the type of the primary display controller. Test its memory, verify the check sum of any ROM installed there, and test its functions. After this test, the display can be used to report errors.

Check that the memory size agrees with that recorded in the CMOS chip. Unless this is a warm boot, thoroughly test all installed memory. Clear all memory.

Test various instructions specific to the 80286. Test the 8042 Keyboard Controller chip. Test and initialize the diskette and disk drives. Test the CMOS clock; use it to set the BIOS clock. Take a census of the parallel and serial ports. Set up communication with the 80287 Numeric Coprocessor if it is installed.

Verify the check sums of any custom ROM chips and execute their custom test routines.

Report problems discovered during testing.

Execute the bootstrap loader to load the operating system.

As you read through the test routines, you will encounter instructions with comments identifying them as numbered checkpoints. They are executed in roughly numerical order. These simply monitor progress through the POST by outputting the corresponding number to a port that can be connected to special testing equipment. The checkpoints will probably not help you understand the POST, so they will not be mentioned again.

Starting the POST

When the 80286 receives a reset signal—for example, when you turn on the PC/AT power switch—it begins its execution cycle in real mode, with the Instruction Pointer (IP) and segment registers initialized as follows:

```
CS = hex F000      DS = 0
IP = hex FFF0      SS = 0
                   ES = 0
```

The first instruction executed is thus located at segment:offset address CS:IP = F000:FFF0. In the PC/AT, this location is near the end of the BIOS ROM. The code there is found in the BIOS listing file ORGS, page 5-175:

```
        db      0eah            ; hard code jump
        dw      offset reset    ; offset
        dw      0f00h           ; segment
        db      '01/10/84'      ; release marker
        org     01ffeh
        db      0fch            ; this pc's id
code    ends
        end
```

This code sets up the very last sixteen bytes of PC/AT main memory as follows:

segment:offset hex f000:	content (hex)
fff0	**ea**
fff1, fff2	**5b,e0** = offset e05b
fff3,fff4	**00,f0** = segment f000
fff5...fffc	ascii codes for '01/10/84'
fffd	**0**
fffe	**fc** (PC/AT signature)
ffff	**ad** (for checksum)

You can use the **debug** instruction **d f000:fff0** to verify this. The byte **ea** is the instruction code for a far jump instruction; the next four bytes give the target offset and segment f000:e05b. To determine this offset, note that **reset** is a label on page 5-166 in the ORGS file, and refers to the same location as label **start**. The label **start** is public, and its offset **e05b** in the BIOS segment is given in the second ROS Map table on page 5-24. The next eight bytes identify the BIOS release date. At address f000:fffe on all PCs is found a signature, identifying the model. The byte **fc** signifies that this is a PC/AT. Your programs can inspect these locations to determine the PC model and the BIOS version. The last byte **ad** is determined not by the assembler, but by the ROM code builder, so that the checksum of the last 64K segment of main memory is zero.

Thus the second instruction executed after the 80286 is reset is located at address f000:e05b, corresponding to the label **reset** in the ORGS listing file. The instruction at that location is a near jump to offset 00a6, corresponding to the assembly code **jmp start_1** at the label. **start_1** is a public label at BIOS offset 00a6, defined on page 5-33 in the listing file Test 1; it is the starting point of POST test routine TEST.01.

Just before the **reset** label, at offset e000, is the BIOS copyright notice. Just after **reset** are some constants misleadingly called a stack. (You can't use read only memory for a stack!) After these constants you will find text for some messages. One of these is familiar. Most of the others will appear only when something fails. To get an idea of what the POST does, turn off your PC/AT, unplug the keyboard, then turn it on; you'll see another of these messages.

You will notice that two other events occur immediately when you turn on the PC/AT power switch. The fixed disk drive motor is turned on, and its red light indicates activity. Second, a reset signal causes the 8042 Keyboard Controller chip to perform its own POST, which includes flashing the three keyboard indicator lights.

BIOS equations and data area

At the beginning of the first BIOS listing file, Test 1, you will find about two pages of equations, followed by about three pages of data area definitions.

The equations are assembler directives that let you use symbolic names for numerical constants. Most of the equations are of four types:

symbolic names for the input/output ports used by the BIOS to communicate with other equipment (for example, equation **status_port equ 64h** gives a symbolic name to the keyboard status port hex 64);

symbolic names for constants that can appear in input ports or memory locations to indicate certain conditions (for example, equation **bad_bat equ 080h** gives a name to the code that will be used somewhere to indicate a bad CMOS battery);

symbolic names for codes to be sent to output ports to control other equipment (for example, **kb_reset equ 0ffh** names the command that the BIOS sends the 8042 chip to cause a keyboard reset);

codes for certain keys (for example, **del_key equ 83** lets the BIOS refer by name to the **Del** key instead of using the extended ASCII code 83 that is used by the 8042).

The first BIOS data area consists of the 256 two word interrupt vectors stored in locations 0000:0000 to 0000:03ff. Some of these locations are given names on page 5-29 so that the BIOS can refer to them easily. Next, a temporary stack for the POST is set up in locations 0030:0000 to 0030:00ff. This overlaps the interrupt vector area, but that part is not in use during the POST.

The main BIOS data area, used throughout PC/AT real mode operation, is set up next in locations 0040:0000 to 0040:00ff. These variables are used to keep track of the status of various equipment. (For example, the directive **kb_buffer dw 16 dup(?)** reserves sixteen words in this area for the keyboard buffer, a circular queue that stores a two-byte code for each of the last fifteen keys struck. Because of the sequence of assembly code statements, this buffer occupies locations 0040:001e to 0040:003f.)

The BIOS sets up one of the video display areas, b800:0000 to b800:4000 (normally the memory on a Color/Graphics adaptor) with the name **regen**. It handles the other video display areas differently.

Finally, you will notice another IBM copyright notice at the beginning of listing file Test 1, that is stored at the beginning of the BIOS ROM at locations f000:0000 to f000:002b.

First battery of POST tests

Recall that the POST routines start at label **start_1** near the beginning of listing file Test 1. Before considering the test routines, however, note that just ahead of this label is some code that will read some special test code if special test equipment is attached. Several provisions for this occur throughout the POST with references to "mfg test"; they will not be mentioned further here.

The first several POST routines are rather straightforward, concerned with functions of the CPU and other chips that must be verified before any more involved tests can be trusted. Failure of any of these tests results merely halts the CPU, with no identification of the failure except the checkpoint number that can only be read by "mfg test" equipment. These routines test the following aspects of the PC/AT:

TEST.01	Flags register, conditional jump instructions
TEST.02	Shutdown byte in CMOS memory
TEST.03	BIOS checksum
TEST.04,05	8253 Timer chip
TEST.06-09	8237 Direct Memory Access (DMA) Controller
TEST.10	8042 Keyboard Controller

A few more involved aspects of these routines are described next.

In TEST.01 just after label **c7a** there are some conditional jump instructions that select different actions depending on "shutdown" status. If this code has not been entered through a "shutdown," control is transferred directly to label **c7**, bypassing code at labels **c7b** and **c7c**. Just after label **c7b** a conditional jump bypasses initialization of the two 8259A Intrerrupt Controllers, going directly to **c7c**, if it had been entered through a "shutdown request 9." In this section you are following the POST process after turning on the PC/AT power switch; this does *not* produce a "shutdown" situation, so these considerations may be ignored. Later, you will see that "shutdown" conditions are produced by re-entering real mode from protected mode. That technique is discussed in Section 10.2.

Just before label **sft_rst** in TEST.01, a conditional jump turns off both color and monochrome displays unless this code was entered via a soft (i.e., warm) boot. Again, you are following the POST process after a *cold* boot, so you can ignore warm boot considerations. Later, you will see how the two processes differ.

TEST.03 uses a procedure **ros_checksum** at the beginning of listing file Test 3 to verify the 64K BIOS ROM check sum. This procedure is used later to verify other check sums.

Unfortunately, the *PC/AT Technical reference manual* does not give enough information about the Timer and DMA Controller chips to explain TEST.04 through TEST.09, and that level of detail is beyond the scope of this book. You will have to consult other texts for this information, for example, reference [26].

Memory testing and census; setting up interrupts

The next POST testing and initialization routines can be more elaborate because the first battery of tests has verified some of the most basic operations of the basic aspects of the CPU and some of the auxiliary chips. These are devoted to counting and testing memory and setting up some of the interrupt services. Here is a summary of events.

TEST.11 Test the first 64K memory segment, using procedure **stgtst_cnt**, listed in file Test 6. Display any errors via *both* the Color/Graphics and Monochrome video controllers. The redundancy compensates for the fact that these haven't been tested yet. Enter an endless loop if an error was found (label **c31_n**).

Clear this memory segment to zeroes.

TEST.11A Test the descriptor table registers and instructions. The assembly language here is messy because it was written for an assembler that recognizes only 8086 instructions. The new 80286 instructions are simulated.

Initialize the two 8259A Interrupt Controller chips (label **c37a**).

Initialize interrupt vectors hex 0 through f to point to a dummy service routine at label **d11** in listing file Test 4, and initialize BIOS interrupt vectors hex 10 through 1f (except for the resident BASIC interrupt vector 18 and the graphics character set vector 1f). The values of these vectors are found at label **vector_table** near the end of the BIOS in listing file ORGS.

TEST.12 Test the CMOS battery, then the CMOS memory itself via a checksum.

TEST.13 Enter protected mode. (The technique for doing this is discussed in Section 10.2.) Determine the amount of base memory installed (up to 640K), and clear it to zeroes. Set the CMOS bytes that indicate the base memory size (see page 1-52 of the *Technical Reference* manual), and set the memory size word at address 0040:0013 in the BIOS data area.

TEST13A Perform essentially the same functions as TEST.13, but for extended memory above the 1 MB limit. Halt (at label **shut8** in file Test 1) if an addressing test fails.

You may wonder if these routines produce the memory count that appears on your screen during the POST. Patience! You haven't got that far yet!

Strangely, part of the listing file Test 6 is missing from the *PC/AT Technical Reference* manual. The omitted part contains some critical routines, including about half of the procedure **stgtst_cnt** mentioned earlier. This performs the same sort of test as the first half, filling memory with solid patterns of ones (hex ffff) instead of alternating ones and zeroes (hex 5555 and aaaa). You can look at the missing part of Test 6 by using the **debug** utility to disassemble the code in locations f000:1a8a through f000:1c2b.

After TEST13A, the POST executes a "shutdown" to get out of protected mode, arriving at label **shut1** on page 5-47 in file Test 1.

Display controller, Timer, and Interrupt Controller checkout

This section of the POST begins with some tests to determine the type of primary display you are using. The Setup program recorded in the CMOS memory your answer to a question about this, and you had to confirm it by setting a switch inside the system unit. The POST first checks if you indicated a Color/Graphics display or a Monochrome display. If neither, it checks for display controller ROM in the 32K following address c000:0000, by looking for the signature word hex aa55 at certain locations. This ROM would be on a display controller board different from the usual type.

Near label **norm1** the POST checks the keyboard for an indication that it should perform the "mfg" test, which requires special test equipment. We ignore this and go on to the next routines, which test the display memory and controller.

Routines TEST.14 through TEST.16 check out whatever display memory is installed, as well as certain other aspects of the display controllers. The memory is tested by the same routine, **stgtst_cnt**, used in TEST.11 to check the first 64K segment, and any ROM installed on a display controller is tested by the same check sum routine that was used in TEST.03 for the BIOS ROM. Errors are reported by a speaker beeping routine listed in file Test 4.

Routines TEST.17 and TEST.18, listed in file Test 2, check out the 8253 Timer and 8259A Interrupt Controller chips. Since the display has been tested, these and following routines report errors by screen messages, using procedures **e_msg** and **prt_hex** listed in files Test 4 and Test 3 and the standard BIOS Interrupt hex 10 service to print strings listed in file ORGS.

The memory count; protected mode and keyboard tests

Now it is about 3.5 seconds since the POST began, and time for TEST.19, the extensive memory checking that produces the familiar **KB OK** counting on your screen. The test is bypassed if this is a warm boot. Like TEST.13, this routine is executed in protected mode. First, the POST prints the message **64KB OK**, since it has already checked the first 64K thoroughly. Then it counts twice upward through the memory, checking first its presence, then its integrity. The **KB OK** messages are output to both color and monochrome displays simultaneously by procedure **prot_prt_hex**, listed in file Test 3. Error information is retained until the POST executes a "shutdown" to return to real mode. Checking 512K requires about 6.5 seconds.

If an error was detected, the POST returns to label **shut3**on page 5-59 of file Test 2, where it writes an error message. Otherwise, it returns to label **shut2** just below, then jumps immediately to routine TEST.20 at label **post7** in file Test 7.

Routine TEST.20 performs protected mode tests of the Flags register and instructions

```
lldt    ltr    pusha    verr    lsl    arpl
sldt    str    popa     verw    lar    bound
```

It's not clear why these instructions are singled out for testing. "Shutdown" to real mode leads the POST to label **shut6** or **shut7** just before TEST.21 on page 5-60 of file Test 2. Any errors are reported by the code at **shut6**.

TEST.21 checks out the 8042 Keyboard Controller, using procedures **kbd_reset** and **c8042** in files Test 4 and Test 7. The former performs the keyboard reset that blinks the three indicator lights.

Remaining initializations: diskette and fixed disk drive tests

The remaining initializations and tests are intermingled, so perhaps the best overview is provided by the following rough schedule of events, starting near label **f7a** in file Test 2.

Initialize the remaining interrupt vectors, referring to the table at label **vector table** in the file ORGS. The ROM BASIC interrupt hex 18 vector is set to f600:0000.

Reset the fixed disk drive if this is a warm boot. (Turning on the power does a reset during a cold boot.)

(Routine TEST.23) Test and recalibrate diskette drive **a:**. You see the drive light turn on.

Initialize some parameters for the keyboard, printer, serial port, and timer.

Test the CMOS clock operation.

Determine if the memory and display controller tests recorded any error conditions in CMOS memory, and write appropriate error messages if so.

Initialize the diskette and disk drive controller, using routines **dskette_setup** and **disk_setup** in BIOS listing files Diskette and Disk.

(Routine TEST.22) Check for the presence of ROM modules in the memory region c800:0000 to e000:0000. When a module is recognized by its hex 55aa signature, test its check sum by using the same procedure used in routine TEST.03 to test the BIOS ROM, then call a custom test procedure located at a standard location in the ROM module.

Display a message if the keyboard has been locked.

Determine what parallel and serial ports are present, and record that in the BIOS data area. Apparently, this is the step that causes your printer to chatter if it's turned on. Enable keyboard interrupts (i.e., turn on the keyboard).

If procedure **e_msg** has reported no error, then beep once and skip the rest of this step. Otherwise, beep twice. If the keyboard was locked, instruct the user to unlock it. Tell the user to touch **F1** to resume, then use the BIOS hex 16 service to poll the keyboard until that happens.

Clear the screen, and clear the memory used earlier for descriptor tables in protected mode.

Use procedure **set_tod** at the end of the listing file BIOS to set the BIOS clock from the CMOS clock.

Set up communication with the 80287 Numeric Coprocessor if it is installed.

Clear the soft (i.e.,warm) boot flag if it was set. The warm boot process is described later.

Test for the custom ROM signature at address e000:000; if it's present, test the check sum, and call a custom test or initialization routine at a standard ROM location.

This long series of tests and initializations finally arrives at the end of listing file Test 2. There, the last POST instruction **int 19h** invokes the *bootstrap loader:* the instructions that start loading the operating system or else jump to the resident BASIC system. The bootstrap is described below.

Warm boots

At several places in the POST, the succession of events depends on whether a warm or cold boot is taking place. How can the system distinguish them? At label **k29** on page 5-118 in file Keyboard, the BIOS keyboard interrupt hex 16 service routine recognizes the **Ctrl-Alt-Del** keystroke combination, and stores hex 1234 in the reset flag at address 0040:0072. Normally, this flag contains zero. Thus the POST can recognize the flag and act accordingly. The main difference between warm and cold boots is that the warm boot bypasses the memory tests, saving about 13 seconds per megabyte of memory. You may recall that routine TEST.11 cleared the first 64K memory segment, destroying this flag. The POST cleverly saves the reset flag in register BX during the memory clearing operation and restores it just after!

The bootstrap loader

The bootstrap loader is the Interrupt hex 19 service routine. It reads the *boot record* of an operating system then jumps to the code in that record. The boot record code loads the rest of the operating system.

The POST set the interrupt vectors from the **vector_table** at the end of the BIOS in file ORGS. By inspecting this table, you will find that the bootstrap vector points to label **boot_strap** on page 5-169 of the same file. There you will find a jump to label **boot_strap_1**. Detective work in the ROS map indicates that this last label is near the end of file Test 6. Unfortunately, the end of that file was omitted from the published BIOS listing. You can look at the missing part of Test 6 by using the **debug** utility to disassemble the code in locations f000:1a8a through f000:1c2b.

Here is the sequence of events in the bootstrap loading process:

Clear a 512 byte memory buffer at 0000:7c00.. 7dff.

Try four times at most to reset the diskette drive. If successful, use the BIOS interrupt hex 13 service to read sector 1 from head 0 on drive **a:** into the buffer cleared above. Look at the first word read. If it is zero, or if it is the same as the next ten words, display an error message and halt. Otherwise, jump to the first instruction in the buffer.

If the diskette drive was not available (nonexistent, door open, or no diskette inserted), then try at most three times to read sector 1 from head 0 on drive **c:** into buffer. If successful, look at the last word read. If it is hex aa55, then jump to the first instruction in the buffer. Otherwise, try drive **c:** again.

If it was not possible to boot from drive **c:** either, then issue interrupt hex 18 to enter the ROM BASIC system. When you leave ROM BASIC you will try again to boot from drive **c:**.

10.2 Assembly language access to protected mode

Concepts

∗ What facilities do the BIOS and DOS provide for using protected mode?   ∗ How does the POST enter protected mode?   ∗ How does it leave?

Some of the main distinguishing features of the 80286 CPU are its virtual memory management, task management, and protection systems. These are only accessible through protected mode operation. However, this mode is not supported yet by DOS, or in fact by any popular software. It is accessible via the BIOS Interrupt hex 15 Function hex 89 routine. However, once you have entered protected mode, you're completely on your own unless you have some special software. Not even the BIOS services are available in protected mode.

In Section 10.3, you will see how you can use BIOS Interrupt hex 15. In the present section, you will see how the BIOS manages the transition. Entering protected mode via an assembly language program is fairly straightforward. However, returning to real mode is mysterious; tricks are required. In the last section, you saw that the POST enters and leaves protected mode several times. The stratagem it uses is described next.

Let's follow the POST when it first enters protected mode, just before routine TEST.13, as listed in BIOS file Test 1. First, there is some code to set a return address; ignore that for a while. Next, procedure **sysinit1** is invoked. This routine, listed in file Sys Init, first performs several initializations required no matter what you want to do in protected mode. The first initialization has to do with the Interrupt Descriptor Table (IDT). Conceivably, you could assume that no interrupts will occur while you're in protected mode; thus, ignore that initialization for a while.

Clearly, **sysinit1** must set up a Global Descriptor Table (GDT) and initialize register GDTR to point to it. Procedure **gdt_bld**, listed in file GDT_BLD, is called to build the table, then **sysinit1** executes instruction **lgdt** to set GDTR. File GDT_BLD is somewhat mysterious because it refers to many symbols that must have been defined by **equ** statements omitted from the BIOS listing. However, enough information is given in the machine code listing to decipher it.

The POST functions with no local segments, forgoing task management, hence **sysinit1** does not bother to set up a local descriptor table.

Since **sysinit1** is used in situations where interrupts may occur after entering protected mode, it calls procedure **sidt_bld**, listed in file SIDT_BLD, to build the IDT. The special POST protected mode service routines for Interrupts 0 through hex 38 are listed in file Test 5; **sidt_bld** refers to their addresses to build the IDT. These routines are not for general use; they serve only to test protected mode operation.

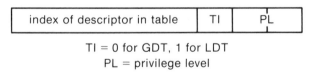

TI = 0 for GDT, 1 for LDT
PL = privilege level

Figure 10.2.1 Selector format

After setting up the descriptor tables, **sysinit1** executes instruction **lmsw** to set the low order bit of the Machine Status Word (MSW), which puts the 80286 in protected mode. After the **lmsw** instruction, one more instruction is ready for execution, but the CS:IP registers are corrupt because they held a segment:offset rather than a protected mode selector:offset instruction address. Thus, the next instruction after **lmsw** must load the CS:IP registers with the selector:offset address of the instruction to follow. This is a far jump instruction: all a far jump does is to alter these registers. Its machine code is set up as follows:

byte 0   code hex ea for far jump with direct
            addressing,
bytes 1, 2 offset of the following instruction in the BIOS
            code segment,
bytes 3, 4 selector for the descriptor of the BIOS code
            segment in the GDT.

The offset is obtained directly from the assembly language statements. To see
how the selector is determined, recall the selector format, shown in Figure
10.2.1. Apparently, on entry to protected mode, the current privilege level is
initialized automatically to 0, the greatest privilege. Since no jump instruction may change privilege level, the privilege level in the BIOS code segment
descriptor must be set at 0 as well, and the PL bits in the selector must also be
set at 0. Now you can determine the selector: in the GDT layout in listing file
GDT_BLD, the ninth code segment descriptor refers to the BIOS code segment, hence the selector index is 8; shift this left three bits, and you get hex
0040, the value of bytes 3 and 4 of the far jump instruction near the end of
sysint1.

From this point, the program will execute in protected mode. The next thing
the POST does is to load the Data Segment and Stack Segment Registers DS
and SS with appropriate selectors.

Once in protected mode, can you return to real mode? It might seem logical
that clearing the low order bit of the MSW should return the CPU to real
mode. However, this could defeat the protection system: once in real mode,
whatever program is running has uncontrolled access to the entire memory.
In fact, *there is no way to return to real mode without resetting the 80286!* In
effect, you must turn it off, then on again.

This inability to return seems to contradict the observation that the POST
enters and leaves protected mode at will. What magic is going on here? The
POST resorts to trickery based on the presence of the other components of the
PC/AT motherboard. Part of the problem is solved by storing the address at
which execution will resume in real mode *before* resetting, then retrieving it
afterward. Several PC/AT components have memory. One of them, moreover,
is unaffected by resetting the CPU: the CMOS chip. Before it enters protected
mode, the POST stores in the CMOS an index into a jump table in ROM,
which it will use during booting to find its place again.

Preparing for entrance to protected mode just before routine TEST.13 in
listing file Test 1, the POST stores the appropriate jump table index, byte 01,
at CMOS memory address hex 0f. This requires outputting hex 80 plus the
CMOS address to port hex 70, then outputting byte 01 to port hex 71. The
POST then sets up the descriptor tables and enters protected mode as described above. How it resets the CPU when TEST.13 is complete is detailed
below. But recall that after reset the CPU executes the boot process, restarting the POST.

Following the POST as described in Section 10.1, you saw that in routine
TEST.01 just after label **c7a** there are some conditional jumps to select different actions depending on "shutdown" status. "Shutdown" refers to the re-

set process. Just how the POST determines that a "shutdown" has taken place is detailed below. The POST retrieves the jump table index from the CMOS chip by outputting hex 80 plus the CMOS address to port hex 70, then inputting the index from port hex 71. Then it resets the CMOS byte to indicate index 0. The retrieved index is used with the table at label **branch** to jump back to one of eleven different return addresses at labels **shut0** through **shuta**. Index 0 causes the POST to proceed as in a warm or cold boot: no shutdown has occurred. Index 9 is also treated slightly differently, because it represents a return not from part of the POST but from the BIOS Interrupt hex 15 service routine; **shut9** is a label in that routine in file BIOS 1.

There are two remaining mysterious steps in the shutdown process. First, how does the BIOS tell the CPU to reset itself? No 80286 instruction does that! Second, how does the POST tell that a reset has taken place?

Follow the POST action in routine TEST.13 near label **sd2** on page 5-47 of the listing file Test 1. The test routine has completed its work in protected mode. The comment there reads, "Cause a shutdown". Follow the jump to label **proc_shutdown** at the end of file Test 3. The instructions there output hex fe to port hex 64 and halt. What is going on?

Outputting to port hex 64 sends a command to the 8042 Keyboard Controller chip. One bit of one of the other 8042 ports is connected to the reset line of the 80286. The command hex fe causes the 8042 to send a signal on this line, causing the CPU to reset. The halt instruction after label **proc_shutdown** gives the 8042 time to obey this command. You can try this sequence with **debug**: execute one at a time the instructions at label **proc_shutdown** (address f000:174c) or assemble and execute instructions

```
mov al,feh
out 64h
```

You'll shut yourself down!

How can the POST determine whether the 8042 has in fact caused a CPU reset? Another effect of command hex fe is to set bit 2 of port hex 64. Evidently, this is cleared after a cold boot; after a warm boot it could be set or not. In routine TEST.01 just after label **c7a**, the POST inputs from this port. If input bit 2 is set, then this is not a cold boot: the conditional jumps previously described discriminate between a warm boot and a shutdown. On the other hand, if input bit 2 is zero, then this is not a shutdown, and the jump table is bypassed.

The PC/AT BIOS method for leaving protected mode is involved, perhaps humorously so. But it is certainly *protected*. Access to the input/output instructions required is controlled by the IOPL setting: underprivileged programs cannot execute them. Moreover, only the indices to the jump table are stored in the CMOS, not the addresses themselves, so any alteration of the index produces a jump back to one of only eleven locations in the POST, not a jump into some other part of memory where some hidden assailant might lurk.

10.3 BIOS services

Concepts

* BIOS interrupts. Where are the service routines? * Dot matrices for Color/Graphics characters * Special interrupts not handled by the BIOS * Conflicts between 80286 and BIOS interrupts * BIOS keyboard processing; keyboard input services * BIOS video services; new write string function * Equipment check and base memory size * Disk and diskette services; "diskette change line" * Serial and parallel port services; new joystick support * Clock/calendar and timer services

---

This section gives an overview of the PC/AT BIOS services, with special attention to those that were not provided by earlier PC models. Discussion of the services concerning the PC/AT extended memory and protected mode operation, however, is placed later in Section 10.4. The earlier PC BIOS services have been considered already in Section 7.3. Figure 10.3.1 provides a detailed picture of all PC/AT BIOS services, and shows you how to find the service routines for the various interrupts in the BIOS listing section of the *PC/AT Technical Reference* manual.

Included at the bottom of Figure 10.3.1 are the addresses of three tables in the BIOS ROM. The BIOS handles these addresses just like interrupt vectors. If you need to change certain display or diskette parameters, you merely place the appropriate table somewhere in RAM and alter the vector to point to it. You are especially invited to construct a table of dot matrices for displaying chr(128).. chr(255) on a Color/Graphics adapter. No such table is supplied with the BIOS, nor with DOS; you must direct vector hex 1f to point to your table. The dot matrix table for the first 128 characters is included at label **crt_char_gen** in the BIOS listing file ORGS; from it you can determine the appropriate table format.

The column in Figure 10.3.1 labeled "Origin" indicates only the *expected* origin of the interrupts. All of them can of course be executed by any software. Some of the interrupts originate from hardware via various Interrupt Request (IRQ) lines to the 8259A Interrupt Controller chips. In some of these cases the hardware is unspecified, leaving the possibility for you to hook up optional equipment to the 8259As for interrupt control and to write appropriate service routines. Your software will then have to install the routines as extensions of the operating system and set the appropriate vectors to point to them.

Redirected interrupt vectors A number of BIOS interrupt service routines merely redirect service requests elsewhere. Moreover, some of the BIOS

Hardware interrupts

Number	Name	Origin		BIOS label/listing file	Ultimate server
0	Divide by 0	80286		D11/Test 4	DOS
1	Single step	80286		D11/Test 4	DOS (user)
2	NMI	Hardware		NMI_int_1/BIOS	BIOS (user)
3	Breakpoint	80286		D11/Test 4	DOS (user)
4	Overflow	80286		D11/Test 4	DOS (user)
6	Invalid Opcode	80286		D11/Test 4	(user)
7	80287 not present	80286		D11/Test 4	(user)
8	Timer ticks	8253	via IRQ0	Timer_int_1/BIOS 2	BIOS
9	Keyboard	8042	via IRQ1	Kb_int_1/Keyboard	BIOS
b	COM2	COM2	via IRQ3	D11/Test 4	(user)
c	COM1	COM1	via IRQ4	D11/Test 4	(user)
d	LPT2	LPT2	via IRQ5	D11/Test 4	(user
e	Diskette	Diskette	via IRQ6	Disk_int_1/Diskette	BIOS
f	LPT1	LPT1	via IRQ7	D11/Test 4	DOS (user)
70	Real Time Clock (RTC)	RTC	via IRQ8	RTC_int/BIOS 2	BIOS
71	Redirected IRQ2	Hardware	via IRQ9	Re_direct/Test 4	Int hex a server
72	IRQ10	Hardware	via IRQ10	D11/Test 4	(user)
73	IRQ11	Hardware	via IRQ11	D11/Test 4	(user)
74	IRQ12	Hardware	via IRQ12	D11/Test 4	(user)
75	IRQ13	80287	via IRQ13	Int_287/Test 4	Int 2 server
76	IRQ14	Disk	via IRQ14	D11/Test 4	HD int/Disk
77	IRQ15	Hardware	via IRQ15	D11/Test 4	(user)

Interrupts generated by other interrupts

Number	Name	Origin	BIOS label/listing file	Ultimate server
5	Print Screen	Int 9 server	Print_screen_1/BIOS 2	BIOS
a	Old IRQ2	Int hex 71 server	D11/Test 4	(user)
1b	Ctrl-Break	Int 9 server	Dummy_return_1/Test 4	DOS
1c	User timer service	Int 8 server	Dummy_return_1/Test 4	BIOS
19	Bootstrap loader	Int 9 server	Boot_strap_1/Test 6	DOS (BIOS)
4a	Alarm	Int hex 70 server		(user)

Software interrupts

Number	Name	Origin	BIOS label/listing file	Ultimate server
10	Video service	(user)	Video_IO_1/Video	BIOS
11	Equipment check	(user)	Equipment_1/BIOS	BIOS
12	Base memory size	(user)	Memory_size_determine_1/BIOS	BIOS
13	Diskette/Disk service	(user)	Diskette_IO_1/Diskette	DOS
14	RS 232 service	(user)	RS232_IO_1/RS 232	BIOS
15	Miscellaneous	(user)	Cassette_IO_1/BIOS 1	BIOS
16	Keyboard service	(user)	Keyboard_IO_1/Keyboard	BIOS
17	Printer service	(user)	Printer_IO_1/Printer	BIOS
18	Resident BASIC	(user)		BASIC
1a	Time of day	(user)	Time_of_day_1/BIOS 2	BIOS

Table addresses

Number	Name	BIOS label/listing file
1d	Video parameters	Video_parms/ORGS
1e	Diskette parameters	Disk_base/ORGS
1f	Matrices for graphics characters 128..255	CRT_char_gen/ORGS

Figure 10.3.1 BIOS interrupt vectors

interrupt vectors are changed by DOS just after it's loaded. Also, a number of service routines are mere dummies: when these interrupts are used, users are expected to redirect the vectors toward custom service routines. In Figure 10.3.1, the "Ultimate server" column reflects this situation, as follows:

entry	meaning
(user)	To use this interrupt, users must redirect the vector from the BIOS dummy service routine d11.
BIOS	The BIOS provides a partial service, but users (user) may have to redirect the vector in order to add additional service.
DOS	DOS redirects this vector to its own service routine.
DOS (user)	DOS redirects this vector to its own dummy routine.

When DOS is loaded, it redirects vectors hex 13 and 76 to its own disk/diskette service routines. It also redirects the bootstrap vector hex 19 to a DOS routine, which just resets vectors 13 and 19 to their original BIOS values, then executes Interrupt 19.

Older models of the PC had only one 8259A chip, hence only eight IRQ lines. Installing a second requires disabling one of the lines on the first, so that it can be used to communicate with the second. IBM chose to disable IRQ2. This move would normally disable optional equipment that uses IRQ2. However, the previous IRQ2 line is now connected to the second chip as IRQ9. To compensate for this, the BIOS directs the corresponding interrupt vector hex 71 toward the service routine for vector hex a, which used to service the IRQ2 interrupts.

The Non-Maskable Interrupt 2 (NMI) is used to report and request action for certain equipment failures. The BIOS routine, found at label **NMI_int_1** in listing file BIOS, only deals with main memory parity failures. However, for historical reasons, certain other interrupt service requests may be directed to this routine. In the earlier PC models, the 8087 Numerical Coprocessor chip used the NMI to report abnormalities to the CPU. An 80287 coprocessor in the PC/AT, however, will use interrupt hex 75. In order to run older software packages on the PC/AT, the BIOS Interrupt hex 75 service routine merely transfers control to the NMI service routine. Thus, software packages that use the 80287 should redirect the NMI vector toward a routine that checks if the service request is from a coprocessor or a parity error, handles any coprocessor requests, and passes parity error reports on to the original BIOS NMI routine.

Interrupt 5: Print Screen or Bound instruction exception? A somewhat similar situation arises with Interrupt 5. Although Intel clearly reserved this 8088 interrupt for special treatment in future CPUs, IBM used it in the PC for the BIOS Print Screen service. This usage persists with the PC/AT, since its BIOS was designed for compatibility with the earlier ones.

The BIOS routine is found at label **print_screen_1** in the BIOS listing file BIOS 2. Intel designed the 80286 to execute this interrupt to signal an exception condition for the **bound** instruction: the instruction has tested an index against upper and lower bounds and found it out of range. When that situation arises in your PC/AT, the result is startling: you get a free hard copy of the screen! If you want to use the **bound** instruction you must install a custom Interrupt 5 service routine and redirect vector 5 to it. The routine must determine whether the interrupt originated from a **bound** instruction or from **int 5**. In the former case, it should take action appropriate for the **bound** exception; in the latter, it should transfer to the original BIOS Interrupt 5 routine. Both instructions push their address on the stack, so the custom service routine can easily determine the origin of the interrupt.

Other conflicts There are three other conflicts like the one between the Print Screen and **bound** exception interrupts. The 80286 uses Interrupt hex 8 for the **lidt** instruction exception, and 9 and d for the 80827 and 80286 segment overrun exceptions. These are rare error conditions. The **lidt** instruction is used only in preparing to enter protected mode (see Section 9.3), and this interrupt only occurs to signal one particular error. The segment overrun errors occur when an instruction attempts to access a word with an address whose offset is ffff. (It isn't clear whether the high order byte should come from offset 0000 in the current or next higher segment.) Nevertheless, if they ever come into play, these interrupts conflict with the BIOS functions described in Figure 10.3.1. Robust software should make a provision for them like that described earlier for the **bound** interrupt.

Keyboard interrupts When you strike or release a key, the 8042 Keyboard Controller chip causes the 8259A Interrupt Controller to issue Interrupt 9. The BIOS Interrupt 9 service routine **kb_int_1**, listed in file Video, interprets and processes keystroke codes sent by the 8042. Because there are several types of keystrokes, keyboard handling is logically complex. It is necessary to appreciate some of the distinctions in order to use the BIOS services.

The Interrupt 9 service routine first updates bytes at labels **kb_flag** and **kb_flag_1** in the BIOS data area. These keep track of the status of the various hold, toggle, and shift keys listed below:

Hold key	*Toggle keys*	*Shift keys*
Ctrl-NumLock	**CapsLock**	**Alt**
	Ins	**Ctrl**
	NumLock	**left Shift**
	ScrollLock	**right Shift**

For example, ordinary keystrokes cause the hold-state bit in **kb_flag_1** to be cleared, but **Ctrl-NumLock** sets it. On detecting this special keystroke, the service routine enters a loop, repeatedly testing this bit until it is turned off. What turns it off? A later request for the same interrupt service for an ordinary keystroke! Thus, all processing stops until you strike an ordinary key.

If you strike one of the toggle keys, the service routine changes a bit in the **kb_flag** byte as shown in Figure 10.3.2. These bits are all cleared by the POST, so they presumably reflect your current intention. Processing a toggle keystroke includes updating the keyboard indicator lights, if necessary.

To understand how the BIOS handles shift keys, you must remember that the 8042 regards as "keystrokes" both the act of *striking* a key and that of *releasing* it. When either event occurs for a shift key, the service routine adjusts the appropriate bit in **kb_flag** as shown in Figure 10.3.2.

For most other keystrokes (not releases), the service routine places two bytes in a circular queue at label **kb_buffer** in the BIOS data area called the *keyboard buffer:* the keystroke's ASCII code and a "scan code" that indicates precisely which key was struck. These codes were described in Section 7.3. For example, the **A** key with scan code 31 yields ASCII code 65 for the uppercase letter or 97 for lowercase, depending on the **CapsLock** and **Shift** bits in **kb_flag**. The buffer can hold fifteen keystroke codes. When it fills, no new keystrokes are recorded there, and the routine beeps the speaker.

Certain special keystrokes, however, are not placed in the buffer but trigger the service routine to take immediate special action by executing other interrupts:

Trigger	*Interrupt (hex)*	*Interrupt name*
Ctrl-Alt-Del	19	Bootstrap
Shift-PrtSc	5	Print Screen
Ctrl-Break	1b	Ctrl-Break
SysReq	15 (with AH = 85)	System Request

The Bootstrap Interrupt causes a warm boot, as described in Section 11.1. The Print Screen Interrupt performs that service. (This interrupt conflicts with the 80286 **bound** instruction exception; if you want to use that instruction, you will have to redirect interrupt vector 5 as described earlier.) You may have noticed the absence of **Ctrl-PrtSc** and **ScrollLock** from the above list of special keystrokes. The first of these has no significance to the BIOS; it is

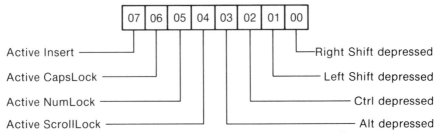

Figure 10.3.2 Toggle and shift key bits in kb_flag

treated specially only by the DOS keyboard service. The **ScrollLock** keystroke just sets a bit in byte **kb_flag**; programs that want to treat it specially may inspect this bit by using a BIOS keyboard service described below.

DOS redirects the **Ctrl-Break** vector from the dummy BIOS routine to its own server, which is also called whenever DOS is in control and you strike **Ctrl-C**. (This explains the relationship of these keystrokes: since DOS uses the BIOS keyboard service, **Ctrl-Break** and **Ctrl-C** are both recognized when DOS is in control, or when your program uses the appropriate DOS function. The DOS **Ctrl-Break** interrupt service routine terminates the current program and invokes the DOS command processor **command.com**. If your program bypasses DOS but uses the BIOS service, then **Ctrl-Break** is effective but not **Ctrl-C**. If it bypasses even the BIOS, communicating directly with the 8042, then both—in fact all—special keystrokes are disabled unless your program handles them specifically.)

The PC/AT SysReq key When the keyboard interrupt routine detects a **SysReq** keystroke, it sets AH = hex 85 and AL = 0 or 1 to indicate that you struck or released the key, then executes instruction **int 15h**. The BIOS Interrupt hex 15 service routine actually does nothing when it is invoked with AH = 85. If you want special treatment for **SysReq** keystrokes, you must write your own routine and redirect vector 15 there. Your routine must first check AH, execute your code if AH = 85, or else transfer to the original BIOS Interrupt 15 routine.

BIOS software interrupt services The remaining BIOS interrupts, invoked by software, provide programmers many indispensible services relating to control of the hardware. Most of these services were already available in the earlier models of the PC. Since they have been discussed already in Section 7.3, they are just summarized here. The BIOS software interrupt services new with the PC/AT are discussed in detail.

Interrupt hex 10 video services The video routine, listed in BIOS file **Video**, provides a number of services depending on the value of register AH when you execute the interrupt. Figure 10.3.3 is a catalog of available services. A Pascal program illustrating use of the scrolling function was shown earlier in Figure 7.3.3.

AH	Service	Description
0	Set video mode	AL = mode. See list below.
1	Set cursor size	CH,CL = 12,13 sets the standard cursor in the bottom two lines 13,14 of the Monochrome Adapter character matrix.
2	Set cursor location	BH = page (for monochrome). DH,DL = row, column.
3	Find cursor size and location	Requires BH = page. Return DH,DL as above.
4	Find light pen location	AH = 0 means button not pushed. Otherwise, character row, column returned in DH,DL and pixel row, column in CH,BX.
5	Select text page	Page in AL.
6	Scroll a window upward	CH,CL and DH,DL = upper left and lower right row, column. AL = number of lines (0 means all). BH = attribute for blank lines.

7 Scroll a window downward.......... See Service 4.

8 Find attribute and character.......
   at cursor level   Requires BH = page. Return attribute and character in
                                       AH, AL.

9 Set attribute and character   BH = page. AL, BL = character, attribute. Setting BL bit 7
   at cursor location................ replaces current attribute by its exclusive disjunction
                                       with BL bits 0..6 . CX = number of repetitions of the
                                       character in AL.

a Set character at cursor location... Like Service 9, but use the current attribute.

b Set palette...................... Color Graphics Adapter text or 320×200 four color mode
                                       only. BL = color value or palette number. BH = 0 sets text
                                       border or graphics background color. BH = 1 sets the active
                                       palette.

c Color a dot...................... Color Graphics Adapter graphics mode. DX ,CX = row, column.
                                       AL = color number. Setting AL bit 7 erases the dot by
                                       replacing the current color by its exclusive disjunction
                                       with AL bits 0..6.

d Find the color of a dot........... Color Graphics Adapter graphics mode. Requires DX, CX = row,
                                       column. Returns color in AL.

e Write a character in TTY style..... AL, BL = character, foreground color for graphics mode.
                                       Starts at the cursor location, does carriage return, line
                                       feed, and scroll if necessary.

f Find current video status.......... AL = mode (see list below). AH = screen width for text
                                       mode. BH = active page.

10..12 Reserved

13 Write string at cursor location.... New service. See the text for a complete description.

Video modes supported by BIOS

AL = mode	adapter	text or graphics	color or monochrome	columns (width)	rows	pages
0	Color/Graphics	text	monochrome	40	25	8
1	Color/Graphics	text	16 colors	40	25	8
2	Color/Graphics	text	monochrome	80	25	4
3	Color/Graphics	text	16 colors	80	25	4
4	Color/Graphics	graphics	4 colors	320	200	1
5	Color/Graphics	graphics	monochrome	320	200	1
6	Color/Graphics	graphics	monochrome	640	200	1
7	Monochrome	text	monochrome	80	25	1

Figure 10.3.3. BIOS video services

New video service: write a string There is one new PC/AT video service
selected by setting AH = hex 13: write a string starting at a given location.
The string entries may be just the characters, or it may consist of alternating
characters and attributes. You have the option of moving the cursor to the
string's end or not. Figure 10.3.4 shows the required register setup.

Interrupt hex 11 equipment check Executing this interrupt merely loads
AX with the word **equip_flag** from the BIOS data area. Its bits are set dur-

Register	Content
AH	hex 13
AL	Set bit 0 if you want to move the cursor. Set bit 1 if the string consists of alternating characters and attributes.
BH	Active page number (text modes only).
BL	Attribute, unless AL indicates that the string contains the attribute codes.
CX	String length.
DH, DL	Starting location row, column.
ES:BP	Address of the first string character.

Figure 10.3.4 Registers for BIOS Interrupt hex 10 write string function 13

ing the POST to indicate some of the equipment installed in your PC/AT, as shown in Figure 10.3.5; it reflects the information stored in the CMOS chip when you ran the **setup** program.

Interrupt hex 12 base memory count Interrupt hex 12 returns in AX the number of contiguous functioning 1K base memory blocks: from 256 to 640. This is merely the number stored at label **memory_size** in the BIOS data area, determined by memory tests during the POST. Extended memory with physical addresses above one MB is ignored.

Interrupt hex 13 disk and diskette services Applications programmers normally use higher level DOS services for interacting with the disk and diskette input/output system, so they rarely need information about the low-level services provided by this interrupt. Therefore, the list in Figure 10.3.6 gives only the briefest summary of these services, which are

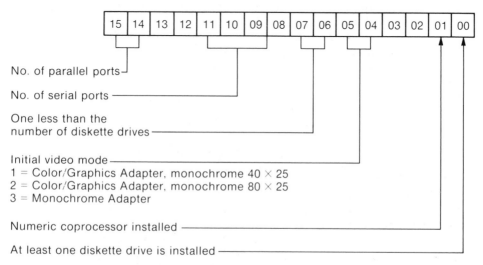

Figure 10.3.5 Equipment data returned in AX by interrupt hex 11

selected by the value of AH when the interrupt is executed. For detailed
information, consult the BIOS listing files Diskette and Disk and the
chapter on the Fixed Disk and Diskette Adapter in the *PC/AT Technical
Reference* manual. These routines serve the high capacity drive **a:**, a standard drive **b:**, the standard fixed disk drive **c:**, and a second fixed disk
drive. The BIOS refers to those as drives 0, 1, hex 80, and hex 81, respectively. It is possible to modify the drive characteristics tables to use other
types of drives.

This part of the BIOS is of course quite different from the corresponding
code for earlier PCs. Many of the new features are due to the need for handling new types of drives, using parameter tables. One other complication is
introduced: since it is possible to use a standard diskette in a high capacity
drive, some method for detecting when diskettes are changed is mandatory.
PC/AT diskette drives have a "diskette change line" that is activated in this
circumstance, and the BIOS can determine its status.

Interrupt hex 14 serial communication services The BIOS provides
primitive support for the serial communications ports: four functions selected
by the value of AH when Interrupt hex 14 is executed. For each of these, DX
= 0 or 1 selects the serial port conventionally named COM1 or COM2. Addresses of these ports are stored at label **RS232_base** in the BIOS data area.
Each service returns in AH a port status byte reflecting current conditions in
the port. You can find the details of serial port operation in the BIOS listing
file RS232 and in the chapter on the Serial/ Parallel Adapter in the *PC/AT
Technical Reference* manual. Figure 10.3.7 is a brief list of the available serv-

AH	Interrupt hex 13 Function
0	Reset a disk drive or the diskette system.
1	Return the system status after the last operation.
2	Read into a memory buffer from given sectors.
3	Write to given sectors from a memory buffer.
4	Verify given sectors against a memory buffer.
5	Format a given track.
8	Return the drive parameters.
9	Initialize drive pair characteristics.
a	Read long (lower level than Function 2).
b	Write long (lower level than Function 3).
c	Seek
d	Reset a disk drive (equivalent to Function 0).
10	Test whether drive is ready.
11	Recalibrate a drive.
14	Execute controller diagnostics.
15	Determine drive type.
16	Check the diskette change line status.
17	Set the drive type.

Figure 10.3.6 BIOS Interrupt hex 13 disk and diskette functions

ices. A Pascal program illustrating use of one of these services was shown earlier in Figure 7.3.5.

These BIOS routines support only *polling* techniques for handling serial ports. That is, to send data, you must determine that the port can accept data for transmission and wait if necessary. Similarly, to process received data, you must inquire first if the port has received a byte, waiting if necessary. Moreover, you must process a received byte quickly before another appears in the port.

The 8250 serial communications chips used on PC compatible expansion boards can request interrupts, and are in fact connected to an 8259A Interrupt Controller Chip on the mother board: COM1 via line IRQ4 and COM2 via IRQ3. For example, the 8250 can request an interrupt for COM1 service when this port receives a byte. If that interrupt is enabled, then the 8259A will execute interrupt hex c, transferring control to a service routine that may store the byte in a memory buffer. The BIOS, however, does not provide that service. If you need that level of support, you'll have to provide it some other way. (Commercial packages are available—for example, reference [1].)

Interrupt hex 16 keyboard services Under the heading "Keyboard interrupts" you saw how the BIOS processes keystrokes, updating a byte called **kb_flag** that tells the status of various toggle and shift keys, and storing keystroke information in a buffer until it's needed. The software interrupt hex 16 keyboard services let you inspect **kb_flag** and the keyboard buffer, and remove entries from the buffer once you've processed them. The individual bits in **kb_flag** have been described in Figure 10.3.2. Figure 10.3.8 is a list of these services, which are selected by the value in AH when the interrupt is executed. A Pascal program illustrating use of one of these services was shown earlier in Figure 7.3.6.

Interrupt hex 17 printer services The low-level BIOS printer services should really be named "parallel communications" services, since they can

AH	Interrupt hex 14 Functions
0	Initialize a port. You may set the number of data bits per transmitted byte, the number of stop bits, the parity checking method, and the BAUD rate.
1	Send the byte in AL. If it can't be sent, AH bit 7 is set.
2	Receive a byte and put it in AL. If no byte is received before the time out limit expires, set AH bit 7. The time out limit is stored at label **RS232_time_out** in the BIOS data area; it is initialized by the POST.
3	Return the port status in AX. The AH byte was mentioned above. The AL byte can report the status of a modem attached to the port.

Figure 10.3.7 BIOS Interrupt hex 14 serial communications functions

AH	Interrupt hex 16 Functions
0	Read the next character and remove it from the keyboard buffer. Place the scan code in AH and the ASCII code in AL. If the buffer is empty, wait.
1	Inspect the keyboard buffer. If it's empty, set ZF = 1; otherwise, set ZF = 0 and copy the scan and ASCII codes into AH and AL. Do not remove the data from the buffer.
2	Return the **kb_flag** byte in AL.

Figure 10.3.8 BIOS Interrupt hex 16 keyboard functions

be used to communicate with other parallel devices. Moreover, as high-level printer software becomes more common, programmers have less need to use these services for printer control. The three services are selected by the value in AH when the interrupt is executed. All three inspect the value in DX to select the appropriate parallel port: DX = 0, 1, 2 selects the port commonly named LPT1, LPT1, or LPT3. The port addresses are stored at label **printer_base** in the BIOS data area. All three services also return a port status byte in AH. For the meaning of its bits, consult the BIOS listing file Printer and the chapter on the Serial/Parallel Adapter in the *PC/AT Technical Reference* manual. Figure 10.3.9 is a list of the services.

ROM BASIC interrupt hex 18 Executing instruction **int 18h** causes immediate entry into the ROM BASIC system. While this is conceivably of some use, it is an unattractive route to BASIC because there's no straightforward way back. (ROM BASIC is independent of the existence of an operating system, so it has no **system** command.)

New interrupt hex 15 joystick support You can request BIOS joystick services—new to the PC/AT—by executing interrupt hex 15 (the "miscellaneous" interrupt) with AH = hex 84. Two services can be selected by the value in DX. The DX = 0 function reports in AL bits 4..7 the settings of four switches on the Game Adapter. The DX = 1 function reports in registers AX,BX, CX, DX the x and y values of joysticks A and B in this order: Ax, Ay, Bx, By. Consult the documentation for the Game Adapter for details of this hardware. Both services set the Carry Flag to indicate that no adapter is func-

AH	Interrupt hex 17 functions
0	Send the character in AL. If it can't be printed before the time out limit expires, the routine sets AH = 1. The time out limit is initialized by the POST and stored in the BIOS data area.
1	Initialize port.
2	Read port status.

Figure 10.3.9 BIOS Interrupt hex 17 printer functions

tioning. The assembly code for the joystick service is located at label **joy_stick** in listing file BIOS 1.

CMOS and 8253 timer and clock/calendar services The 8253 Timer chip causes hardware Interrupt 8 to be executed about 18.2 times each second. This time interval is called a *tick*. The BIOS service routine, found at label **timer_int_1** in listing file BIOS 2, increments a double word tick counter, restarting it each 24 hours (and recording the restart), then executes Interrupt hex 1c. The tick counter and restart indicator are stored at labels **timer_low**, **timer_high**, and **timer_ofl** in the BIOS data area. The BIOS supplies a dummy hex 1c service routine, and you are invited to write your own and redirect to it the hex 1c vector, thus taking advantage of the timer. For example, you could determine the time and display it somewhere on the screen.

The BIOS provides a number of other services relating to this timer and to the more elaborate one on the CMOS chip. Offered by the Interrupt hex 15 and 1a routines, these services are selected by the value in AH when the interrupt is executed. Figure 10.3.10 provides an overview. The Interrupt 1a assembly code is found following label **time_of_day_1** in BIOS listing file BIOS 2; the Interrupt 15 code at labels **event_wait** and **wait** in file BIOS 1. Hex 1a functions 2, 4, and 6 set the Carry Flag if the clock is not operating; service 6 and the hex 15 services also set it to indicate that the alarm is already active.

The first two Interrupt hex 1a functions were offered by the earlier PCs. Interrupt hex 1a Function 0 loads registers AL and DX, CX with a restart indicator and the low and high order words of the tick counter. Thus the number of seconds since your machine was last booted is normally given by the formula

$$(DX + 2^{16}*CX)/18.2$$

Normally, AL = 0. However, if the tick counter proceeds undisturbed for 24 hours, it is restarted at 0 and this interrupt will set AL = 1. Function 1 allows you to reset the tick counter to any value you wish by loading appropriate values into DX and CX before the interrupt.

It's remarkable that the earlier PCs had no clock that continued running when the power was off or the system rebooted. Of course, expansion board manufacturers provided them, and now the PC/AT has an elaborate battery-powered timer on its CMOS chip, with convenient BIOS routines to help you use it.

Interrupt hex 1a functions 2 and 3 let you read or set the CMOS clock. Hours, minutes, and seconds are returned or set using registers CH, CL, and DH as in this example:

```
Set  AH = 2.
Execute Interrupt  hex 1a.
Observe that  CH,CL,DH = hex 17,45,23.
Conclude that the time is  17:45:23.
```

Interrupt AL = hex	Function AH = hex	Timer	Description
1a	0	8253	Read the system clock.
1a	1	8253	Set the system clock.
1a	2	CMOS	Read the CMOS clock.
1a	3	CMOS	Set the CMOS clock.
1a	4	CMOS	Read the calendar.
1a	5	CMOS	Set the calendar.
1a	6	CMOS	Set the alarm clock.
1a	7	CMOS	Disable the alarm clock.
15	83	CMOS	Set the CMOS alarm.
15	86	CMOS	Wait.

Figure 10.3.10 BIOS Interrupt hex 1a and 15 clock/calendar functions

Comments in the BIOS listing indicate that there is some facility for enabling and disabling daylight savings time; it's not clear how that works. Note that this clock reading is actually less precise than the tick counter: the BIOS reports CMOS time correct to the second, but a tick is $1/18.2 = 0.055$ sec. The CMOS clock is actually much more precise, but these particular services don't take advantage of that.

Services 4 and 5 for Interrupt hex 1a let you read or set the CMOS calendar. The century, year, month, and day are returned or set via registers CH, CL, DH, and DL as in this example:

```
Set  AH = 4.
Execute Interrupt  hex 1a.
Observe that  CH, CL, DH, DL  =  hex 19, 85, 03, 16.
Conclude that the date is  1985 March 16.
```

A complete Pascal program illustrating use of this service was shown already in Figure 7.2.2. Although the CMOS calendar also keeps track of the day of the week, the BIOS service does not provide it.

Services 6 and 7 for Interrupt hex 1a let you set or cancel an alarm. The following two fragments of assembly language code set an alarm at 18:52:00, then cancel it:

	Set the alarm	*Cancel it*
	mov ch,18h	mov ah,7h
	mov cl,52h	int 1ah
	mov dh,00h	
	mov ah,5h	
	int 1ah	

What happens when the alarm goes off? The CMOS chip causes the 8259A Interrupt Controller to execute Interrupt hex 4a. You must provide your own service routine for that interrupt, and redirect the hex 4a vector to it. (You can easily test this with **debug**: assemble and execute the little program to set the alarm, then set the hex 4a vector equal to the ROM BASIC hex 18 vector. At 18:52:00 you will suddenly enter BASIC!).

Two additional CMOS timer interrupts, far more precise, are provided by the BIOS Interrupt hex 15 service routine. They are selected by the value in AH when the interrupt is executed. Interrupt hex 15 Function 83 is an alarm whose resolution is about one millisecond. You don't set it for a particular time of day, but rather for a certain period. When that period has elapsed, the high order bit of a specified byte in memory will be set. You must clear this bit, of course, before setting the alarm, and it is your responsibility to inspect it periodically to detect when the alarm has occurred. To use this service, express the alarm period in microseconds as a 32-bit double word, and place the high order word in CX and the low order word in DX. Load the address of the alarm byte in ES:BX, set AH = 83, AL = 0, and execute instruction **int 1ah**. While the BIOS documentation suggests that invoking this service with AL = 1 should cancel the alarm, inspection of the code seems to indicate otherwise. Figure 10.3.11 is an IBM Pascal program that illustrates the use (and failure) of this interrupt service. It uses the IBM software interrupt mechanism described in Section 7.2.

```
{$include:'IBMintrp.int'}
program alarmtst(input,output);
uses IBMintrp;
{This program sets an alarm about 86.5 sec ahead. You have
the option of cancelling it immediately. When the alarm goes
off, it sets the high order bit of an alarm byte. You can repeat
the test up to 100 times. For each test a different alarm byte
is used. It is cleared and displayed, then the alarm is set.
You are given the opportunity to wait a while, then the byte is
displayed again. If you wait less than the alarm period, the byte
is unchanged; if you wait long enough, it will change. If you
opt to cancel the alarm, the test should leave the byte
unchanged, but it doesn't.}


var
  i      : 1..100;
  alarm  : array [1..100] of byte;      ! New byte for each test.
  answer : char;
  r1,r2,r: reglist;                 ! Registers for setting and can-
                                    ! celing alarm, and for garbage.
begin {alarmtst}
  for i := 1 to 100 do
    begin
      writeln('**********************************************');
      writeln('Event wait test');
      alarm[i] := 0;                ! Clear the byte.
      writeln('Alarm byte = ',alarm[i]:8:2);   ! And display it.
```

```
  with r1 do
    begin                                    ! AH = function.
      ax : = #8300;                          ! AL = 0 to set.
      es : = (ads alarm[i]).s;               ! ES: BX = alarm
      bx : = (ads alarm[i]).r;               ! byte address.
      cx : = 100;                            ! CX, DX = 100 *
      dx : = 0                               ! 64K microsec
    end;
  r2     : = r1;                             ! AL = 1 to
  r2. ax  : = #8301;                         ! cancel alarm.
  write('Cancel immediately [y,n] or quit [q]?');
  readln(answer);
  if answer = 'q' then break;
  intrp(#15,r1,r);
  writeln('The alarm was set for 6.5 seconds.');
  if answer = 'y'
    then
      begin
        intrp(#15,r2,4);
        writeln('Then it was canceled.')
      end;
  writeln('Wait a while, then touch the enter key.');
  readln;
  writeln('Now, alarm byte = ';alarm[i]:8:2)
  end
end. {alarmtst}
```

Figure 10.3.11 Pascal program to test BIOS Interrupt hex 15 Function 83 alarm service

Interrupt hex 15 Function 86 allows you to delay for a period that can be specified with a precision of about one millisecond. You can't do that with the other timer services, because their finest resolution is one tick = 0.055 sec. A typical use of this service is to send a break signal over a serial communication line: you must hold a particular voltage on the line for a period comparable to the time it takes to transmit a character, which is often far shorter than one tick. To use this service, load the delay period into registers CX and DX as for Function hex 83, set AH = 86, and execute instruction **int 1a**.

Note that although the delay periods for these two Interrupt hex 15 timer services are specified in microseconds, the precision is only about one millisecond. The CMOS chip actually causes the 8259A Interrupt Controller chip to execute Interrupt hex 70 about 1000 times per second. The BIOS Interrupt hex 70 service routine, located at label **RTC_int** in BIOS listing file BIOS 2, just decrements a counter and sets an alarm bit when it reaches zero. This accounts for the behavior of the Interrupt hex 15 alarm service hex 83 routine; the hex 86 delay routine merely clears an alarm bit and watches it until it changes.

Interrupt hex 15 services for multitasking Several BIOS hex 15 functions, selected by the value of AH when the interrupt is executed, are intended for use by a multitasking operating system. No services are provided; the operating system must provide custom services. The documentation in the *PC/AT Technical Reference* manual is meager and confusing; for a clearer picture, we'll have to wait for such operating systems to appear. Here is a list of the services:

AH	Name
80	Device open
81	Device close
82	Program terminate
90	Device busy
91	Interrupt complete

The "device open" interrupt is evidently intended to perform whatever services are required to mark a device as open to one task and unavailable to others.

The "device busy" interrupt is to be used to tell the operating system that a task is waiting to use some device. The device is identified in the registers, so that the operating system can put the task in a queue and transfer control to some other task. The "interrupt complete" interrupt will be used when a device has finished serving a task, so that the operating system can maintain the queue. These two interrupts have been installed already at the appropriate places in the BIOS. Of course, their service routines are dummies. For example, "device busy" is executed when a program requests keyboard Service 0—read a character from the buffer—and no character is ready. In a multitasking situation, an operating system may switch to another task at this point, but it must make sure that the next keystrokes go to the proper task. "Interrupt complete" is executed at the end of the keyboard Interrupt 9 routine. Similar pairs are found in the disk/diskette service routines, but not in the video routines, even though there are frequent waits for horizontal and vertical retrace periods.

10.4 Using extended memory

Concepts

∗ Determining the size of extended memory   ∗ Moving data to and from extended memory using a high level language   ∗ Entering protected mode operation using a high level language

BIOS Interrupt hex 15 services include three that have to do with protected mode operation. They are selected by the value in AH when the interrupt is executed, as follows:

AH (hex)	Interrupt hex 15 service
87	Move data to and from extended memory.
88	Determine extended memory size.
89	Enter protected mode operation.

These services are discussed below, in the order 88, 87, 89.

Determining extended memory size Service hex 88 merely reads into AX two bytes from CMOS memory. At boot time, the POST verified that these reflected the amount of functioning memory installed above the 1-MB standard memory address limit. You request this service by setting AH = 88 and executing instruction **int 15h**. The interrupt returns with AX = the extended memory size in kilobytes.

Moving data to and from extended memory Service hex 87 seems fairly simple to request. You must first initialize

```
AH = 87;
ES:SI = the segment:offset address of the Global Descriptor
        Table  (GDT)  to be used once the interrupt service
        routine enters protected mode;  (This table contains
        three byte physical addresses of the source and
        target buffers between which data will be moved.)
CX = the number of words to move.
```

Executing Interrupt hex 15 will then move the data from the source to the target buffer. On return, AH will contain a status code, as follows:

AH	Status
0	Successful move
1	RAM parity error
2	Exception error (probably a bad GDT)
3	Address line 20 failed

Moreover, ZF = 1 indicates success and CY = 1 indicates failure.

The only difficulty is setting up the GDT according to specifications. Rather than describe these details in the abstract, then present an example, it seems easier to describe the construction of some IBM Pascal data structures and routines that will implement this interrupt.

The first problem is to set up three-byte physical addresses. In IBM Pascal you can use real mode segment:offset addresses directly, but you must define a data type for protected mode physical addresses, then develop a procedure for converting known segment:offset addresses to equivalent physical addresses. The standard IBM segment:offset address type is defined as

```
type
  adsmem = record
               s,r: word          ! s  is the segment
             end                  ! r  is the offset
```

It seems reasonable to define a type for physical addresses as follows:

```
type
  ad3mem = record
               hi,md,lo: byte     ! high, medium, and
             end                  ! low order bytes
```

Commented code for a Pascal function **ad3** to convert an address **a** of type **adsmem** to an equivalent one of type **ad3mem** is shown in Figure 10.4.1.

A GDT must be constructed for the interrupt service routine to use in protected mode. It requires six descriptors:

0: The first descriptor in a GDT is always all zeros—a dummy target for null selectors.
1: The next descriptor in a GDT always describes the GDT itself as a data segment. The service routine merely needs a dummy descriptor here; it will initialize it properly.
2: The descriptor for the source buffer, which will constitute a single segment.
3: The descriptor for the target buffer.

```
function ad3(const a: adsmem)
        : ad3mem;

{This function returns the three byte PC/AT physical address of
type ad3mem equivalent to a segment:offset address of type
adsmem.}

var
  as,ar,long: integer4;              ! Four byte integers
  address   : ad3mem;

begin {ad3}
  as          := bylong(0,a.s);      ! Zeroes followed by a.s
  ar          := bylong(0,a.r);      ! Zeroes followed by a.r
  long        := #10*as+ar;          ! Shift as left 4
                                     ! bits and add ar.
  address.lo := lobyte(loword(long));
  address.md := hibyte(loword(long));
  address.hi := lobyte(hiword(long));
  ad3        := address
end; {ad3}
```

Figure 10.4.1 Pascal function to compute physical addresses

4: A dummy descriptor that the service routine will initialize for its code segment.

5: A dummy descriptor that the service routine will initialize for its stack segment.

Since the buffers must fit in single segments, their length is limited to 32K words. Figure 10.4.2 (a replica of Figure 7.3.2) shows the structure of an individual descriptor.

Byte 7	Byte 6
Access Rights Byte	Byte 4
Byte 3	Byte 2
Byte 1	Byte 0

Format for all entries of a descriptor table

Reserved for future use by Intel	
Access Rights Byte	High order address
Low order bytes of physical base address	
Segment length	

Format for all segment descriptors

Figure 10.4.2 Descriptor formats

Figure 10.4.3 shows commented code for an IBM Pascal function **at_movel** that moves words from a buffer starting at **source_address** to another at **target_address**. The number of words to move is given by the variable **length**. On return, the value of the function is the status code placed in AX by the Interrupt hex 15 service routine hex 87, or else the value hex ff if **length** was out of bounds. The code first validates **length** and sets up the GDT. Then it sets up variables corresponding to the registers for the interrupt, and uses the IBM Pascal procedure **intrp** to execute the interrupt. This IBM software interrupt mechanism was described in detail in Section 7.2.

```
function at_movel (const source_address: ad3mem;
                   const target_address: ad3mem;
                         length          : word)
        : byte;
```

{This function uses PC/AT Interrupt hex 15 Service hex 87 to
move words from a source buffer to a target buffer, starting at
the lowest address. The buffer addresses are three byte physical
PC/AT addresses. The buffer must be ≤ 32K words long. The
one byte function value is a status code, as follows:

```
          0 :   Successful move
          1 :   RAM  parity error
          2 :   Interrupt exception error
          3 :   Address line  20  failed.
         ff :   Specified buffer length is too great.}
```

```
type
  GDT_index = 0..47;
var
  i: GDT_index;
  GDT: array [GDT_index] of byte;
  registers:  reglist;


begin {at_move1}
  if length = 0
    then
      at_move1 := 0                        ! Nothing to do.
    else if length > 32768 then
      at_move1 := #ff                      ! Length too great.
    else
      begin

        ! Make the  GDT  required by the interrupt service
        ! routine.  There are  6  descriptors,  8  bytes each:
        !
        !   0)  dummy (zeros) required by the  BIOS,
        !   1)  dummy (zeros) required by the  BIOS,
        !   2)  source segment descriptor,
        !   3)  target segment descriptor,
        !   4)  dummy (zeros) required by the  BIOS,
        !   5)  dummy (zeros) required by the  BIOS.

        for i := 0 to 15 do              ! Dummies  0)  and  1)
          GDT[i] := 0;

        GDT[16] := lobyte(2*length);     ! Source descriptor  2)
        GDT[17] := hibyte(2*length);
        GDT[18] := source_address.lo;
        GDT[19] := source_address.md;
        GDT[20] := source_address.hi;
        GDT[21] := #93;                  ! Explained in the text
        GDT[22] := 0;
        GDT[23] := 0;
```

```
GDT[24] : = GDT[16];              ! Target descriptor 3)
GDT[25] : = GDT[17];
GDT[26] : = target_address.lo;
GDT[27] : = target_address.md;
GDT[28] : = target_address.hi;
GDT[29] : = #93;                  ! Explained in text
GDT[30] : = 0;
GDT[31] : = 0;

for i : = 32 to 47 do            ! Dummies 4) and 5)
  GDT[i] : = 0;
                                 ! Set up the PC/AT CPU
with registers do               ! register variables.
  begin
    ax : = #8700;               ! AH = hex 87
    cx : = length;
    ex : = (ads GDT).s;         ! ES:SI = segmnent:offset
    si : = (ads GDT).r;         ! address of GDT.
  end;

intrp(#15,registers,registers); ! Execute the interrupt.
at_movel : = registers.ax
  end
end; {at_movel}
```

Figure 10.4.3 Pascal function to move data using physical addresses (especially for extended memory)

The magic number hex 93 occurs as the sixth byte in the source and target descriptors in Figure 10.4.3. This is the Type and Access byte, reckoned as shown in Figure 10.4.4.

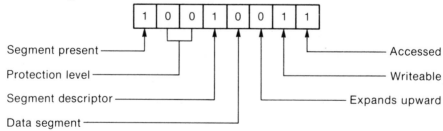

Figure 10.4.4. Type and Access Byte for Interrupt hex 15 Function hex 87 segment descriptors

Figure 10.4.5 shows a complete IBM Pascal program that tests this method. It creates a distinctive array of words on the Pascal heap, displays it, then copies it to extended memory, beginning at physical address $100000 = 16 \char94 5 = 2 \char94 20 = 1$ MB. Since you can't access extended memory directly, you can't immediately verify the copy. Therefore the source buffer is cleared and shown to be empty. The array is copied back from extended memory and shown to be intact.

```
{#include:'IBMintrp.int'}
program testatm2(input,output);
uses IBMintrp;

{This program tests the use of  PC/AT  Interrupt  hex  15  Service
hex 87  to move data between buffers, that may be in extended
memory. In this test, the source buffer is a Pascal array;  the
target is simply a region in extended memory.  First the source
buffer is created on the heap, filled with a distinctive pattern,
then displayed.  Next it is moved to extended memory.  You can't
access it directly there, so to verify the process, the buffer is
cleared and displayed, then the target moved to the source.
Voila!  It reappears!}

type
  buffer_type     = super array [1..*] of word;
  ad3mem          = record
                       hi,md,lo: byte
                    end;

const
  buffer_length = wrd(100);                 ! Short for display
  ad3_target    = ad3mem(#10,#00,#00);      ! 16 ^ 5 = 1 Megabyte

var
  source        : ^ buffer_ type;
  i             : 1..buffer_length;
  ad3_source    : ad3mem;
  ax            : byte;

{Include the code for functions  ad3  and  at_move1  in
Figures  10.4.1  and  10.4.3 ,  declared as follows:

function ad3(const a: adsmem)
        : ad3mem;

function at_move1(const source_address: ad3mem;
                  const target_address: ad3mem;
                        length         : word)
        : byte:}

begin {testatm2}
  new (source,buffer_length);           ! Create source buffer.
  for i := 1 to buffer_length do        ! Fill it.
  source ^ [i] := i;
  writeln('Here is the source buffer:'); ! Display it.
  for i := 1 to buffer_length do
```

```
  writeln(source ˆ [i]);

ad3_source : = ad3(ads source ˆ);           ! Move it.
ax : = at_movel (ad3_source,
        ad3_target,buffer_length);
writeln('I moved it.  Status= ',ax);
for i : = 1 to buffer_length do              ! Clear it.
  source ˆ [i] : = 0;

writeln('I cleared it.  See?');             ! Show that it's gone.
for i : = 1 to buffer_length do
  writeln(source ˆ [i]);

ax : = at_movel (ad3_target,                 ! Move it back.
        at3_source,buffer_length);
writeln('I moved it back. Status=',ax);

writeln('Here it is again:');               ! Display it.
for i : = 1 to buffer_length do
  writeln(source ˆ [i]);
dispose(source,buffer_length)               ! Clean up.
end. {testatm2}
```

Figure 10.4.5 Pascal program to test the technique for moving data between standard and extended memory

The dynamically allocated super array type was used in the program of Figure 10.4.5 so that you need change only one statement—the declaration of the constant **buffer_length**—to change the length of the buffer.

It's instructive to follow the action of the Interrupt hex 15 Service hex 87 routine; its code is found at label **blockmove** in listing file BIOS 1. Although only a single **movsw** instruction is required to move the data, about two pages of overhead code is necessary to arrange the transition to protected mode and back. The first major task is to store in CMOS memory the number of the return address in the jump table that will be used by the POST on returning from protected mode. (Section 10.2 contains a discussion of this return route.) The number 9 is stored in CMOS. The ninth entry in the jump table at label **branch** in listing file Test 1 is the address corresponding to label **shut9** later on in the hex 87 routine.

Next, the routine converts into a physical address the segment:offset GDT address that you supplied in ES:SI, and places it in GDT descriptor number 1—the descriptor for the GDT itself—and in the GDT register. It proceeds similarly to build the descriptors numbers 4 and 5 for the stack and code segments. (This code is a little mysterious because it depends on the definition of the assembly language structure **descr_def**, which is in a file omitted from the BIOS listing.)

One last task remains before entering protected mode: setting up the interrupt descriptor table (IDT). Although external interrupts are disabled during this entire routine (its first instruction is **cli**), errors in the move operation will be signaled by exception interrupts. A predefined IDT is used, found at label **rom_idt** just after this routine. All the selector:offset vectors in this table point to the exception interrupt routine in listing file Test 5, which was also used by the POST while testing the 80286 protected mode instructions. This routine just records the source of the exception and halts if it is serving the POST (not the case here).

The hex 87 service routine now enters protected mode, moves the data, and leaves protected mode, resetting the 80286 by the method described in Section 9.2. To move the data, it must set up DS:SI and ES:DI, then execute a **movsw** instruction. You had long ago stored in CX the number of words for this instruction to move.

Once back at label **shut9** in real mode, the service routine must restore your registers, which it saved at the onset, and ensure that AH contains 0 if the move was successful or else reflects any error signal recorded in protected mode by the exception interrupt routine. Finally, it enables interrupts and returns.

Because this routine turns off interrupts, it could interfere, at least momentarily, with processing of events that use hardware interrupts to request service. (For example, missing a timer tick could disrupt a process triggered by BIOS timer interrupt hex 1c; missing a serial port interrupt could interfere with processing data arriving on a communications line.)

Entering protected mode Interrupt hex 15 Service hex 89 provides a means for entering protected mode and continuing with the currently executing program. (Remember, there's no way to get back!) The technique used is similar to Service hex 87. You must first construct an appropriate GDT, then execute the interrupt. Since this is a permanent transition, the GDT must be more elaborate than the one for the former service. Specifically, it must contain eight descriptors, as follows:

0: the standard dummy descriptor,
1: the descriptor for the GDT itself,
2: a descriptor for your IDT,
3: a descriptor for your data segment,
4: a descriptor for your extra segment,
5: a descriptor for your stack segment,
6: a descriptor for your code segment,
7: a descriptor for the BIOS code segment containing this routine.

You must provide space for all these and initialize all except the last, which this service routine sets up for itself.

Moreover, you must set up an entire IDT, and you must provide this routine with the information necessary for it to reprogram the two 8259A Interrupt Controller chips to find the interrupt descriptors that you want to associate with the IRQ lines. In particular, you must load BH and BL with the IDT offsets corresponding to the descriptors for the interrupts corresponding to

IRQ0 and IRQ8, and the descriptors for IRQ1..IRQ7 and IRQ9..IRQ15 must follow these in order.

Following the service routine code, found at label **x_virtual** in listing file BIOS 1, you will see that the routine turns off interrupts (because the interrupt system will be temporarily in disarray) completes the GDT initialization, loads the GDT and IDT registers, reprograms the 8259As, enters protected mode, loads the segment registers with the corresponding descriptors from the GDT, adjusts the stack so that it can execute a protected mode return instruction, then returns. Your program has the responsibility to turn on interrupts again.

11

Important Topics Not Covered in This Book

Concepts

* What important topics are not covered in this book? * BASIC
* Assembler, librarian, linker * Debuggers * Program editors
* Programming auxiliary chips * Selecting peripheral equipment
* Operating system developments

Ideally, this book would cover everything you might need to know to have complete control of a PC/AT running the DOS operating system, independent of your particular application. Of course, reality never matches the ideal. Considerations of time and space have made it impossible to cover a number of topics. These are listed here, with references to other literature to help you find detailed information.

BASIC

First, no high level language is described. While it can be argued that your choice of high level language always depends on your application, one such language is always available: BASIC. A simple BASIC interpreter is provided in the PC/AT Read Only Memory (ROM), and a more powerful one, BASICA Version 3.0, is shipped with DOS 3.0. BASICA is IBM's adaptatation of the Microsoft GWBASIC interpreter. It is unsuitable for most complex programming tasks because it fails to implement many principles of structured programming, and because BASICA programs run very slowly. However, it has particularly powerful input/output commands to handle keyboard, screen, external files, and the serial and parallel ports, so it is useful for many miscellaneous small programming tasks, particularly those involving peripheral equipment. Many texts are available to introduce you to BASIC; once you are generally familiar with the language, you will find its reference manual, reference [11], very well organized.

General programming tools

Although this book uses assembly language to describe all the 80286 instructions and the PC/AT BIOS, it does not describe

- an *assembler*, for translating assembly language programs to object code,
- a *librarian*, for managing object code files,
- a *linker*, for combining object code files into executable program files.

The standard assembler, librarian, and linker for the PC/AT are produced by the Microsoft Corporation and licensed for distribution by IBM. When this book was written, the most current versions were all shipped with Version 3.0 of the Microsoft Macro Assembler package. The manual for that product [23], while better than earlier versions, is still inadequate. You will find the Intel *ASM86 Language Reference Manual* [4] much more informative on questions of segment allocation, combination, and ordering, and you will need to consult the *DOS 3.0 Technical Reference* manual [15] for information about the structure of executable program files.

Another important programming tool is a *debugger*. This type of utility helps you find program errors by providing these services:

- displaying memory contents in hex format or as characters corresponding to stored ASCII codes;
- disassembling instruction codes, providing at least an approximation of the original assembly language;
- assembling simple assembly language programs;
- installing breakpoints to stop your programs midstream so that you can examine memory and register contents;
- stepping through your program one instruction at a time, displaying current memory and register contents.

Again, no debugger is described in this book. A rudimentary one, called **debug**, is distributed with DOS 3.0. A more elaborate one, **symdeb**, is included in the Microsoft Macro Assembler package, Version 3.0. The latter one can read linker map output files that show which memory locations correspond to public variable names and program line numbers. This allows you to inspect the current values of public variables and install breakpoints at particular lines without having to look up the actual memory locations. Unfortunately, the descriptions of both debuggers, in the *DOS 3.0 Reference* and Macro Assembler manuals, are inadequate and sometimes misleading. Moreover, the versions mentioned do not recognize the instructions peculiar to the 80286—they only handle 8086 instructions.

More elaborate debuggers are available that will execute a program and halt it when certain conditions occur—for example, when a certain byte in memory assumes a certain value. Some will also keep a record of the previous several hundred machine instructions, so that you can investigate what events led to your problem. Some (very expensive) products come with an adapter board that will actually take over your computer and simulate the action of your misbehaving program, retaining control when it crashes on your machine. This is a great help when the effect of a bug is to destroy your means of discovering what is happening.

Editors

This book does not describe any *program editor*. A very rudimentary editor called **edlin** is shipped with DOS 3.0 and described in the *DOS 3.0 Technical Reference* manual. It's not really useful for large editing tasks, but sometimes its very *lack* of special features is helpful—you can use **edlin** to manipulate characters that you can't touch with some editors because they are used to control the editing process. Moreover, **edlin** will manipulate lines up to 253 characters long—longer than some generally more powerful editors admit.

Editors are available that are particularly suited for programming. Some actually detect syntax errors for particular languages, thus saving compilation time. In the end, choice of an editor is very personal; the author originally chose his word processor because it was equally suited for editing programs and for processing text like this book.

Programming auxiliary chips

Although this book describes in great detail the process of programming the Intel 80286 CPU, it rarely mentions the related task of programming the auxiliary chips. Occasionally you may find it necessary to deal with them, particularly if you must write or adapt software to control external equipment. On the PC/AT motherboard you have noted the following chips:

```
Intel      8042     Keyboard Controller
Intel      8237A    Direct Memory Access  (DMA)   Controller
Intel      8254-2   Timer Chip
Intel      8259A    Interrupt Controller
Intel      80287    Numerical Coprocessor
Motorola 146818     Clock and   CMOS Chip
```

You will find other programmable chips on various adapter boards: for example,

```
INS        8250     Universal Asynchronous Receiver/Transmitter
                    Chip   (UART)
Intel      8255     Peripheral Interface
Motorola 6845       Video Controller
```

The chips are programmed by sending various codes to CPU output ports, which are connected to appropriate input ports or registers of the chips. Some details of these chips are found in the *PC/AT Technical Reference* manual [20]. Texts [3] and [26] consider some of them in depth. Reference [21] has an excellent treatment of the 6845 Video Controller chip. Finally, the huge data catalog [8] is a major source of information on the Intel chips.

Selecting peripheral equipment

Several other topics relating to peripheral equipment are not covered in this book because the information is constantly changing:

```
selecting a display controller
selecting a  CRT  display
selecting a printer or other input/output device
selecting network hardware and software
acquiring additional memory
```

You can find up-to-date surveys of feasible equipment selections in current PC-oriented periodicals. Often, however, they provide only sparse technical information. To obtain more, you need to find deeper review articles and the product manuals and ask users. Some of this hardware, notably display controllers and networks, contains chips that you may sometime have to program; to give adequate treatment of the available equipment and techniques for using it might require entire books. One very informative text is available on programming display controllers: [21].

Operating systems

A major omission from this book, but a necessary one, is consideration of operating systems that utilize the unique capabilities of the 80286 CPU. Every author and publisher confronts the general problem: software is a moving target. As this book was taking shape, Microsoft's XENIX three user UNIX based operating system appeared, and DOS continued its evolution. Consideration of these was beyond the scope of this book. In fact, a substantial programmer-oriented treatment of any operating system that supports the multitasking capabilities of the 80286 would require an entire book. That must be left to a future project.

Bibliography

[1] BLAISE COMPUTING INC., *ASYNCH MANAGER: Asynchronous support tools for Pascal programmers,* Blaise Computing Inc., 1985. This product is also available for the C language.

[2] BLAISE COMPUTING INC., *C TOOLS 2: C procedure support for DOS 2.0,* Blaise Computing Inc., 1984. This product is also available for the Pascal language.

[3] Lewis C. EGGEBRECHT, *Interfacing to the IBM personal computer,* Howard W. Sams, 1983.

[4] INTEL CORPORATION, *ASM86 language reference manual,* (Publication No. 121703-002), Intel, 1982.

[5] INTEL CORPORATION, *iAPX 286 programmer's reference manual including the iAPX 286 numeric supplement,* (Publication No. 210498-002), Intel, 1984.

[6] INTEL CORPORATION, *iAPX 286 Operating systems writer's guide,* (Publication No. 121960-001), Intel, 1983.

[7] INTEL CORPORATION, *iAPX 86, 88 user's manual,* (Publication No. 210201-001), Intel, 1981.

[8] INTEL CORPORATION, *Microsystem components handbook,* (Two volumes, Publication No. 230843-002), Intel, 1985.

[9] INTERNATIONAL BUSINESS MACHINES CORPORATION, *BASIC handbook: General programming information,* (Publication No. 6361129), IBM, 1984.

[10] INTERNATIONAL BUSINESS MACHINES CORPORATION, *BASIC quick reference,* (Publication No. 6361724), IBM, 1984.

[11] INTERNATIONAL BUSINESS MACHINES CORPORATION, *BASIC reference,* (Publication No. 6025010), IBM, 1984.

[12] INTERNATIONAL BUSINESS MACHINES CORPORATION, *Disk Operating System Version 3.00 application setup guide,* (Publication No. 6137811), IBM, 1984.

[13] INTERNATIONAL BUSINESS MACHINES CORPORATION, *Disk Operating System Version 3.00 quick reference card,* (Publication No. 6322668), IBM, 1984.

[14] INTERNATIONAL BUSINESS MACHINES CORPORATION, *Disk Operating System Version 3.00 reference,* (Publication No. 6322666), IBM, 1984.

[15] INTERNATIONAL BUSINESS MACHINES CORPORATION, *Disk Operating System Version 3.00 technical reference,* (Publication No. 6322677), IBM, 1984.

[16] INTERNATIONAL BUSINESS MACHINES CORPORATION, *Disk Operating System Version 3.00 user's guide,* (Publication No. 6322670), IBM, 1984.

[17] INTERNATIONAL BUSINESS MACHINES CORPORATION, *Pascal compiler fundamentals and Pascal compiler language reference,* (Publications No. 1502396 and 6361111), IBM, 1984.

[18] INTERNATIONAL BUSINESS MACHINES CORPORATION, *Personal Computer AT guide to operations,* (Publication No. 1502241), IBM, 1984.

[19] INTERNATIONAL BUSINESS MACHINES CORPORATION, *Personal Computer AT installation and setup,* (Publication No. 1502491), IBM, 1984.

[20] INTERNATIONAL BUSINESS MACHINES CORPORATION, *Personal Computer AT technical reference,* (Publication No. 1502494), IBM, 1984.

[21] Gary KANE, *The CRT controller handbook,* Osborne/McGraw-Hill, 1980.

[22] Robert LAFORE, *Assembly language primer for the IBM PC and XT,* New American Library, 1984.

[23] MICROSOFT CORPORATION, *Macro assembler user's guide and reference manual,* (Part No. 016-014-009), Microsoft, 1984.

[24] MICROSOFT CORPORATION, *Microsoft MS-DOS operating system: Programmer's reference manual,* Microsoft, 1984.

[25] Peter NORTON, *MS-DOS and PC-DOS user's guide,* Robert J. Brady Co., 1984.

[26] Murray SARGENT III and Richard L. SHOEMAKER, *The IBM personal computer from the inside out,* Addison-Wesley, 1984.

[27] Leo J. SCANLON, *IBM PC assembly language: A guide for programmers,* Robert J. Brady Co., 1983.

[28] Mitchell WAITE, John ANGERMEYER, and Mark NOBLE, *DOS primer for the IBM PC & AT,* New American Library, 1984.

INDEX

RELATED BOOKS OF INTEREST FROM BRADY

Inside the IBM PC: Revised and Enlarged
Peter Norton

The new edition of the "Bible" of the IBM PC family and the inner workings of each machine. Ideal for new users, power users, and programmers alike, this classic book covers the operating system, 8088 and 80286 microprocessors, ROM, BASIC, Pascal, and Assembly language. Peter Norton is the best-known independent authority on the IBM PC, a contributing editor to *PC Magazine* and *PC-Week*, and creator of the Norton Utilities.

☐ Book: 1985/420pp/0-89303-583-1/$19.95

The Hidden Power of Lotus 1-2-3: Using Macros
Richard W. Ridington and Mark M. Williams

Details the problem-solving and practical ways to expand the capabilities of Lotus 1-2-3 and use its special features. Includes the basics of getting started, spreadsheets, steps for writing macros, and numerous sample applications.

☐ 1984/350pp/paper/D5173-2/$19.95
☐ Book Diskette 1984/D5181-5/$49.95
☐ Diskette 1983/D519X-1/$30.00

Understanding and Using dBASE II
Robert Krumm

This easy-to-use guide succinctly explains the fundamental concepts behind computerized information systems. Emphasizes techniques for organizing your records, adding records, using command files, creating loops, formatting input and output, and using dBASE II with spreadsheets.

☐ 1984/350pp/paper/D9160-5/$18.95

TO ORDER: Enclose a check or money order with this coupon, or include credit card information. Add $2.00 for postage and handling. You may also order by calling 800-624-0023 (0024 in New Jersey).

Name _____

Address _____

City/State/Zip _____

Charge my credit card instead: ☐ MasterCard   ☐ Visa

Account # _____ Expiration Date _____

Signature _____

Dept. Y   Y6692-BB

Prices subject to change without notice